Robert Ferguson

Surnames as a Science

Robert Ferguson

Surnames as a Science

ISBN/EAN: 9783337035051

Printed in Europe, USA, Canada, Australia, Japan

Cover: Foto ©Suzi / pixelio.de

More available books at **www.hansebooks.com**

SURNAMES AS A SCIENCE

BY

ROBERT FERGUSON, M.P.,

F.S.A., F.S.A. (SCOT.);

AUTHOR OF "THE TEUTONIC NAME-SYSTEM."

LONDON:

GEORGE ROUTLEDGE AND SONS,

BROADWAY, LUDGATE HILL,

NEW YORK: 9, LAFAYETTE PLACE.

1883.

TO

MRS. R. H. DANA (*née* LONGFELLOW),

OF BOSTON, MASS.,

IN MEMORY OF EARLY AND VALUED FRIENDSHIP, AND OF DAYS

NOT TO BE FORGOTTEN, PASSED AT CRAGIE HOUSE,

THIS LITTLE VOLUME IS INSCRIBED

BY THE AUTHOR.

PREFACE.

THAT portion of our surnames which dates back to Anglo-Saxon times, and so forms a part of the general system by which Teutonic names are governed, is distinctly a branch of a science, and as such has been treated by the Germans, upon whose lines I have generally endeavoured to follow.

It has been a part of my object to show that this portion of our surnames is a very much larger one than has been generally supposed, and that it includes a very great number of names which have hitherto been otherwise accounted for, as well as of course a great number for which no explanation has been forthcoming.

Nevertheless, while claiming for my subject the dignity of a science, I am very well aware that the question as to how far I have myself succeeded in treating it scientifically is an entirely different one, and one upon which it will be for others than myself to pronounce an opinion.

This work is of the nature of a supplement to one which I published some time ago under the title of *The Teutonic Name-system applied to the Family-names of France, England, and Germany* (Williams and Norgate), though I have been obliged, in order to render my system intelligible, to a certain extent to go over the same ground again.

I will only say, in conclusion, that in dealing with this subject—one in which all persons may be taken to be more or less interested—I have endeavoured as much as possible to avoid technicalities and to write so as to be intelligible to the ordinary reader.

ROBERT FERGUSON.

MORTON, CARLISLE.

CONTENTS.

CONTRACTIONS.

A.S. ...	... Anglo-Saxon.	O.G.	... Old German.
O.N. ...	... Old Northern.	O.H.G.	... Old High German.

SURNAMES AS A SCIENCE.

CHAPTER I.

THE ANTIQUITY AND THE UNSUSPECTED DIGNITY OF SOME OF OUR COMMON NAMES.

As some things that seem common, and even ignoble, to the naked eye, lose their meanness under the revelations of the microscope, so, many of our surnames that seem common and even vulgar at first sight, will be found, when their origin is adequately investigated, to be of high antiquity, and of unsuspected dignity. *Clodd*, for instance, might seem to be of boorish origin, and *Clout* to have been a dealer in old rags. But I claim for them that they are twin brothers, and etymologically the descendants of a Frankish king. *Napp* is not a name of distinguished sound, yet it is one that can take us back to that far-off time ere yet the history of England had begun, when, among the little kinglets on the old Saxon shore, "Hnaf ruled the Hôcings." [1] *Moll; Betty,*

---

[1] From the old Saxon fragment called the "Traveller's Song." Hnaf is no doubt from the Ang.-Sax. *cnafa, cnapa*, son, boy, the Anglo-Saxons often representing *c* by a (no doubt aspirated) *h*.

B

Nanny, and *Pegg* sound rather ignoble as the names
of men, yet there is nothing of womanliness in their
warlike origin. *Bill* seems an honest though hardly
a distinguished name, unless he can claim kinship
with Billing, the "noble progenitor of the royal house
of Saxony." Now Billing, thus described by
Kemble, is a patronymic, "son of Bill or Billa," and I
claim for our Bill (as a surname) the right, as
elsewhere stated, to be considered as the progenitor.
Among the very shortest names in all the directory
are *Ewe*, *Yea*, and *Yeo*, yet theirs also is a pedigree
that can take us back beyond Anglo-Saxon times.
Names of a most disreputable appearance are *Swearing*
and *Gambling*, yet both, when properly inquired into,
turn out to be the very synonyms of respectability.
Winfarthing again would seem to be derived from
the most petty gambling, unless he can be rehabili-
tated as an Anglo-Saxon Winfrithing (patronymic of
Winfrith.) A more unpleasant name than *Gumboil*
(*Lower*) it would not be easy to find, and yet it
represents, debased though be its form, a name borne
by many a Frankish warrior, and by a Burgundian
king fourteen centuries ago. Its proper form would
be Gumbald (Frankish for Gundbald), and it signifies
"bold in war." Another name which wofully belies
its origin is *Tremble*, for, of the two words of which it
is composed, one signifies steadfast or firm, and the
other signifies valiant or bold. Its proper form is
Trumbald, and the first step of its descent is *Trumbull*. A name which excites anything but agreeable
associations is *Earwig*. Yet it is at any rate a name
that goes back to Anglo-Saxon times, there being an

Earwig, no doubt a man of some consideration, a witness to a charter (*Thorpe*, p. 333). And the animal which it represents is not the insect of insidious repute, but the sturdy boar so much honoured by our Teuton forefathers, *ear* being, as elsewhere noted, a contraction of *evor*, boar, so that Earwig is the "boar of battle." Of more humiliating seeming than even Earwig is *Flea* (vouched for by Lower as an English surname). And yet it is at all events a name of old descent, for Flea—I do not intend it in any equivocal sense, for the stem is found in Kemble's list of early settlers—came in with the Saxons. And though it has nothing to do with English "flea," yet it is no doubt from the same root, and expresses the same characteristic of agility so marvellously developed in the insect.

Even *Bugg*, if he had seen his name under this metaphorical microscope, might have felt himself absolved from changing it into Howard, for Bugg is at least as ancient, and etymologically quite as respectable. It is a name of which great and honourable men of old were not ashamed; there was, for instance, a Buga, minister to Edward of Wessex, who signs his name to many a charter. And there was also an Anglo-Saxon queen, Hrothwaru, who was also called Bucge, which I have elsewhere given reasons for supposing to have been her original name. There are moreover to be found, deduced from place-names, two Anglo-Saxons named respectively Buga and Bugga, owners of land, and therefore respectable. In Germany we find Bugo, Bugga, and Bucge, as ancient names of men and women in the *Altdeutsches*

Namenbuch. And Bugge is at present a name both among the Germans and the Scandinavians, being, among others, that of a distinguished professor at Christiania. As to its origin, all that we can predicate with anything like confidence is that it is derived from a word signifying to bend, and of the various senses thus derived, that of ring or bracelet (O.N. *baugr*) seems to me the most appropriate. The bracelet was of old an honourable distinction, and the prince, as the fountain of honour, was the "bracelet-giver." [1]

My object then at present is to show that many of our short and unpretending names are among the most ancient that we have, being such as our Saxon forefathers brought with them when they first set foot upon our shores, and such as we find whenever history gives us a yet earlier glimpse of the Teuton in his home. *Bass,* for instance, whose red pyramid to-day stamps authenticity on many a bottle, was in ancient times a well-known potter's name on the beautiful red Samian ware of the Romans. The seat of this manufacture was on the banks of the Rhine, and in the long list of potters' names, mostly of course Roman, there are not a few that are those of Germans or of Gauls. And there is one interesting case, that of a lamp found along the line of the Roman wall, in which the German potter, one Fus, has asserted his own nationality by stamping his ware with the print of a naked human foot, within which is inscribed his name, thus proving, by the play upon his name, that

[1] Stark also adduces an instance in the eleventh century of Buggo as a contraction of Burchard.

fus meant "foot" in the language which he spoke.
Little perhaps the old potter thought, as he chuckled
over his conceit, that when fifteen centuries had passed
away, his trade-mark would remain to attest his
nationality.

But to return to Bass, let us see what can be
done to bridge the gulf between the princely
brewers of to-day and the old potter on the banks
of the Rhine. And first, as to Anglo-Saxon England,
we find Bass as a mass-priest, and Bassus as a
valiant soldier of King Edwin in the Anglo-Saxon
Chronicle, as also a Bassa in the genealogy of the
Mercian kings. Basing, the Anglo-Saxon patronymic,
"son of Bass," occurs about the twelfth century, in
the *Liber Vitæ*. And Kemble, in his list of Anglo-
Saxon "marks," or communities of the early settlers,
finds Bassingas, *i.e.* descendants or followers of Bass,
in Cambridgeshire and in Notts, while Mr. Taylor finds
offshoots of the same family on the opposite coast in
Artois. In Germany we find many instances of Bass,
and its High German form Pass, from the seventh
century downwards. And in the neighbourhood of the
Wurm-See, in Bavaria, we find, corresponding with our
Bassings, a community of Pasings, *i.e.* descendants or
followers of Pass. We may take it then that our name
Pass is only another form of *Bass*, both names being
also found at present in Germany. As to the origin
of the name, for which no sufficient explanation
is to be found in the Old German dialects, Foerstemann has to turn to the kindred dialect of the Old
Northern, where he finds it in *basa*, anniti, to strive
contend.

Thus far we have had to do with Bass as a name of Teutonic origin. But it appears to have been a Celtic name as well, for Bassa, a name presumably Welsh, occurs in the pathetic lament of Llywarch, written in the sixth century, the name being, on the authority of the late Dr. Guest, still retained in Baschurch near Shrewsbury. The name Bass, then, or Pass, on Roman pottery might be either that of a German or of a Gaul, but more probably the former, especially as we find also Bassico, a form more particularly German, and some other forms more probably Teutonic.

Before parting with Bass, I may refer to one in particular of his progeny, the name *Basin*, formed from it by the ending *en* or *in*, referred to in a subsequent chapter. The original of our Basin has been supposed to have been a barber, the mediæval leech, but I claim for him a different origin, and connect his name, which is found as Basin in Domesday, with the name Basin of a Thuringian king of the fifth century.

Let us take another of our common surnames, *Scott.* This has been generally assumed to have been an original surname derived from nationality, and we need not doubt that it has been so in many, perhaps in most, cases. But Scott, as a man's name, is, not to say older than the introduction of surnames, but as old probably as the name of the nation itself. To begin with England, it occurs in the thirteenth century, in the *Liber Vitæ*, where it is the reverse of a surname, Scott Agumdessune (no doubt for Agemundessune). I do not think, however, that Agumdessune is here a surname, but only an individual description, an earnest of surnames that were to be. For there is another Scott who signs about the same time, and it might be necessary to distinguish between these two men. There is in the same record yet another Scott, described as " Alstani filius," who, in the time of William the Conqueror, " for the redemption of his soul, and with the consent of his sons and of all his friends," makes a gift of valuable lands to the Church. Scott again occurs in an Anglo-Saxon charter of boundaries quoted by Kemble, " Scottes heal," *i.e.* " Scot's hall." And Scotta occurs in another in " Scottan byrgels," *i.e.* " Scotta's burial mound." In Germany Scot occurs in the ninth century in the Book of the Brotherhood of St. Peter at Salzburg, where it is classed by Foerstemann as a German name, which seems justified by the fact that Scotardus, a German compound (*hard*, fortis), occurs as an Old Frankish name in the time of Charlemagne. In Italy, where, as I shall show in a subsequent chapter, the Germans have left many Teutonic names behind them, we find a Scotti, duke of Milan, in the middle ages, whose name is probably due to that cause. Scotto is a surname at present among the Frisians, while among the Germans generally it is most commonly softened into Schott.

Scot however, as a man's name, seems to have been at least as common among the Celts as among the Teutons ; Gluck cites four instances of it from ancient, chiefly Latin, authors, in only one of which, however, that of a Gaul, is the particular nationality distinguished. As to the origin of the name, all that

can be said is that it is most probably from the same
origin, whatever that may be, as the name of the
nation ; just as another Celtic man's name, Caled,
signifying hard, durus, is probably from the same
origin as that of Caledonia, "stern and wild."

Lastly, among the names on Roman pottery, we
have Scottus, Scoto, and Scotni, the last being a genitive, " Scotni manû." Of these three names the first is
the Latinisation of Scott ; the second has the ending in
o most common for men's names among the old Franks,
but also found among the Celts ; the third, as a genitive,
presumably represents the form Scotten, the ending in
en, hereafter referred to, running through the whole
range of Teutonic names, but being also found in Celtic.
Upon the whole, then, there does not seem anything
sufficiently distinctive to stamp these names as either
Teutonic or Celtic. I may observe that all these
three forms, *Scott, Scotto,* and *Scotten,* are found in
our surnames, as well as *Scotting,* the Anglo-Saxon
patronymic, which assists to mark the name as in
Anglo-Saxon use. We have also *Scotland,* which has
been supposed to have been an original surname
derived from nationality, and so I dare say it may
be in some cases. But Scotland appears as a man's
name in the *Liber Vitæ* about the twelfth or thirteenth
century, and before surnames begin to make their
appearance. Scotland again occurs as the name of
a Norman in the *Acta Sanctorum,* where it seems
more probably of Frankish origin, and cannot at any
rate be from nationality. The fact seems to be that
land, terra, was formed into compounds, like *bald,* and
fred, and *hard,* without reference perhaps to any

particular meaning. Similarly we find Old German, apparently Frankish, names, Ingaland and Airland (more properly Heriland), which might account in a similar way for our surnames *England* and *Ireland.*

Let us take yet one more name, *Gay*, a little more complicated in its connections than the others, and endeavour to trace it up to its origin. " Nay! but what better origin can we have," I can fancy the reader saying at starting, " than our own word ' gay,' French *gai ?* " I would not undertake to say that our name is not in any instance from this origin, but what I say is that a proved Anglo-Saxon *name* is better than any assumed *word*, however suitable its meaning may seem to be. Moreover, the same Anglo-Saxon word will account, not only for Gay, but for a whole group of names, *Gay, Gye, Gedge, Gage, Kay, Key, Kegg, Kedge, Cage,*—all variations, according to my view, of one original name. It must inevitably be the case that a name dating back to a remote antiquity, and in use over a wide area, must be subject to many phonetic variations. And it matters nothing to etymology, so long as her own strict rules are complied with, if some of these names have not a single letter in common. Given, then, an Anglo-Saxon name Gagg, Gegg, with its alternative form Cagg, Keg, and we get from it all the forms that are required. For the English ear is averse, as a matter of euphony, to a final *g*, and while it most commonly changes it into *y* (which is in effect dropping it), as in A.S. *dag*, Eng. *day*, A.S. *cæg*, Eng. *key*, it also not unfrequently changes it into *dg*, as in A.S. *bricg*, Eng. *bridge*, &c. To come, then, to the Anglo-Saxon names concerned, Kemble, in his list of original settlers, has both Gagingas, *i.e.* descendants or followers of Gag, and Cægingas, *i.e.* descendants or followers of Cæg. And the Anglo-Saxon names cited below, one of them the exact counterpart of Gay, are deduced from place-names of a later period. The Old German names do not, in this case, throw any light upon the subject, as, on account of the stem not being so distinctly developed as it is in Anglo-Saxon, they have been placed by Foerstemann to, as I consider, a wrong stem, viz. *gaw*, patria.

> *Anglo-Saxon names.*—Gæcg, Geagga, Geah, Cæg, Ceagga, Ceahha (Gæging, Gaing, *patronymics*).
> *Old German names.*—Gaio, Geio, Kegio, Keyo, Keio.
> *Present German.*—Gey, Geu.
> *Present Friesic.*—Kay, Key.
> *English surnames.*—Gay, Gye, Gedge, Gage, Kay, Key, Kegg, Kedge, Cage.

As to the origin and meaning of the word, I can offer nothing more than a somewhat speculative conjecture. There is a stem *gagen*, *cagen*, in Teutonic names, and which seems to be derived most probably from O.N. *gagn*, gain, victory. We find it in Anglo-Saxon in Gegnesburh, now Gainsborough, and in Geynesthorn, another place-name, and we have it in our names *Gain, Cain, Cane*. It is very possible, and in accordance with the Teutonic system, that *gag* may represent the older and simpler form, standing to *gagen* in the same relation as English *ward* does to *warden*, and A.S. *geard* (inclosure), to , *garden.*

As in the two previous cases, so also in this case, there is an ancient Celtic name, Geio, to take into account, and to this may be placed the names *Keogh* and *Keho,* if these names be, as I suppose, Irish and not English. Also the Kay and the Kie in *McKay* and *McKie.* Lastly, in this, as in the other two cases, there is also a name on Roman pottery, Gio, which might, as it seems, be either German or Celtic. Can there be any connection, I venture to inquire, between these ancient names, Celtic or Teutonic, and the Roman Gaius and Caius? Several well-known Roman names are, as elsewhere noted, referred by German writers to a Celtic origin.

It will be seen then that, in the case of all the three names of which I have been treating, there is an ancient Celtic name in a corresponding form which might in some cases intermix. And there are many more cases of the same kind among our surnames. *Wake,* for instance, may represent an ancient name, either German or Celtic; for the German a sufficient etymon may be found in *wak,* watchful, while for the Celtic there is nothing, observes Gluck, in the range of extant dialects to which we can reasonably refer it. So *Moore* represents an ancient stem for names common to the Celts, the Germans, and the Romans, though at least as regards the Germans, the origin seems obscure.[1]

---

[1] So at least Foerstemann seems to think, observing that we can scarcely derive it from Maur, Æthiops, English "Moor." Nevertheless, seeing the long struggle between the Teutons

Now it is quite possible, particularly in the case of such monosyllabic words as these, that there might be an accidental coincidénce between a Celtic and a Teutonic name, without their having anything in common in their root. It is possible, again, that the one nation may have borrowed a name from the other, as the Northmen, for instance, sometimes did from the Irish or the Gael, one of their most common names, Niel(sen), being thus derived ; while, on the other hand, both the Irish and the Gael received, as Mr. Worsaae has shown, many names from the Northmen. So also the Romans seem to have borrowed names from the Celts, several well-known names, as Plinius, Livius, Virgilius,[1] Catullus, and Drusus, being, in the opinion of German scholars, thus derived.

But though no doubt both these principles apply to the present case, yet there is also, as it seems to me, something in the relationship between Celtic and Teutonic names which can hardly be accounted for on either of the above principles. And I venture to throw out the suggestion that when ancient Celtic names shall have been as thoroughly collected and examined as, by the industry of the Germans, have been the Teutonic, comparative philology may—

and the Moors in Spain, it seems to me that such a derivation would be quite in accordance with Teutonic practice. See some remarks on the general subject at the end of Chapter IV.

[1] So that we may take it that Virgilius, as the name of a Scot who became bishop of Salzburg in the time of Boniface, was his own genuine Celtic name, and not derived from that of the Roman poet.

'perhaps within certain lines—find something of the same kinship between them that it has already established in the case of the respective languages. Meanwhile, I venture to put forward, derived from such limited observations as I have been able to make, certain points of coincidence which I think go some way to justify the opinion expressed above. In so doing I am not so much putting forward etymological views of my own, as collecting together, so as to shape them into a comparison, the conclusions which have, in various individual cases, been arrived at by scholars such as Zeuss. There are, then, four very common endings in Teutonic names,—*ward*, as in Edward, *ric*, as in Frederic, *mar*, as in Aylmar, and *wald*, as in Reginald (= Reginwald). The same four words, in their corresponding forms, are also common as the endings of Celtic names, *ward* taking the form of *guared* or *guaret*, the German *ric* taking generally the form of *rix* (which appears also to have been the older form in the German, all names of the first century being so given by Latin authors), *wald* taking the form of *gualed* or *gualet*, and *mar* being pretty much the same in both. Of these four cases of coincidence, there is only one (*wald* = *gualet*) which I have not derived from German authority. And with respect to this one, I have assumed the Welsh *gualed*, order, arrangement, whence *gualedyr*, a ruler, to be the same word as German *wald*, Gothic *valdan*, to rule. But we can carry this comparison still further, and show all these four endings in combination with one and the same prefix common to both tongues. This prefix is the Old German *had*, *hat*, *hath*, signifying war, the corresponding word to which is in Celtic *cad* or *cat*. (Note that in the earliest German names on record, as the Catumer and the Catualda of Tacitus, the German form is *cat*, same as the Celtic. This seems to indicate that at that early period the Germans so strongly aspirated the *h* in *hat*, that the word sounded to Roman ears like *cat*, and it assists perhaps to give us an idea of the way in which such variations of tongues arise.)

I subjoin then the following names which, *mutatis mutandis*, are the same in both tongues, and which, judging them by the same rules which philology has applied to the respective languages, might be taken to be from some earlier source common to both races :—

Ancient German Names.	*Ancient Celtic Names.*
Hadaward.	Catguaret (*Book of Llandaff*).
Haduric.	Caturix (*Orelli*).
Hadamar (Catumer, *Tacitus*).	Catmôr (*Book of Llandaff*).
Hadold (= Hadwald).	Catgualet (*British king of Gwynedd*, A.D. 664).
Catualda, (*Tacitus*).	Cadwalladyr (*British king*) (Catgualatyr, *Book of Llandaff*).

In comparing Catualda with the British Cadwalladyr I am noting an additional point of coincidence. Catualda is not, like other Old German names, from *wald*, rule, but from *walda*, ruler. There is only one other Old German name in the same form, Cariovalda,[1] also a very ancient name, being of the first

---

[1] This name, that of a prince of the Batavi, is considered by the Germans to be properly Hariovalda, from *har*, army, and

century. This then may represent the older form, though this is not what I wish at present to note, but that Catualda is the counterpart of the* British Cadwalladyr, which also is not from *gualed*, rule, but from *gualedyr*, ruler.

In suggesting that this coincidence may be confined within certain lines I mean to guard against the assumption that it would, as in the case of the language, be found to pervade the whole system, many of the formations of which may be of a more recent time. There are some other stems, considered by the Germans to be in coincidence, to only one of which I will refer at present, the Old Celtic *tout*, Welsh *tûd* = the Gothic *thiuda*. Hence the name Tudric, of a British king of Glamorgan, would be the counterpart of that of the Gothic king Theuderic, or Theoderic. I will take one more instance of a name presumed to be common to the Germans and to the Celts as an illustration of the manner in which—men's names being handed down from generation to generation without, even in ancient times, any thought of their meaning—a name may survive, while the word from which it was originally derived has perished out of the language, or is retained in a sense so changed as hardly to be recognised. The German name in question is that of Sigimar, the brother of Arminius, dating from the first century of our era, a name which we still have as *Seymore*,

---

hence is another instance of an initial *h* being represented among the Romans by a *c*. The name is the same as the Anglo-Saxon Harald, and as our present name *Harold*.

and in its High German form Sicumar we have as *Sycamore*, intermediate Anglo-Saxon names being found for both. The prefix *sig* is taken, with as much certainty as there can be in anything of the kind, to be from *sig*, victory ; the ending *mar*, signifying famous, is a word to which I have already referred as common both to the Germans and to the Celts. Segimar was also an ancient Celtic name, but while the ending *mar* has a meaning to-day in Celtic speech, the prefix *seg* is a word of which they are hardly able to render any account. Only in the Old Irish (which seems to contain some of the most ancient elements) Gluck, finding a word *seg* with the meaning of the wild ox, *urus*, deduces from it the ancient meaning of strength (Sansc. *sahas*, vis, robor), and infers an original meaning akin to the German.

It happens, perhaps yet more frequently, that a German name, which cannot be explained by anything within the range of Teutonic dialects, may find a sufficient etymon from the Celtic. That is to suppose that a word originally common to the Teutonic and the Celtic, has dropped out of the former, and been retained only in the latter. Thus there is a word *arg, arch*, found in many Teutonic names, and from which we have several names, as *Archbold, Archbutt, Archard, Argent, Argument*, for which the meaning that can be derived from the German seems very inadequate, but for which the Irish *arg*, hero or champion, seems to offer as good a meaning as could be desired. So also *all*, from which, as elsewhere shown, there are a number of names, in its Teutonic sense of *omnis*, does not seem to give by any means so satisfactory a result as in its Celtic sense of "great" or "illustrious." Many other instances might be adduced on both sides to show the way in which a word has dropped out of the one language and been retained in the other.

Before passing from this part of the subject, I may be allowed to adduce an illustration—a striking one I think, albeit that the name in this case is not that of a man but of a dog—of the way in which a name may be retained in familiar use, though the word from which it is derived has perished out of the language, though the language itself has passed out of use among us for more than a thousand years, and though the word itself is only used in a sort of poetical or sentimental sense. Who has not heard, in verse or in prose, of the "poor dog *Tray*"? And yet who ever heard, excepting in books, of a dog being called Tray, a word which conveys no meaning whatever to an English ear? What then is the origin, and what is the meaning, of the name? It is, I venture to think, the ancient British name for a dog, which is not to be found in any living dialect of the Celtic, and which is only revealed to us in a casual line of a Roman poet :—

> Non sibi, sed domino, venatur *vertragus* acer,
> Illæsum leporem qui tibi dente feret.
> > *Martial.*

The British *vertrag* must have been something of the nature of a greyhound, though, from the description of his bringing back the game unmangled to his master, perhaps capable of a higher training

C

than the greyhound generally attains to. Now the
ver in *vertrag* is in the Celtic tongues an intensitive,
and as prefixed to a word, gives the sense of pre-
eminence. The ancient British word for a dog in
general must have been *trag*, a word of which we
find a trace in the Irish *traig*, foot, allied, no doubt,
to Gothic *thragjan*, Greek τρεχειν, Sanscrit *trag*, to
run. The ancient British name then for a dog, *trag*,
signified the "runner," and with the intensitive prefix
ver, as in *vertrag*, the "swift runner." [1]   And *trag* is,
I take it, the word from which, *g* as usual in English
becoming *y*, is formed our word Tray.

It may be of interest, in connection with the
antiquity of our names, to take a few of the oldest
Teutonic names of which history gives us a record,
and endeavour to show the relationship which they
bear to our existing surnames. It will be seen that
not only have we the representatives of these ancient
names, but also in certain cases names which represent
a still more ancient form of the word.

And first let us take the name, dating back to the
first century of our era, of the old German hero
Arminius, brought before us with such magnanimous
fairness by Tacitus. The old idea, let me observe,
that Armin is properly *herman*, leader or warrior,
has long been given up by the Germans. The name,
of which the most correct form is considered to be
Irmin, is formed from one single word of which the
root is *irm*, and the meaning of which is, as Grimm
observes, entirely obscure. We have then as English
surnames *Armine*, *Ermine*, and *Harmony*, the last,

[1] For this explanation of *vertragus* I am indebted to Gluck.

no doubt, a slight corruption, though, as far as the prefix of *h* is concerned, it is as old as Anglo-Saxon times, for we find " Harmines den," Harmine's valley, in a charter quoted by Kemble. Then we have compounded with *gar*, spear, and corresponding with an O.G. Irminger—*Arminger, Irminger*,[1] and again as a corruption, *Iremonger*. And, compounded with *hari*, warrior, and corresponding with an O.G. Irminhar, we have *Arminer*. And, as a Christian name of women, one at least of our old families still retains the ancient name *Ermentrude*, the ending *trude*, as found also in *Gertrude*, being perhaps from the name Thrud, of one of the *Valkyrjur*, or battle-maidens of Odin. The French also, among the many names derived from their Frankish ancestors, have *Armingaud, Armandet*, and *Ermingcard*, corresponding with the ancient names Irmingaud, Irmindeot, and Irmingard. And *Irminger*, as I write, comes before me in the daily papers as the name of a Danish admiral. But Irmin is not the oldest form of the name,—" the older and the simple form," observes Foerstemann, " runs in the form Irm or Irim," and with this also we can claim connection in our family names. For we have the simple form as *Arms* and *Harme ;* and as compounds we have *Armiger*, corresponding with an O.G. Ermgar ; *Armour*, with an O.G. Ermhar ; and *Armgold*, with an O.G. Ermegild. Lastly, I may observe that both Irm and Irmin are found also by Stark as ancient Celtic names. And certainly there is no stem more likely than this, of the origin of which

---

[1] There was an English admiral of this name, though I do not know of it at present.

all trace is lost in the darkness of the past, to be one that is older than the Arian separation.

The name Sigimar, of the brother of Arminius, I have already shown that we have, not only in its own form as *Seymore*, but also in its High German form as *Sycamore*, the Anglo-Saxon names from which they may be taken to be more immediately derived being also found in the chapter on place-names. And I have also shown that we have the name Cariovalda (or Harwald) of a prince of the Batavi, of the first century, in our *Harold*.

There was another old hero of the German race, not so fortunate as Arminius in finding an historian in a generous foe, whose name only comes before us in a line of Horace :—

Occidit Daci Cotisonis agmen.

Cotiso must have been a leader of some High German tribe, perhaps somewhere on the Upper Danube, and he must have made a gallant stand against the Roman arms, inasmuch as his final over-throw is deemed by the Roman poet a worthy subject on which to congratulate his imperial patron. Cotiso is a High German form of another name, Godiso or Godizo, elsewhere referred to, and hence may be represented, I venture to think, in our names *Godsoe* and *Goddiss*, while Cotiso itself may be represented in our *Cottiss*, the ancient vowel-ending being in our names, as I shall show in the next chapter, sometimes dropped and sometimes retained.

Another name which goes back to the first century of our era is Arpus, that of a prince of the Catti in

Tacitus. The Eorpingas, descendants or followers of Eorpa, were among the original settlers, and seem to have confined themselves to Norfolk, where alone we have any traces of them. The name may perhaps be referred to Anglo-Saxon *eorp*, wolf, though other derivations have also been proposed. We have the name at present as *Earp* (the name of a member of the House of Commons), and also as *Harp*. Upon this stem is formed the name Arbogastes (*gast*, guest) of a Frankish general under the Emperor Gratian in the fourth. century ; and *Arbogast* is still ·a family name among the French.

Lastly, let us take the name of the German king, Ariovistus, brought before us by Cæsar. The proper form of this name, there seems little doubt, is Arefastus, as found in some other O.G. names. There was also an Arfast, bishop of East Anglia, in the time of William the Conqueror. And Arfast is a present name among the Frisians, according to Outzen, who compares it—rightly, as it seems to me— with the old name Ariovistus. The corresponding name Arinfast (*aro, arin*, eagle) was also in ancient use among the Danes. It seems to me that our name *Harvest* may easily be a corruption of Arfast ; it has generally no doubt been derived from a man's having been born at such a season, but I distrust, as a general rule, as elsewhere stated, derivations of this kind.

In connection with the subject of the antiquity of Teutonic names generally, and of English names as derived from them, I shall have, in a subsequent chapter, to refer to the names of original settlers in England as deduced by Kemble from ancient charters, and compare them with names of a similar kind found in Germany. The coincidence that will be found in these names at that early period, from England and Friesland in the north to Bavaria in the south, will, I think, be a very strong argument to show that these names could not have originated within the Teutonic area itself, and so dispersed themselves over it in its length and breadth, but that they must have been brought with them by the Teutonic invaders from their earlier homes

CHAPTER II.

CLUE TO SOME OF THE ANCIENT FORMS
REPRESENTED IN ENGLISH NAMES.

So long as our surnames are treated as if each name were something standing apart by itself, very little progress can be made in their elucidation ; it is by collation and comparison that, in this as in any other science, definite results are to be obtained. And a moderate amount of attention to the forms in which these names appear, and to the various endings prevalent among them, will enable many names, otherwise unrecognisable, to be brought within the pale of classification and of possible explanation.   I am of course referring to that portion of our surnames— a much larger one according to my judgment than is generally acknowledged—which dates back to Anglo-Saxon times, and so forms a part of the general system by which Teutonic names are governed.

I shall have, in the course of this work, frequently to refer to the Teutonic system, and to names which do, or do not, according to my judgment, enter into it.   And I will therefore, before going further, endeavour to explain what I mean by the Teutonic system. There is, then, a class of words which, at a time of remote antiquity, have been adopted as stems upon which, in some cases by a sort of phonetic accretion, in some cases by the addition of a diminutive ending, in some cases by forming a patronymic, in some cases by taking in another word as a compound, a number of other names have been formed. Thus, when we find such a group of names as *Dill, Dilly, Dillow, Dillen, Dilling, Dilke, Dilwyn*, or as *Budd, Budden, Buddle, Budding, Buddrich, Budmore*, we may take it that these are all ancient names, of which *Dill* and *Budd* are respectively the stems. And whenever we find a group of names with ·endings· such as it is my object in the present chapter to explain, and in compounds such as will be dealt with in a succeeding chapter, we shall be warranted in assuming the antiquity of the group.

The endings in *a, ay, ah, ey, ie, o, oe, ow.*

And in the first place, let us take the endings in *a, i,* and *o,* of which the above are nothing more than arbitrary variations of spelling. Now ancient Teutonic names formed of one single word had commonly, though not invariably (and the same thing applies also to ancient Celtic names), a vowel-ending in *a, i,* or *o ;* this ending is in our names sometimes dropped and at other times retained. (It is to be observed, however, that even in Anglo-Saxon times it is not an unfrequent thing to find the same name variously with and without a vowel-ending, of which some instances may be noted in Chapter V.) Thus

we have *Abbe*, *Abba*, and *Abbey*, we have *Bell*, *Belly*,
and *Bellow*, we have *Earl* and *Early*, we have *Dand*,
Dandy, and *Dando*, we have *Brand* and *Brandy*, we
have *Todd* and *Toddy*, we have *Dane* and *Dana*,
we have *Marr*, *Marry*, and *Marrow*. These are all
ancient names, variously with and without the vowel-
ending, and it will be readily seen how apt the
addition is to disguise the name, and to give it the
appearance of something else.

The question now to consider is—What is the value
and meaning of this vowel-ending, which was only
given to simple names and never to compounds ? It
might be, in some cases, used simply as a sort of
euphonic rounding-off of a name which might seem
meagre and insignificant without something of the
sort. We ourselves appear to use *s* in the same
manner in the case of some very short names, such as
Wills and Epps, in which the final *s* may perform the
same service that was rendered by the vowel-ending.
But there is also another principle which I think
obtains, and which, indeed, may be the guiding
principle in such cases. In Anglo-Saxon (and the
same principle applied to other Teutonic dialects), the
addition of *a* to a word implied connection with it.
Thus, from *scip*, a ship, is formed *scipa*, one connected
with a ship, a sailor. Now, going back to the remote
origin of names, there were many cases in which
a man took a name from an abstraction, such as war,
peace, glory, victory, or from a weapon, as the sword
or the spear, and it is obvious that in such cases he
required something to connect his name with it, and
this is, as it seems to me, what was effected by the

ending in question. And the principle is still a living one among us, and we form names daily in accordance with it, though we no longer use the ending in *a*, which has been superseded by that in *i*.[1] A connection with anything whatever is expressed by this ending, as when a stupid person is called "Duncey," one with a remarkable nose "Nosey," or one with a halting gait "Stumpy." The French seem to have retained their old ending, and, when they form names of this sort, to do it with the ending in *o* (*eau*) which appears to be in accordance with the genius of their language, as that in *i* (*ey*) is with that of ours.

Of these three endings, that in *a* is the one which was in use among the Goths, in such names as Cniva, Totila, Ulfila. And the same was also the case among the Saxons, a branch of the same Low German stock, in such names as Anna, Ella, Penda, Dodda. The ending in *i* was also common among the Old Saxons, and, if we may judge by the *Liber Vitæ* of Durham (which might naturally be supposed to contain a large proportion of Northern names), was also prevalent in the ancient Northumbria. We have in that record the names Alli, Arni, Bynni, Betti, Cyni, Diori, Elsi, Paelli, Tidi, Tilli, Terri, all of which are found in our present names *Alley*, *Arney*, *Binney*, *Betty*, *Kinney*, *Deary*, *Elsey*, *Paley*, *Tidy*, *Tilley*, *Terry*. The ending in *o* was that which

---

[1] How or when this change took place is a question that awaits solving, but I observe that, in 1265, the Countess of Montford, giving names (or sobriquets) to her servants, calls one of her messengers Treubodi (trusty messenger), and not Treuboda, as the Anglo-Saxon form would have been.

was in favour among the Franks and the High Germans generally, the oldest instance on record being
probably that of Cotiso, p. 20. This is the usual
ending in French names (so far as they are of Old
Frankish origin, and come under this head), the form
being generally *eau*, as in *Baudeau, Godeau, Fredeau,*
representing the ancient names Baldo, Godo, Fredo.
Hence our names ending in *o* may be taken to be, to
some extent, names of Old Frankish origin come to
us through the Normans. But the number of such
names is larger than could reasonably be accounted for
in such a way, and in point of ·fact, we meet occasionally with such names at a much earlier period. The
Frisians certainly seem to have had names in this
form, and it is a question whether such names may
not be partly due to them. It must be observed,
then, that names with these three various endings
represent the stem just the same as those that are
without it.

The ending in *an, en, in,* or *on.*

This ending runs through the whole range of Teutonic names, and is common in English surnames.
Hence we have *Doran, Lingen, Bolden, Hannen,
Farren,* the names on which they are formed being
represented in *Dore, Ling, Bold, Hann, Farre.* As
to the value and meaning of this ending, we have
nothing more to guide us than its parallel use in the
languages most nearly concerned, where it is what
may be called formative. That is to say, it is a form
of speech which is used to form the endings of words,
not adding anything to the meaning, but forming a

kind of euphonic rounding-off of the word. Thus from A.S. *wearda* is formed *warden*, from *geard* (inclosure) is formed *garden*, from *Brytta* is formed Briton, from *mægd*, maid, is formed *maiden*. Cf. also the old word *ratten* for *rat*, still used in provincial speech. In many cases in Teutonic names we have words thus formed, and also the simpler forms on which they have been founded, *e.g.* we have *bero*, bear, and also *berin*, we have *aro*, eagle, and also *arin* (= A.S. *earn*), both forming the stems on which a number of other names have been built. I take the ending in *en*, then, to be most probably a kind of phonetic accretion, adding nothing to the sense, but sometimes representing a secondary word, and starting a stem on its own account.

The ending in *ing*.

This is the Anglo-Saxon and ancient German patronymic, as in *Browning*, "son of Brown," *Dunning*, "son of Dunn," *Winning*, "son of Winn." It must have been superseded during, or very soon after, Anglo-Saxon times, by the patronymic in *son*, inasmuch as no names of Scriptural origin appear to be formed with it. Hence we have such names as *Bulling, Burning, Canning, Gambling, Halling, Harding, Hopping, Loving, Manning, Swearing, Telling, Walking, Willing*, some of which have been popularly supposed to be from the present participle. All of the above except two, *Swearing* and *Gambling*, are found in the list of early Saxon settlers, and of these two (which are found in after Anglo-Saxon times) *Swearing*, which corresponds with an Old German

Suaring, finds its stem in an Anglo-Saxon name Sweor, signifying important, honourable ; and *Gambling* (properly Gamling) is the patronymic of an A.S. and O.N. name, Gamol, signifying "old," probably in the honorific sense of old descent. From this origin, I take it, are also our names *Farthing* and *Shilling*, the former from the stem *fard*, or *farth*, signifying "travel," found in several ancient names, and which I rather take to be the same as *ford*, found in the Fordingas among the early settlers. And *Shilling*, which corresponds with a present German *Schilling*, is probably the same as the Scilling in the "Traveller's Song," a supposed contraction of Scilding, from A.S. *scyld*, shield, in which case our name *Shield* would be the parent of *Shilling*. I have referred at the beginning of this book to the curious-looking name *Winfarthing* (quoted from Lower) as perhaps a corruption of an A.S. Winfrithing, though it is a case in which I do not feel much certainty, finding one or two other such names as *Turnpenny*, which may have been sobriquets.

The ending in *el* or *il*.

This ending in Teutonic names may be taken, as a general rule, to be a diminutive, though in a few cases it may be more probably, like that in *en*, formative. Thus in the list of early A.S. settlers we have Bryd(ingas) and we have Brydl(ingas), representing the words *bride* and *bridle*. Now, as German writers have taken the word *brid* in ancient names to mean "bridle," comparing it with French *bride*, it would seem probable that, in the above A.S. name, Brydl is

not a diminutive, but the extended word "bridle."
However, as a general rule, it may be presumed to be
a diminutive, and in such sense I take the following,
premising that this, as well as all other diminutives,
except *kin,*lin*, and *et*, is subject to a vowel-ending just
the same as simple forms. We have *Bable*, corresponding with an A.S. Babel, and an O.G. Babilo ; *Ansell* and
Anslow (Ansilo), corresponding with an O.G. Ansila ;
Mundell and *Mundella*, with a Gothic Mundila ;[1] *Cos-
tall*, *Costello*, and *Costly*, with an O.G. Costila. *Costly*
is properly Costili, with the ending in *i*, as also
Brightly is Brightili, and some other names with an
adverbial look may be similarly explained.

The ending in *ec* or *ic*.

This ending, with rare exceptions, may also be
taken to be a diminutive. The oldest instance on
record is stated by Stark as that of the Vandal
general Stilicho in the fourth century, though, as
found on Roman pottery (in the names Bassico
and Bennicus), it may be still older. It seems
rather singular that, though, according to Grimm,
this ending was more particularly in favour among
the Saxons, not a single instance of it occurs among
the names of our early settlers, nor indeed any other
form of diminutive except that in *el*, though the form
in question is not uncommon in after Anglo-Saxon
times. This diminutive is still in living use among
us, at least in Scotland, where a " mile and a

---

[1] This name appears as Μουνδιλας in Procopius, but, judging
by the present pronunciation of Greek, it would sound as
Mundila.

bittock" (little bit) has proved a snare to many a
tourist. We have *Willock*, *Wilkie*, and *Wilke*, corresponding with an O.G. Willico, and an A.S. Uillech;
Lovick and *Lubbock*, corresponding with O.G. Liuvicho;
Jellicoe, corresponding with O.G. Geliko, Jeliko, and an
A.S. Geleca, some of these examples being with, and
some without, the vowel-ending.

The ending in *lin.*

This ending, which is also a diminutive, is probably
formed from that in *el*, by the addition of *en*. It is found
in Foerstemann's list as early as the fifth century, but,
as found on Roman pottery, must probably be still
older. We have *Bucklin*, corresponding with a
Buccellin, general of the Alemanni in the sixth
century, and with a Buccellan on Roman pottery.
Also *Tomlin*, corresponding with an O.G. Domlin;
Applin, with an O.G. Abbilin; *Franklin*, with an O.G.
Francolin; *Papillon*, with an O.G. Babolen, &c. This
form of diminutive never takes a vowel-ending.

The ending in *kin.*

This diminutive ending is formed from that in *ec* by
the addition of *en*. It is the youngest-born of all, not
being found, unless in rare cases, before the tenth
century. And it is one that is still in living use both
in England and in Germany, in the latter country
more especially. We have *Wilkin*, corresponding with
an O.G. Williken, and an O.N. Vilkinr; *Godkin*, with an
O.G. Gotichin; *Hipkin*, with an O.G. Ibikin or Ipcin;
and *Hodgkin*, with an A.S. Hogcin.

The ending in *et*.

There is an ending in *d* or *t* in O.G. names, which may be taken, though perhaps not with anything like certainty, to have the force of a diminutive. Hence might be such a name as *Ibbett*, corresponding with O.G. names Ibed and Ibet, from an unexplained stem *ib;* also our names *Huggett*, *Howitt*, and *Hewitt*, corresponding with an Anglo-Saxon Hocget, and an O.G. Huetus, from the stem *hog*, *hug*, signifying study or thought. But some other endings are so liable to intermix, and particularly the common one *had*, war, that there is very seldom anything like certainty.

The ending in *es* or *is*.

I take this ending also to be diminutive, and to be possibly akin to our *ish*, as in blue-*ish*, which, as signifying a "little blue," seems to have the force of a diminutive. Hence we have *Riches*, corresponding with an O.G. Richizo, and a present French *Richez ;* and *Willis*, corresponding with an O.G. Willizo. Then we have *Godsoe*, corresponding with an O.G. Godizo, of which Cotiso, mentioned in Horace (p. 20), is a High German form ; and *Abbiss*, corresponding with the name, Abissa, of the son of Hengest, from, as supposed, Gothic *aba*, man. And we have *Prentiss*, corresponding with an A.S. Prentsa ·(= Prentisa), respecting which I have elsewhere suggested that the name should be properly Pentsa. Another name which I take to be from this ending is *Daisy*. There is an A.S. Dægsa, which as Dagsi, with the alternative ending in *i*, would give us *Daisy*. We have another name, *Gipsy*, which I take to be from Gibb or Gipp (A.S. *geban*, to give) with this ending. This ending in *is* is naturally very apt to be corrupted into *ish*, and it is from this source, I take it, that we have such names as *Radish, Reddish, Varnish, Burnish,* and *Parish,* the two last of which we have also in their proper form as *Burness,* and *Parez* or *Paris.*

The ending in *cock.*

This ending is not one that enters into the Teutonic system, unless so far as it may turn out to be a corruption of something else. I have not met with it earlier than A.D. 1400, nor do I know of anything to make me think that it is much older. There has been at different times a good deal of discussion as to its origin in *Notes and Queries* and elsewhere. Mr. Lower has supposed it to be a diminutive, for which I do not think that any etymological sanction can be found, unless indeed we can suppose it to be a corruption of the diminutive *eck* or *ock* before referred to, which seems not impossible. But on the whole I am disposed to agree with the suggestion of a writer in *Notes and Queries* that *cock* is a corruption of *cot,*—not, however, in the sense which I suppose him to entertain, of *cot* as a local word, but of *cot* as an ancient ending, the High German form of *gaud* or *got,* signifying, as supposed, "Goth." So far as the phonetic relationship between the two words *cock* and *cot* is concerned, we have an instance, among others, in our word *apricot,* which was originally *apricock.*

D

I am influenced very much in coming to the above conclusion by finding *coq* as a not unfrequent ending in French names, as in *Balcoq* and *Billecoq*, also in *Aucoq*, *Lecoq*, *Videcocq*, *Vilcocq*, which latter seem to be names corresponding with our *Alcock*, *Laycock*, *Woodcock*, and *Willcock*. They might all be formed on Teutonic stems, if we suppose *Lecoq* and *Laycock* to have lost a *d*, like *Lewis* and *Lucas*, from *leod*, people. Now, that the ending *gaud*, with its alternative forms *got*, *caud*, *cot*, is present in French names as well as in English will be clearly seen from the following. From the Old German Faregaud we have *Faragut*, and the French have *Farcot ;* from the O.G. Benigaud they have *Penicaud*, and we have *Pennycad ;* from the O.G. Ermingaud they have *Armingaud*, and from Megingaud they have *Maingot ;* from the O.G. Aringaud we have *Heringaud*, from Wulfegaud we have *Woolcot*, from Adogoto we have *Addicott*, and from Madalgaud we have *Medlicott.* I am also disposed on the same principle to take *Northcott*, notwithstanding its local appearance, to represent the O.G. name Nordgaud, and in this case we have also the name *Norcock* to compare.

Presuming the above derivation to be the correct one, the question then arises,—Has this ending come to us through the French, or has the corruption proceeded simultaneously in both countries? That the latter has been the case, the French *Videcocq*, as compared with our *Woodcock*, goes some way to show, the one having the High German form *vid* or *wid*, and the other the Saxon form *wud.* I may also mention, as being, so far as it goes, in accordance with the above theory, that we have a number of names both in the form of *cot* and *cock*, as *Adcock* and *Addicot, Alcock* and *Alcott, Norcott* and *Norcock, Jeff-cock* and *Jeffcott.* I do not, however, desire to come to a definite conclusion, though, as far as I am able to carry it, the inquiry seems in favour of the view which I have advocated. But the whole subject will bear some further elucidation.

CHAPTER III.

THE subject of the relative antiquity of simple names (*i.e.* those formed from one single word) and of compound names is one which has occupied a good deal of the attention of the Germans. And the conclusion at which some of them at least seem to have arrived, and which perhaps has been stated the most distinctly by Stark, is that the compound names are the older of the two. And the principal ground upon which this conclusion is based seems to be this, that in a very great number of cases we find that a simple name was used as a contraction of a compound name, just as we use Will for William, and Ben for Benjamin. Stark, in particular, has gone into the subject with German thoroughness, and produced a most complete list of instances of such contractions, such as Freddo for Fredibert, Wulf for Wulfric, Benno for Bernhard ; and among the Anglo-Saxons, Eada for Edwine, and Siga for Siwerd, &c., from which he seems to arrive at the general conclusion that simple names are in all cases contractions of compound names.

Nevertheless, I must say that it seems to me that to assume the compound to be older than the simple looks very much like something that is contrary to first principles, and indeed the very fact that simple names are so often used in place of compounds appears to me to show that they are more natural to men, and that men would generally adopt them if they could. I cannot but think then, going back to the far remote origin of Teutonic names, that the vocabulary of single words must have been exhausted before men began to take to the use of compounds. When this period arrived, and when the confusion arising from so many men being called by the same name could no longer be endured, some other course required to be adopted. And the course that was adopted was—I put this forward only as a theory— when the range of single names was exhausted, to *put two names together.* The number of changes that could be thus introduced was sufficient for all purposes, and there is, as I believe, no established case of a Teutonic name being formed of more than two words. From this point of view Teutonic names would not be translatable, or formed with any view to a meaning, and this is, as it seems to me, what was in fact the case, as a general rule, though I should be very far from laying it down as a universal principle. If names were formed with a view to a meaning, it does not seem very probable that we should have a name compounded with two words, both of which signify war; still less with two words, one of which signifies peace and the other war. "Bold in war" might have a meaning, but "bold in peace," if it means anything,

seems satirical. In point of fact, there was a certain
set of words on which the changes were rung in
forming names without any apparent reference either
to meaning or congruity. Thus we find that the early
Frankish converts in the time of Charlemagne, the
staple of whose names was German derived from their
heathen ancestors, adopted not a few words of
Christian import from the Latin or the Hebrew, and
mixed them up with the old words to which they had
been accustomed in their names. Thus a woman
called Electa, no doubt meaning "elect," calls her son
Electardus (*hard*, fortis) ; thus from *pasc* (passover) is
formed Pascoin (*wine*, friend) ; from the name of
Christ·himself is formed Cristengaudus (*gaud*, Goth.)
Now these are three of the common endings of German
names, but no one can suppose that any sense was
intended to be made out of them here, or that they
were given for any other reason than that they were
the sort of words out of which men had been
accustomed to form their names. Indeed, the idea
present to the minds of the parents seems to have
been in many cases to connect the names of their
children with their own, rather than anything else, by
retaining the first word of the compound and vary-
ing the second. Thus a man called Girveus and his
wife Ermengildis give their children the names of
Giroardus, Girfridis, Gertrudis, Ermena, and Ermen-
gardis, three of the names connecting with that of the
father, and two with that of the mother. In the case
of a man called Ratgaudus and his wife Deodata,
the names of four of the children are Ratharius,
Ratgarius, Ratrudis, and Deodatus, the names of two

other children being different. Many other instances might be given of this sort of yearning for some kind of a connecting-link in the names of a family. Now the people by whom these names were given were common peasants and serfs, so that the case was not one like that of the Anglo-Saxon kings of Northumbria, among whose names the prefix *os*, signifying "semideus," and expressive of a claim to a divine lineage, was of such frequent recurrence. It may be a question then whether, while the former word of the compound connected with the father or the mother, the latter part did not sometimes connect with some other relative whose name it was desired to commemorate, giving the effect that is now frequently expressed by a Christian name and a surname. Again, when we look at the remote origin of these names, when we find in the opening century of our era, and who can tell for how many centuries before, precisely the same names that have been current in all these centuries since, we can hardly doubt that some of these names, derived from words that had long died out from the language, must have been used even in ancient times without any more thought of their meaning than parents have now when they call a child Henry or John. I desire, however, to put forward the above theory as to the origin of compound names rather with a view of raising the question than of expressing a definite conclusion.

The vowel ending in *a*, *i*, or *o*, to which I have referred as in general use in the case of simple names was not used in the case of compounds, unless indeed it happened to be an original part of the second word as in Frithubodo, from *bodo*, messenger. Only in the case of women, to mark the sex, the ending in *a* was given. And in the case of some names, such as *Gertrud*, in which the second part is a word that could only be given to a woman, as no vowel-ending was required, so none was given.

I now proceed to give a list of the principal compounds occurring in English names, with the ancient forms corresponding. I have been obliged, as a matter of necessity, to compare our names more frequently with Old German than with Anglo-Saxon equivalents, on account of the former having been collected and collated—a work which it remains for some one of our well qualified Anglo-Saxon scholars to do with regard to the latter.

The meanings which I have assigned for these names are such as have been most generally adopted by the German writers who have made a special study of the subject. But it must be borne in mind that this study is one in which there is no context by which conclusions can be verified, and that in the vast majority of cases we have nothing more to go upon than a reasonable presumption.

Adal, athel, ethel, " noble."

(*Hard*, fortis), Old Germ. Adalhard—Ang.-Sax. Ethelhard—Eng. *Adlard*. (*Helm*), O.G. Adalhelm—Eng. *Adlam*. (*Hari*, warrior), A.S. Ethilheri—Eng. *Edlery*. (*Stan*, stone), A.S. Æthelstan—Eng. *Ethelston*.

Ag, ac, ec, " point, edge."

(*Hard*, fortis), O.G. Agihard—Eng. *Haggard*. (*Hari*, warrior), O.G. Agiher, Egiher—Eng. *Agar, Eager*. (*Leof*

• dear), O.N. Eylifr — Eng. *Ayliffe*. (*Man*, vir), O.G. Egiman—A.S. Æcemann—Eng. *Hayman, Aikman*. (*Mund*, protection), A.S. Agemund—Eng. *Hammond*. (*Ward*), O.G. Eguard—A.S. Hayward—Eng. *Hayward*.

Agil, Ail, of uncertain meaning, but perhaps formed on the previous stem *Ag*.

(*Gar*, spear), O.G. Egilger, Ailger—Eng. *Ailger*. (*Hard*, fortis), O.G. Agilard, Ailard—Eng. *Aylard*. (*Man*), O.G. Aigliman—Eng. *Ailman*. (*Mar*, famous), O.G. Agilmar, Ailemar—Eng. *Aylmer*. (*Ward*, guardian), O.G. Agilward, Ailward—Eng. *Aylward*. (*Wine*, friend), A.S. Aegelwine— Eng. *Aylwin*.

Alb, Alf, signifying " elf."

(*Hard*, fortis), O.G. Alfhard—Eng. *Alvert*. (*Hari*, warrior), A.S. Ælfhere—O.G. Alfheri, Albheri — Eng. *Alvary, Albery, Aubrey*. (*Rad, red*, counsel), O.G. Alberat— A.S. Alfred—Eng. *Alfred*. (*Run*, mystery), O.G. Albrun[1]— Eng. *Auberon*.

Ald, signifying " old."

(*Bert*, famous), O.G. Aldebert—Eng. *Aldebert*. (*Hari*, warrior), A.S. Aldheri—Eng. *Alder, Audrey*. (*Gar*, spear), A.S. Eldecar (Moneyer of Edmund)—Eng. *Oldacre* (?). (*Rad*, red, counsel), O.G. Aldrad—Eng. *Aldred, Eldred*. (*Rit*, ride), O.G. Aldarit—Eng. *Aldritt*. (*Ric*, rule), O.G. Alderich, Olderich, Altrih—Eng. *Aldrich, Oldridge, Altree*. (*Man*, vir), A.S. Ealdmann—Eng. *Altman*.

Amal, of uncertain meaning.

(*Gar*, spear), O.G. Amalgar—Eng. *Almiger*. (*Hari*, warrior), O.G. Amalhari, Amalher—Eng. *Ambler, Emeler*.

---

[1] Hence I take to be the name of the fairy king Oberon. Albruna was also the name of a "wise woman" among the ancient Germans referred to by Tacitus.

Angel, signifying "hook, barb" (?).

(*Bert,* famous), O.G. Engilbert—Eng. *Engleburt.* (*Hard,* fortis), O.G. Englehart—Eng. *Engleheart.* (*Hari,* warrior), O.G. Angelher—Eng. *Angler.* (*Man*), O.G. Angilman— Eng. *Angleman.* (*Dio,* servant), O.G. Engildeo—A.S. Angeltheow—Eng. *Ingledew.* (*Sind,* companion), O.G. Ingilsind—Eng. *Inglesent.*

Ans, High Germ. form of A.S. *os,* "semi-deus."

(*Hard,* fortis), O.G. Ansard—Eng. *Hansard.* (*Hari,* warrior), O.G. Ansher — Eng. *Anser.* (*Helm*), O.G. Anshelm—Eng. *Anselme, Hansom.*   •

Ark, Arch (see page 16).

(*Bald,* bold), Eng. *Archbold.* (*Bud,* envoy), O.G. Argebud—Eng. *Archbutt.* (*Hard,* fortis), O.G. Archard— Eng. *Archard.* (*Hari,* warrior), O.G. Erchear—Archere, *Roll of Battle Abbey*—Eng. *Archer.* (*Rat,* counsel), O.G. Archarat—Eng. *Arkwright* (?). (*Mund,* protection), O.G. Argemund—Eng. *Argument.*

Aud, Aut, High Germ. form of A.S. *ead,* "prosperity."

(*Hari,* warrior), O.G. Authar—Eng. *Auther.* (*Ric,* rule), O.G. Audricus—Eng. *Auterac.* (*Ram,* raven), O.G. Audram— Eng., *Autram, Outram.*

All (see page 16).

(*Frid,* peace), O.G. Alufrid—Eng. *Allfrey.* (*Gar,* spear), A.S. Algar—Eng. *Alger.* (*Hard,* fortis), A.S. Ealhard— Eng. *Allard.* (*Mar,* famous), O.G. Alamar—Eng. *Almar.* (*Mund,* protection), A.S. Ealmund—O.G. Alamunt—Eng. *Almond, Alment.* (*Noth,* bold), A.S. Ælnoth—Eng. *Allnut.* (*Ward*), O.G. Aloard—A.S. Alwerd—Eng. *Allward.* (*Wid,* wood), O.G. Aluid—Eng. *Allwood.* (*Wig, wi,* war), A.S.

Alewih—Eng. *Allaway*.[1] (*Wine*, friend), O.G. Allowin—Eng. *Alwin*.

Al, el, probably "foreigner." *ξενο* -

(*Bod*, envoy), O.G. Ellebod—Eng. *Albutt*. (*Gaud*, Goth), O.G. Eligaud—Eng. *Allgood, Elgood*. (*Gar*, spear), O.G. Elger—Eng. *Elgar*. (*Hard*, fortis), O.G. Eleard—Eng. *Ellard*. (*Hari*, warrior), O.G. Elier—Eng. *Ellery*. (*Mar*, famous), O.G. Alimer—Eng. *Elmore*. (*Mund*, protection), Elmund, *Domesday*—Eng. *Element*. (*Wine*, friend), Elwin, *Lib. Vit.*—Eng. *Elwin*. (*Wood*), Elwod, *Lib. Vit.*—Eng. *Elwood*. (*Gern*, eager), O.G. Aligern—Eng. *Hallgreen*.

Ad, at (Gothic, *atta*), "father."

(*Gis*, hostage), O.G. Atgis—Eng. *Atkiss*. (*Gaud*, Goth), O.G. Adogoto—Eng. *Addicott*. (*Hari*, warrior), O.G. Adohar—Eng. *Adier*. (*Mar*, famous), O.G. Adamar—Eng. *Atmore*. (*Ric*, rule), A.S. Ætheric—Eng. *Attridge*. (*Rid*, ride), O.G. Atharid—Eng. *Attride*. (*Wulf*), A.S. Athulf—Eng. *Adolph*.

An, han (O.H.G. *ano*), "ancestor."

(*Fred*, peace), O.G. Enfrid—Eng. *Henfrey*. (*Gar*, spear), O.G. Anager, Eneger—Eng. *Hanger, Henniker*. (*Man*, vir), O.G. Enman—Eng. *Hanman, Henman*. (*Rad*, counsel), O.G. Henred—Eng. *Hanrot*. (*Wald*, rule), O.G. Anawalt —Eng. *Anhault*.

Arm, of uncertain meaning.

(*Gar*, spear), O.G. Ermgar—Eng. *Armiger*. (*Gild*, value ?) O.G. Ermegild—Eng. *Armgold*. (*Had*, war), O.G. Ermhad —Eng. *Armat*. (*Hari*, warrior), O.G. Ermhar—Eng. *Armour, Armory*. (*Rad*, counsel), O.G. Ermerad—Eng. *Ormerod*.

---

[1] Probably also A.S. Haluiu—Eng. *Halloway*.

Armin, of uncertain meaning

(*Gar,* spear), O.G. Irminger—Eng. *Irminger, Arminger*
(*Hari,* warrior), O.G. Irminhar—Eng. *Arminer.*

* *Arn, ern* (A.S. *earn*), "eagle."

(*Hari,* warrior), O.G. Arnheri—Eng. *Harnor.* (*Helm*),
O.G. Arnhalm—Eng. *Arnum.* (*Wald,* rule), O.G. Arnoald
—Eng. *Arnold.* (*Wulf*), O.G. Arnulf—Eng. *Arnulfe.*

Ask, ash, perhaps in the sense of "spear."

(*Bert,* famous), A.S. Æscbyrht—Eng. *Ashpart.* (*Hari,*
warrior), A.S. Æschere—Eng. *Asher.* (*Bald,* fortis), Eng.
Ashbold. (*Man,* vir), A.S. Æscmann—Aschmann, *Hund.*
Rolls—Eng. *Ashman.* (*Mar,* famous), A.S. Æscmer—Eng.
Ashmore. (*Wid,* wood), O.G. Asquid—Ascuit, *Domesday*
—Eng. *Asquith, Ashwith.* (*Wine,* friend), A.S. Æscwine—
Eng. *Ashwin.* (*Wulf*), O.G. Ascolf—Eng. *Ascough.*

A.S. *beado,* "war."

(*Hari,* warrior), O.G. Bathari—Eng. *Badder, Bather.*
(*Hard,* fortis), A.S. Badherd—Beadheard, *Lib. Vit.*—Eng.
Beddard. (*Man,* vir), Badumon, *Lib. Vit.*—Eng. *Badman.*
(*Ric,* rule), O.G. Betterich—A.S. Bædric—Eng. *Betteridge.*
(*Ulf,* wolf), O.G. Badulf—Eng. *Biddulph.*

Bald, "fortis."

(*Hari,* warrior), A.S. Baldhere—Eng. *Balder, Boldery.*
(*Ric,* rule), O.G. Baldric, Baldrih—Eng. *Baldridge, Baldry.*
(*Wine,* friend), A.S. Baldwine—Eng. *Baldwin.*

A.S. *band, bend,* "crown, chaplet."

(*Hard,* fortis), O.G. Pantard—Eng. *Pindard.* (*Hari,*
warrior), A.S. Pender—Eng. *Pender.* (*Rad,* counsel), O.G.
Bandrad—Eng. *Banderet, Pendered.*

A.S. *ben*, "wound."

(*Gar*, spear), O.G. Benegar—Eng. *Benger.* (*Gaud*, Goth), O.G. Benegaud—Eng. *Pennycad.* (*Hari*, warrior), O.G. Beniher—Eng. *Benner.* (*Man*, vir), Eng. *Beneman*, A.D. 1535, *Penman.* (*Nid*, strife), O.G. Bennid—Eng. *Bennet.*

A.S. *bera*, "bear."

(*Gar*, spear), O.G. Bereger [1]—Eng. *Berger.* (*Grim*, fierce), O.G. Peragrim—Eng. *Paragreen.* (*Hard*, fortis), O.G. Berhard—Eng. *Barehard.* (*Hari*, warrior), O.G. Beriher—Eng. *Berrier.* (*Helm*), O.G. Perrhelm—Eng. *Perriam.* (*Land*, terra), O.G. Perelant—Eng. *Purland.* (*Man*, vir), O.G. Berman—Eng. *Burman, Perman.* (*Mar*, famous), O.G. Bermar—Eng. *Barmore, Paramore.* (*Rat*, counsel), O.G. Perratt—Eng. *Perrott.* (*Dio*, servant), O.G. Peradeo—Eng. *Purdue.* (*Ward*), O.G. Beroward—Eng. *Berward.* (*Wise*, sapiens), O.G. Berois (= Berwis)—Eng. *Barwise.*

Berin, bern, "bear."

(*Gar*, spear), O.G. Beringar—Eng. *Berringer.* (*Hard*, fortis), O.G. Berinhard—Eng. *Bernard.* (*Hari*, warrior), O.G. Bernher, Pernher—Eng. *Berner, Pirner.* (*Wald*, rule), O.G. Berneold—Eng. *Bernold.* (*Kel*, for *Ketil*), O.N. Biornkel—Eng. *Barnacle.*

Bil, supposed to mean "mildness, gentleness."

(*Frid*, peace), O.G. Bilfrid—Eng. *Belfry.* (*Grim*, fierce), O.G. Biligrim, Pilgrim—Eng. *Pilgrim.* (*Mar*, famous), O.G. Belemar—Eng. *Billamore, Belmore.* (*Gard*, protection), O.G. Biligard—Eng. *Billiard.* (*Mund*, protection), O.G. Pilimunt—Eng. *Belment.* (*Wald*, rule), Biliald, *Lib. Vit.*—Eng. *Billyald.*

---

[1] Here probably the name Biracrus, on Roman pottery, corresponding with an O.G. form, Berecar.

Bert, " bright, illustrious."   *þran*

(*Ram,* raven), O.G. Bertram—Eng. *Bertram.* (*Land,*
terra), O.G. Bertland—Eng. *Brightland.* (*Mar,* famous),
A.S. Brihtmar—Eng. *Brightmore.* (*Rand,* shield), O.G.
Bertrand—Eng. *Bertrand.* (*Ric,* rule), O.G. Perhtric—
A.S. Brihtric—Partriche, *Hund. Rolls*—Eng. *Partrick,
Partridge.* (*Wine,* friend), A.S. Brihtwine—Eng. *Bright-
wine.*

Black, blake, signifying " brightness."

(*Hari,* warrior), O.G. Blicher—Eng. *Blacker, Blaker.*
(*Man*), A.S. Blæcman (genealogy of the kings of North-
umbria), Blacman (Moneyer at Norwich)—Blaecmon, *Llb.
Vit.*—Blacheman, *Domesday*—Eng. *Blackman, Blakeman.*
(*Wine,* friend), Eng. *Blackwin.*

Bod, bud, " envoy."

(*Gar,* spear), O.G. Baudochar—Eng. *Bodicker.* (*Hari,*
warrior), O.G. Botthar—Boterus, *Domesday*—Eng. *Butter,
Buttery.* (*Gis,* hostage), O.G. Boutgis, Boggis—Eng.
Boggis. (*Mar,* famous), O.G. Baudomir—Eng. *Bodmer.*
(*Ric,* rule), O.G. Buttericus, Bauderich—Eng. *Butterick,
Buddrich.* (*Rid, rit,* " ride "), O.G. Bodirid, Buotrit—
Eng. *Botright.*

Boll, bull (prob. M.H.G. *buole*), " friend."

(*Gar,* spear), O.G. Pulgar—Eng. *Bulger.* (*Hard*),
Pollardus, *Domesday*—Eng. *Bullard, Pollard.* (*Hari,*
warrior), O.G. Bolheri—Eng. *Buller.* (*Mar,* famous), A.S.
Bulemær—Eng. *Bulmer.*

Burg, signifying " protection."

(*Hard*), A.S. Burghard—Eng. *Burchard.* (*Hari,* warrior),
O.G. Burghar—Eng. *Burger.* ,(*Wald,* rule), O.G. Burgoald
—Eng. *Purgold.* (*Wine,* friend), Eng. *Burgwin.*

Ball, *bale*, signifying " bale, woe."

(*Frid*, peace), O.G. Palfrid—Eng. *Palfrey*. (*Mar*, famous), O.G. Ballomar, Belimar—Eng. *Balmer*, *Bellmore*.

Coll, signifying "helmet."

(*Brand*, sword), A.S. Colbrand—Eng. *Colbran*. (*Biorn*, bear), O.N. Kolbiorn—Eng. *Colburn*. (*Man*, vir), A.S. Col man—Eng. *Colman*. (*Mar*, famous), A.S. Colomôr—Eng *Collamore*. (*Hard*), A.S. Ceolheard—Eng. *Collard*.

Cost, *cust*, " skill, science " (Germ. *kunst*).

(*Hard*), O.G. Custard—Eng. *Custard*.

Dag, " day," in the sense of brightness, glory.[1]

(*Bald*, bold), O.G. Tagapald—Daegbald, *Lib. Vit.*—Eng. *Daybell*. (*Bern*, bear), O.G. Tagapern—Eng. *Tayburn*. (*Burg*, protection), O.G. Tagabirg—Eng. *Tackabarry*. (*Gisil*, hostage), O.G. Daigisil—Eng. *Daggesell*. (*Hari*, warrior), O.G. Daiher—Dacher, *Lib. Vit.*—Eng. *Dagger*, *Dacker*, *Dayer*. (*Helm*), O.G. Dachelm—Eng. *Dacombe*. (*Mund*, protection), O.G. Dagamund—A.S. Daiemond—Eng. *Daymont*. (*Mar*, famous), O.G. Dagemar—Dagemar on Roman pottery—Eng. *Damer*.

Dall, *dell*, as supposed, " illustrious.'

(*Bert*, famous), O.G. Dalbert—Talbercht, *Lib. Vit.*—Eng. *Talbert*. (*Fare*, travel), O.G. Dalferi—Eng. *Telfer*. (*Hari*, warrior), O.G. Dealher—Eng. *Deller*. (*Man*), O.G. Dalman —Eng. *Dalman*, *Tallman*. (*Wig*, *wi*, war), Daliwey, *Hund. Rolls*—Eng. *Dalloway*.

[1] Or perhaps of beauty, like a Celtic stem *tac*, found in names of men, and perhaps a corresponding word.

Dan, den, of uncertain meaning, perhaps, " Dane."
(*Hard*), A.S. Dæneheard—Eng. *Denhard.* (*Gar,* spear),
O.G. Thangar—Eng. *Danger.* (*Wulf*), A.S. Denewulf—
Eng. *Denolf.*

Dar, signifying "spear."

(*Nagel,* nail), A.S. Dearnagel—Eng. *Darnell.* (*Gund,*
war), O.G. Taragun—Eng. *Darrigon.* (*Wine,* friend), O.G.
Daroin—Eng. *Darwin.*

Dear, "carus."

(*Leof,* dear), A.S. Deorlaf—Eng. *Dearlove.* (*Man,* vir),
Dereman, *Domesday*—Eng. *Dearman.* (*Môd,* courage),
A.S. Deormod—Eng. *Dermott.* (*Wine,* friend), A.S.
Deorwyn—Eng. *Derwin.*

Gothic, *thius* (O.H.G. *dio*), "servant."

(*Log, loh,* clean?), O.G. Thioloh—Eng. *Dialogue.* (*Mad,*
reverence), O.G. Deomad—Eng. *Demaid.* (*Man,* vir),
O.G. Dioman—Eng. *Demon.* (*Mund,* protection), O.G.
Thiomunt—Eng. *Diamond.*

Old North. *dolgr,* "foe."

(*Fin,* people's name), O.N. Dolgfinnr—Eng. *Dolphin.*
(*Man,* vir), A.S. Dolemann—Eng. *Dolman.*

A.S. *dôm* (O.H.G. *tuom*), "judgment."

(*Gis,* hostage), O.G. Domigis, Tomichis—Eng. *Tomkies.*
(*Hard,* fortis), O.G. Domard—Eng. *Dummert.* (*Hari,*
warrior), O.G. Domarius—Domheri, *Lib. Vit.*—Eng. *Dum-
mer.*

A.S. *dugan,* to be "doughty."

(*Man,* vir), O.G. Dugiman, Tugeman—A.S. Ducemann—
Eng. *Tugman, Duckman.* (*Mar,* famous), O.G. Daumerus

—Eng. *Dugmore.* Probably from the noun, *duguth,* virtue, A.S. Dogod—Eng. *Doggett, Dugood.*

Erl, supposed same as " earl."

(*Bad,* war), O.G. Erlebad—Eng. *Hurlbat.* (*Bert,* famous), O.G. Erlebert—Eng. *Hurlburt.* (*Hari,* warrior), O.G. Erleher—Eng. *Hurler.* (*Wine,* friend), O.G. Erliwin, A.S. Herlawine—Eng. *Urlwin.*

Evor, " boar."

(*Hard,* fortis), O.G. Everhard—Eng. *Everard, Earheart.* (*Rad,* counsel), O.G. Eburrad—Eng. *Evered, Everett.* (*Ric,* rule), O.G. Eburicus—Eng. *Every.* (*Wacar,* watchful), O.G. Eburacar—Eureuuacre, *Domesday*—Eng. *Earwaker.* (*Wig,* war), O.G. Eberwic—A.S. Earwig—Eng. *Earwig.*

Anglo-Saxon *eâd,* " prosperity."

(*Burg,* protection), A.S. Eadburh—Eng. *Edbrook.* (*Gar,* spear), A.S. Eadgar—Eng. *Edgar.* (*Mund,* protection), A.S. Eadmund—Eng. *Edmond.* (*Ric,* rule), A.S. Eadric— Eng. *Edridge.* (*Ward*), A.S. Eadweard—Eng. *Edward.* (*Wig,* war), A.S. Eadwig—Eng. *Edwick.* (*Wulf*), A.S. Eadwulf—Eng. *Edolph.* (*Wacar,* watchful), O.G. Odoacer —A.S. Edwaker—Eng. *Eddiker?*

Far, fare, signifying " travel."

(*And,* life, spirit), O.G. Ferrand, Eng. *Ferrand.* (*Gaud,* Goth), O.G. Faregaud—Eng. *Farragut, Forget.* (*Hari,* warrior), O.G. Feriher—Eng. *Ferrier.* (*Man*), O.G. Faraman—Fareman, *Hund. Rolls*—Eng. *Fairman.* (*Mund,* protection), O.G. Faramund—Eng. *Farrimond* (*Ward*), O.G. Faroard—Eng. *Forward.*

E

Fard, also signifying " travel."

(*Hari,* warrior), A.S. Forthere—Eng. *Forder.* (*Man*), O.G. Fartman—Eng. *Fortyman.* (*Nand,* daring), O.G. Ferdinand—Eng. *Ferdinand.* (*Rad,* counsel), Forthred, *Lib. Vit.,*—Eng. *Fordred.*

Fil, ful, signifying " great."

(*Bert,* famous), O.G. Filibert—Eng. *Filbert.* (*Gar,* spear), —Eng. *Fullagar.* (*Leof,* dear), O.G. Filuliub—Eng. *Fullalove.* (*Man*), O.G. Filiman—Eng. *Filemàn.* (*Mar,* famous), A.S. Fealamar, O.G. Filomor—Eng. *Fillmer,* *Phillimore.* (*Dio, thius,* servant), O.G. Filethius—Eng. *Filldew.*

Frid, free,[1] signifying " peace."

(*Bad,* war), O.G. Fridibad—Eng. *Freebout.* (*Bern,* bear), O.G. Fridubern—Friebern *Domesday*—Eng. *Freeborn.* (*Bod,* envoy), O.G. Frithubodo—Eng. *Freebody.* (*Lind* gentle), O.G. Fridulind—Frelond *Hund. Rolls*—Eng. *Freeland.* (*Ric,* rule), O.G. Frithuric—Eng. *Frederick.* (*Stan,* stone), A.S. Frithestan—Eng. *Freestone.*

Fin, supposed from " the nation."

(*Bog,* bow), Old Norse, Finbogi—Eng. *Finbow.* (*Gar,* spear), Old Norse, Finngeir—Eng. *Finger.*

Gad, of uncertain meaning, perhaps " friend "

(*Man,* vir), A.S. Cædmon—Eng. *Cadman.* (*Leof,* dear), —Eng. *Gatliffe.*

---

[1] As an ending also *frid* commonly becomes *free,* as in Humphrey from Humfrid, Godfrey from Godfred, Geoffry from Galfrid.

Gal, signifying " spirit, cheerfulness."

(*And,* life, spirit), Galaunt, *Hund. Rolls*—Eng. *Galland, Gallant.* (*Frid,* peace), A.S. Galfrid, Gaufrid—Eng. *Geoffry.* (*Hard*), Gallard *Hund Rolls*—Eng. *Gallard.* (*Wig,* war), O.G. Geilwih—Galaway, *Hund. Rolls*—Eng. *Galloway.*

Gand, signifying "wolf."

(*Hari,* warrior), O.G. Ganthar—A.S. Gandar—Eng. *Gander, Ganter.* (*Ric,* rule), O.G. Gendirih, Cantrih—Eng. *Gentery, Gentry, Chantrey.*

Gar, signifying " spear."

(*Bad,* war), O.G. Kerpat—Eng. *Garbett.* (*Bald*), O.G. Garibald, Kerbald—Eng. *Gorbold, Corbould.* (*Brand,* sword), O.G. Gerbrand—Eng. *Garbrand.* (*Brun,* bright), O.G. Gerbrun—Eng. *Gorebrown.* (*Bod,* envoy), O.G. Gaerbod—Gerbode *Lib. Vit.*—Eng. *Garbutt.* (*Hard*), O.G. Garehard—Eng. *Garrard.* (*Hari,* warrior), O.G. Garoheri, Caroheri—Eng. *Carary, Carrier.* (*Lac,* play), O.G. Gerlac —Eng *Garlick.* (*Man*), O.G. Garaman—A.S. Jaruman— Eng. *Garman, Jarman.* (*Mund,* protection), O.G. Gari-mund—Eng. *Garment.* (*Noth,* bold), O.G. Garnot—Eng. *Garnett.* (*Rod,* red), O.G. Kaerrod—Old Norse, Geirraudr Eng. *Garrod.* (*Laif,* relic), O.G. Gerlef—Eng. *Gerloff.* (*Ferhth,* life, spirit), Gerferth, *Lib. Vit.*—Eng. *Garforth.* (*Stan,* stone), O.G. Kerstin—Eng. *Garstin.* (*Wald,* power), O.G. Garold—Eng. *Garrold.* (*Was,* keen), O.G. Gervas— Eng. *Jervis.* (*Wid,* wood), O.G. Gervid—Eng. *Garwood.* (*Wig,* war), O.G. Garavig, Gerwi—Eng. *Garroway, Garvey.* (*Wine,* friend), O.G. Gerwin, Caroin—Eng. *Curwen ?* [1] (*Van,* beauty), O.G. Geravan—Eng. *Caravan.*

---

[1] This name might perhaps be from the Irish Cwaran, whence probably the present *Curran*. This name appears also to have

Gan, gen, supposed to mean " magic, sorcery."

(*Bert,* famous), O.G. Gimbert—Eng. *Gimbert.* (*Had,* war), O.G. Genad—Eng. *Gennett.* (*Hari,* warrior), O.G. Genear, Ginheri—Eng. *Genner, Jennery.* (*Rid,* ride), O.G. Generid—Eng. *Jeannerett.*

Gab, Geb, Eng. " give."

(*Bert,* famous), O.G. Gibert—Eng. *Gippert.* (*Hard*), O.G. Gebahard, Givard—Eng. *Giffard.* (*Hari,* warrior), O.G. Gebaheri—Eng. *Gaffery.*

Gart, cart, signifying " protection."

(*Hari,* warrior), O.G. Gardar, Karthar—Eng. *Garter, Carder.* (*Dio,* servant), O.G. Cartdiuha—Eng. *Carthew.* (*Ric,* rule), A.S. Gyrdhricg—Eng. *Cartridge.*

Gald, gold, " reddere, valere."

(*Birin,* bear), O.G. Goldpirin—Eng. *Goldbourne.* (*Red,* counsel), O.G. Goltered—Eng. *Coulthred.* (*Ric,* rule), O.G. Goldericus—Eng. *Goldrick.* (*Run,* mystery), O.G. Goldrun, Coldrun—Coldrun *Lib. Vit.*—Eng *Calderon.* (*Wine,* friend), O.G. Gildewin—Eng. *Goldwin.*

Geld, gild, probably same as above.

(*Hard*), O.G. Gildard—Eng. *Gildert.* (*Hari,* warrior), O.G. Gelther—Eng. *Gilder.* (*Wig, wi,* war), O.G. Geltwi —Eng. *Gildawie.*

Gisal, gil, " hostage."

(*Bert,* famous), O.G. Gisalbert, Gilbert—Eng. *Gilbert. Brand,* sword), O.G. Gislebrand—Eng. *Gillibrand.* (*Frid,*

been sometimes borrowed by the Northmen, as in the case of Olaf Cwaran.

péace), O.G. Gisalfred—Eng. *Gillford.* (*Hard*), O.G.
Giselhard—Eng. *Gillard.* (*Hari*, warrior), O.G. Gisalhar
—A.S. Gislher—Eng. *Giller, Killer.* (*Had*, war), O.G.
Gislehad—Eng. *Gillett.* (*Helm*), O.G. Gisalhelm—Eng.
Gilliam. (*Man*), O.G. Gisleman—Eng. *Gillman, Killman.*
(*Mar*, famous), O.G. Gisalmer—Eng. *Gilmore.*

God, supposed to mean " Deus." [1] *Theo*

(*Bald*), O.G. Godebald—Godebaldus, *Domesday*—Eng.
Godbold, Godbolt, Cobbold. (*Frid*, peace), O.G. Godafrid—
Eng. *Godfrey.* (*Gisil*, hostage), O.G. Godigisil—Eng.
Godsell. (*Heid*, state, " hood "), O.G. Gotaheid—Eng.
Godhead. (*Hard*), O.G. Godehard—Eng. *Goddard, Good-*
heart. (*Hari*, warrior), O.G. Godehar—Eng. *Goddier,*
Goodyear. (*Laif*, relic), O.G. Godolef—Eng. *Goodliffe.*
(*Lac*, play), O.G. Godolec—Eng. *Goodlake.* (*Land*), O.G.
Godoland—Godland *Lib. Vit.*—Eng. *Goodland.* (*Man*),
O.G. Godeman—Godeman *Lib. Vit.*—Eng. *Godman.*
(*Mund*, protection), A.S. Godemund—Eng. *Godmund.*
(*Niu*, young), O.G. Godeniu—Eng. *Goodnow.* (*Ram*,
raven), O.G. Godramnus—Eng. *Goodram.* (*Rad*, counsel),
O.G. Gotrat—Eng. *Goodred.* (*Rit*, ride), O.G. Guderit—
Godritius *Domesday*—Eng. *Goodwright.* (*Ric*, rule),
Godricus *Domesday*—Eng. *Godrick.* (*Scalc*, servant), O.G.
Godscalc—Eng. *Godskall.* (*Ward*), O.G. Godeward—Eng.
Godward. (*Wine*, friend), A.S. Godwine—Eng. *Godwin.*

Goz, Gos, supposed High Germ. form of *gaud* = Goth.

(*Bald*), O.G. Gauzebald—Eng. *Gosbell.* (*Hard*), O.G.
Gozhart, Cozhart—Eng. *Gozzard, Cossart.* (*Hari*, warrior),

[1] But not in a Christian sense, the stem being much older
than Christian times. There is another stem *gaud*, supposed to
mean Goth, very liable to intermix.

O.G. Gauzer, Cozhere—Eng. *Gozar, Cosier.* (*Lind*, gentle), O.G. Gauzlind—Eng. *Gosland.* (*Mar*, famous), O.G. Gozmar—Eng. *Gosmer.* (*Wald*, power), O.G. Gausoald— Eng. *Goswold.*

Grim, " fierce, terrible."

(*Bald*), O.G. Grimbald—Eng. *Grimbald, Grimble.* (*Hari*, warrior), O.G. Grimhar—Eng. *Grimmer.* (*Mund*, protection), O.G. Grimund—Eng. *Grimmond.* (*Hard*), O.G. Grimhard —Eng. *Grimerd.*

Gund, gun, signifying " war."

(*Bald*), O.G. Gundobald, Gumbald—Eng. *Gumboil.* (*Hari*, warrior), O.G. Gunther, Cundher—Eng. *Gunter, Conder.* (*Ric*, rule), O.G. Gunderih—Eng. *Gundry.* (*Stan*, stone), Old Norse, Gunstein—Eng. *Gunston.*

Hun, probably from " the people."

(*Bald*), O.G. Hunibald—Eng. *Hunibal.* (*Frid*, peace), O.G. Hunfrid, Humfrid—Eng. *Humphrey.* (*Gar*, spear), O.G. Hunger—Eng. *Hunger.* (*Hard*), O.G. Hunard—Eng. *Hunnard.* (*Man*), Huniman *Hund. Rolls*—Eng. *Honeyman.* (*Wald*, power), O.G. Hunewald—Hunewald, *Lib. Vit.*—Eng. *Hunhold.*

Had, hath, signifying " war."

(*Gis*, hostage), O.G. Hadegis—Eng. *Hadkiss.* (*Mar*, famous), O.G. Hadamar—Eng. *Hattemore.* (*Rat*, counsel), O.G. Hadarat—Eng. *Hadrott.* (*Ric*, rule), O.G. Hadaricus —Eng. *Hattrick.* (*Wig*, war), O.G. Hathuwi—Eng. *Hathaway.* (*Wine*, friend), O.G. Hadawin—Eng. *Hadwen.*

Hard, hart, " strong, hardy."

(*Hari*, warrior), O.G. Hardier—Eng. *Harder.* (*Land*, terra), O.G. Artaland—Eng. *Hardland.* (*Man*, vir), O.G.

Hartman—Eng. *Hardman*. (*Mund*, protection), O.G. Hartomund—Eng. *Hardiment*. (*Nagel*, nail), O.G. Hartnagel—Eng. *Hartnoll*. (*Nid*, strife), O G. Hartnit—Eng. *Hartnott*. (*Rat*, counsel), O.G. Hartrat—Eng. *Hartwright*. (*Ric*, rule), O.G. Harderich, Hertrih—Eng. *Hartridge*, *Hartry*. (*Wulf*), O.G. Hardulf—Eng. *Hardoff*. · (*Wig*, war), O.G. Hardwic—Eng. *Hardwick*. (*Wine*, friend), O.G. Hardwin—Eng. *Ardouin*.

Har, her, "army" or "soldier." [1]

(*Bad*, war), O.G. Heripato—Eng. *Herepath*. (*Bert*, famous), O.G. Hariberaht—A.S. Herebritt—Eng. *Harbert*, *Herbert*. (*Bord*, shield), O.G. Heribord—Eng. *Harboard*. (*Bod*, envoy), O.G. Heribod—Eng. *Harbud*. (*Gar*, spear), O.G. Hariker—A.S. Hereger—Eng. *Harker*. (*Gaud*, Goth), O.G. Haregaud—Eng. *Hargood*. (*Land*, terra), O.G. Hariland—Eng. *Harland*. (*Man*, vir), O.G. Hariman—Eng. *Harryman, Harman*. (*Mar*, famous), O.G. Harmar—Eng. *Harmer*. (*Mund*, protection), O.G. Herimund—Eng. *Harmond*. (*Sand*, envoy), O.G. Hersand—Eng. *Hersant*. (*Wald*, rule), A.S. Harald—Eng. *Harold*. (*Ward*), A.S. Hereward—Eng. *Harward*. (*Wid*, wood), O.G. Erwid—Eng. *Harwood*. (*Wig*. war), O.G. Herewig, Hairiveo—Eng. *Harvey*. (*Wine*, friend), O.G. Harwin—A.S. Herewine—Eng. *Harwin*.

Hild, hil, "war."

(*Brand*, sword), O.G. Hildebrand—Eng. *Hildebrand*. (*Gard*, protection), O.G. Hildegard—Eng. *Hildyard*. (*Hari*, warrior), O.G. Hildier—Eng. *Hilder, Hillyer*. (*Man*, vir),

---

[1] As a prefix this may mean "army," but as an ending, where it is often *hari* or *heri* (and perhaps was originally always so), it may be taken, as suggested by Grimm, to mean warrior.

O.G. Hildeman—Eng. *Hillman.* (*Mar*, famous), O.G.
Hildemar—Eng. *Hilmer.* (*Rad*, counsel), O.G. Hildirad
—Eng. *Hildreth.* (*Ric*, rule), O.G. Hilderic—Eng.
Hilridge.

Ing, ink, " son, descendant."

(*Bald*), O.G. Ingobald, Incbald—Eng. *Inchbald.* (*Bert*,
famous), O.G. Ingobert—Eng. *Inchboard.* (*Hari*, warrior),
O.G. Inguheri—Eng. *Ingrey.* (*Ram*, raven), O.G. Ingram
—Eng. *Ingram.* (*Wald*, power), O.G. Ingold—Eng.
Ingold.

Ise, signifying " iron."

(*Burg*, protection), O.G. Hisburg—Eng. *Isburg.* (*Man*),
O.G. Isman—A.S. Hysemann—Eng. *Heasman.* (*Mar*,
famous), O.G. Ismar—Eng. *Ismer.* (*Odd*, dart), Old Norse,
Isodd—Eng. *Izod.*

Isen, signifying " iron."

(*Hard*), O.G. Isanhard—Eng. *Isnard.* (*Hari*, warrior),
O.G. Isanhar—Eng. *Isner.*

Ken, kin, "nobility."

(*Hard*), A.S. Cyneheard—Eng. *Kennard, Kinnaird.*
(*Laf*, relic), A.S. Cynlaf—Eng. *Cunliffe.* (*Mund*, protection),
A.S. Cynemund—Eng. *Kinmonth.* (*Ric*, rule), A.S. Cynric
—Eng. *Kenrick.* (*Ward*), A.S. Cyneweard—Eng. *Kenward.*
(*Wig*, war), Kenewi, *Hund. Rolls*—Eng. *Kennaway.*

Land, "terra."

(*Bert*, famous), O.G. Landbert, Lambert—Eng. *Lambert.*
(*Burg*, protection), O.G. Landburg—Eng. *Lambrook. Frid*,
peace), O.G. Landfrid—Lanfrei *Lib. Vit.*—Eng. *Landfear,
Lanfear, Lamprey.* (*Hari*, warrior), O.G. Landar—Eng.
Lander. (*Ric*, rule), O.G. Landerich—Landric *Domesday*—

Eng. *Landridge, Laundry.* (*Wig,* war), O.G. Lantwih—
Eng. *Lanaway.* (*War,* defence), O.G. Landoar—Eng.
Lanwer. (*Ward*), O.G. *Landward*—Eng. *Landlord?*

Laith, let, "terrible."

(*Hara*), O.G. Lethard—Eng. *Leathart.* (*Hari,* warrior),
O.G. Lethar—Eng. *Leather.* (*Ward*), O.G. Lethward—
Eng. *Lateward.*

Led, lud, "people."

(*Burg,* protection), O.G. Luitburc—Eng. *Ludbrook.*
(*Gar,* spear), O.G. Leodegar—Eng. *Ledger.* (*Gard*), O.G.
Liudgard—A.S. Lidgeard—Eng. *Ledgard.* (*Goz,* Goth),
O.G. Luitgoz, Luikoz—Lucas *Lib. Vit.*—Eng. *Lucas.*
(*Hard*), O.G. Luidhard—Eng. *Liddard.* (*Hari,* warrior),
O.G. Liuthari—A.S. Luder—Eng. *Luther.* (*Man*), O.G.
Liudman—A.S. Ludmann—Eng. *Lutman.* (*Ward*), O.G.
Liudward—Eng. *Ledward.* (*Wig,* war), O.G. Liudwig—
Eng. *Lutwidge.*

Anglo-Saxon *leof,* "dear."

(*Dag,* day), O.G. Leopdag—Luiedai, *Domesday*—Eng.
Loveday. (*Hard*), O.G. Luibhard, Leopard—A.S. Lipperd
—Eng. *Leopard.* (*Hari,* warrior), O.G. Liubheri, Libher—
A.S. Leofer—Eng. *Lover.* (*Lind,* gentle), O.G. Liublind—
Eng. *Loveland.* (*Man*), O.G. Liubman—A.S. Leofmann—
Eng. *Loveman.*[1] (*Mar,* famous), O.G. Liubmar—Eng.
Livemore. (*Ric,* rule), A.S. Leofric—Eng. *Loveridge.* (*Drud,*
friend), O.G. Lipdrud—Eng. *Liptrot.*[2] (*Gaud, goz,* Goth),
O.G. Liobgoz—Eng. *Lovegod, Lovegood.*

[1] Also as a contracted form, Ang.-Sax. Leommann (=Leof-mann, Eng. *Lemon*).
[2] This seems to be a name of an exceptional kind, the ending *drud* being a female one. That our name Liptrot (which I take from Lower), is really from the above origin is rendered the

Mal, signifying to " maul."

(*Hard*), O.G. Mallard—Maularde, *Roll. Batt. Abb.*—Eng.
Mallard. (*Ric,* rule), O.G. Malarich—Eng. *Mallory.*
(*Thius,* servant), O.G. Malutheus—Eng. *Malthus.* (*Wulf*),
O.G. Malulf—Eng. *Maliff.*

Man, as the type of " manliness."

(*Frid,* peace), O.G. Manfrit—Eng. *Manfred.* (*Gar,* spear),
O.G. Mangar—Eng. *Manger.* (*Leof,* dear), A.S. Manlef—
Eng. *Manlove.* (*Gald,* value), O.G. Managold—Eng.
Manigault.

Mar, signifying " famous."

(*Gaud,* Goth), Merigeat *Lib. Vit.*—Eng. *Margot.* (*Gild,*
value), O.G. Margildus—Eng. *Marigold.* (*Wig,* war),
O.G. Merovecus, Maroveus—Eng. *Marwick, Marvey.*
(*Wine,* friend), O.G. Maruin—Mervinus *Lib. Vit.*—Eng.
Marvin.

Mag, may, Goth. *magan,* " valere."

(*Hari,* warrior), O.G. Magher—Eng. *Mager, Mayer.*
(*Had,* war), O.G. Magodius—Magot *Lib. Vit.* — Eng.
Maggot. (*Ron,* raven), O.G. Megiran—Eng. *Megrin.*

Main, also signifying " strength, vigour."

(*Hard*), O.G. Mainard—Eng. *Maynard.*

Mad, med, Anglo-Saxon *math,* " reverence."

(*Hari,* warrior), O.G. Mather—Eng. *Mather.* (*Helm*),
O.G. Madelm—Eng. *Madam.* (*Lac,* play), O.G. Mathlec

more probable by the corresponding name Liebetrut as a present
German name, similarly derived by Foerstemann. But it may
◄ well be that the ending in this case is from a different word to
that which, see p. 19, forms the endings of women's names,
viz. O. H. G. *trut,* amicus, which, as a prefix, enters into several
men's names.

—Eng. *Medlock.* (*Land*), O.G. Madoland—Eng. *Medland.*
(*Man*), O.G. Medeman—Eng. *Maidman, Meddiman.*
(*Wald,* power), O.G. Meduald—Eng. *Methold.* (*Wine,*
friend), Eng. *Medwin.* (*Wig,* war), O.G. Medoveus—Eng.
Meadway.

Madel, medal, " discourse, eloquence."
(*Hari,* warrior), O.G. Madalhar—Eng. *Medlar.* (*Gaud,*
Goth), O.G. Madalgaud—Eng. *Medlicott.*

Mil, mel, of uncertain meaning.
(*Dio,* servant), O.G. Mildeo—Eng. *Mellodew, Melody,
Melloday.* (*Hard*), O.G. Milehard—Eng. *Millard.*

Mald, Anglo-Saxon *meald,* " strife, friction."
(*Wid,* wood), O.G. Maldvit—Maldwith *Domesday*—Eng.
Maltwood.

Ang.-Sax. *môd.* O.H.G. *môt,* "courage."
(*Hari,* warrior), O.G. Muatheri, Modar—Eng. *Mutrie,
Moder.* (*Ram, ran,* raven), O.G. Moderannus—Eng.
Mottram. (*Ric,* rule), O.G. Moderich—Eng. *Mudridge.*

Mark, of uncertain meaning.
(*Hari,* warrior), O.G. Marcher—A.S. Marker—Eng.
Marcher, Marker. (*Leif,* relic), O.G. Marcleif—Eng.
Marklove. (*Wig,* war), O.G. Marcovicus—Eng. *Markwick.*

Old North. *âs,* Ang.-Sax. *ôs,* "semideus."
(*Beorn,* bear), A.S. Osbeorn—Eng. *Osborn.* (*Got,* goth),
A.S. Osgot—Eng. *Osgood.* (*Lac,* play), A.S. Oslac—O.N.
Asleikr—Eng. *Aslock, Hasluck.* (*Man,* vir), O.G. Asman,
Osman—Asseman *Hund. Rolls*—Eng. *Asman, Osman.*
(*Mar,* famous), O.G. Osmer—Osmer, *Domesday*—Eng.
Osmer. (*Ketil*), O.N. Asketil—Eng. *Ashkettle.* (*Mund,*

protection), A.S. Osmond—Eng. *Osmond.* (*Wald*, rule),
A.S. Oswald—Eng. *Oswald.* (*Wine*, friend), A.S. Oswin—
Eng. *Oswin.*

Rad, red, signifying "counsel."

(*Brand*, sword), O.G. Redbrand—Eng. *Redband.* (*Geil*,
elatus), O.G. Ratgeil—Eng. *Redgill.* (*Hari*, warrior), O.G.
Rathere, Rateri—Eng. *Rather, Rattray.* (*Helm*), O.G.
Rathelm—Eng. *Rattham.* (*Leif*, relic), O.G. Ratleib—Eng.
Ratliffe. (*Man*, vir), O.G. Redman—Eng. *Redman.* (*Mar*,
famous), O.G. Radmar, Redmer—Eng. *Radmore, Redmore.*
(*Mund*, protection), O.G. Redemund—Eng. *Redmond.*
(*War*, defence), O.G. Ratwar—Eng *Redwar.* (*Wig*, war),
O.G. Redwi—Eng. *Reddaway.* (*Wine*, friend), A.S. Red-
win—Eng. *Readwin.* (*Bald*, fortis), O.G. Ratbold—Eng.
Rathbold. (*Bern*, bear), O.G. Ratborn, Ratbon—Eng.
Rathbone.

Rag, ray, signifying "counsel."

(*Bald*, fortis), O.G. Ragibald—Eng. *Raybauld, Raybolt.*
(*Hari*, warrior), O.G. Racheri—Eng. *Rarey* (= Ragheri).
(*Helm*), O.G. Rachelm—Eng. *Rackham.* (*Mund*, protection), O.G. Raimond—Eng. *Raymond, Rayment.* (*Ulf*,
wolf), A.S. Rahulf—Raaulf, *Lib. Vit.*—Eng. *Ralph.*

Ragin, rain, same as above.

(*Bert*, famous), O.G. Raginbert, Reinbert—Eng. *Rain-*
bird. (*Bald*, fortis), O.G. Raginbald—Eng. *Raynbold.*
(*Frid*, peace), O.G. Rainfred—Eng. *Rainford.* (*Gar*,
spear), O.G. Raingar, Reginker—Eng. *Ranger, Ranacre.*
(*Hard*, fortis), O.G. Regnard, Rainhard—Eng. *Regnard,*
Reynard. (*Hari*, warrior), O.G. Reginhar—A.S. Reiner—
Eng. *Reyner.* (*Helm*), O.G. Rainelm—Eng. *Raynham,*
(*Wald*, rule), O.G. Reginold—A.S. Reinald—Eng.
Reynolds.

Ric, rich, signifying " rule."

(*Bald,* fortis), O.G. Richbold—Eng. *Richbell.* (*Gard,* protection), O.G. Richgard—Eng. *Ridgyard.* (*Hard,* fortis), O.G. Ricohard—Eng. *Riccard, Richard.* (*Hari,* warrior), O.G. Richer—Richerus, *Domesday*—Eng. *Richer.* (*Man,* vir) O.G. Ricman—Eng. *Rickman, Richman.* (*Mund,* protection), O.G. Richmund—Eng. *Richmond.* (*Wald,* rule), O.G. Ricoald—Eng. *Richold.* (*Wig,* war), O.G. Ricwi—Eng. *Ridgway.*

Ring, perhaps signifying " armour."

, (*Hari,* warrior), O.G. Rincar—Eng. *Ringer.* (*Wald,* rule), A.S. Hringwold—Eng. *Ringold.*

Rod, signifying " glory."

(*Bero,* bear), O.G. Hruadbero—Eng. *Rodber.* (*Bern,* bear), O.G. Roudbirn—Eng. *Rodbourn.* (*Bert,* famous) O.G. Hrodebert—Eng. *Robert.* (*Gar,* spear), O.G. Hrodgar—Eng. *Rodger.* (*Gard,* protection), O.G. Hrodgard—Eng. *Rodgard, Rodyard.* (*Hari,* warrior), O.G. Hrodhari, Rotheri, Rudher—Eng. *Rothery, Rudder.* (*Land*), O.G. Rodland—Eng. *Rolland.* (*Leik,* play), O.G. Rutleich—Eng. *Rutledge.* (*Ram,* raven), O.G. Rothram—Eng. *Rotheram.* (*Man,* vir), O.G. Hrodman—Eng. *Rodman, Roman.* (*Niw,* young), O.G. Hrodni—Eng. *Rodney.* (*Ric,* rule), O.G. Hrodric—Eng. *Rodrick.* (*Wig,* war), O.G. Hrodwig —Eng. *Rudwick.* (*Ulf,* wolf), O.G. Hrodulf—Roolf, *Lib. Vit.*—Eng. *Rolfe.*

Ros, perhaps signifying " horse."

(*Bert,* famous), O.G. Rospert—Eng. *Rosbert.* (*Kel,* contraction of Ketel),[1] Old Norse Hroskel—Eng. *Roskell.*

---

[1] From the mythological kettle of the gods, which enters into many Old Norse men's names.

Rum, O.H.G. hruam, "glory."

(*Bald*, bold), A.S. Rumbold—Eng. *Rumbold.* (*Hari*, warrior), O.G. Rumhar—Eng. *Rummer.*

Sal, perhaps meaning "dark." [1]

(*Hari*, warrior), O.G. Salaher—Eng. *Sellar.* (*Man*, vir) O.G. Salaman—Eng. *Salmon.* (*Wig*, war), O.G. Selwich— Eng. *Salloway.*

Sar, signifying "armour" or anything used for defence.

(*Bod*, envoy), O.G. Sarabot—Eng. *Serbutt.* (*Gaud*, Goth), O.G. Saregaud—Eng. *Sargood.* (*Man*, vir), O.G. Saraman—Eng. *Sermon.* (*Had*, war), O.G. Sarratt—Eng. *Sarratt.*

Sig, signifying "victory."

(*Bald*, bold), A.S. Sigebald — Eng. *Sibbald.* (*Bert*, famous), A.S. Sigiberht, Sibriht—Eng. *Sibert.* (*Fred*, peace), A.S. Sigefred—Eng. *Seyfried.* (*Gar*, spear), A.S. Siggær—Eng. *Segar.* (*Man*), O.G. Sigeman—Eng. *Sickman* (*Suff. Surn.*). (*Mar*, famous), O.G. Sigimar, Sicumar —A.S. Simær, Secmær—Eng. *Seymore, Sycamore.* (*Mund*, protection), O.G. Sigimund—Eng. *Simmond.* (*Wig*, war), O.G. Sigiwic—Eng. *Sedgewick.* (*Wine*, friend), O.G. Sigiwin —Seguin, *Roll Batt. Abb.*—Eng. *Seguin* .

[1] "The Anglo-Saxons seem to have used sallow in the sense of dark. The raven is called sallow both by Cædmon and the author of Judith," *Skeat.* It seems to me, however, a question whether, seeing how frequently the names of nationalities enter into Teutonic men's names, the word contained in the above stem may not be "Salian." This, however, still leaves open the question as to what is the origin of Salian.

Sea, "mare."

(*Bera*, bear), Sebar, *Lib. Vit.*—Eng. *Seaber*. (*Bern*, bear), Old Norse Sæbiorn—Sberne, *Domesday*—Eng. *Seaborn*. (*Bert*, famous), A.S. Sæberht—Eng. *Seabright*. (*Burg*, protection), O.G. Seburg, Seopurc—Seaburch *Lib. Vit.*—Eng. *Seabrook, Seabury*. (*Rit*, ride), O.G. Seuerit—Eng. *Searight, Sievewright*. (*Wald*, rule), O.G. Sewald—Eng. *Seawall*. (*Ward*), O.G. Sæward—Eng. *Seaward, Seward*. (*Fugel*, fowl), A.S. Sæfugl—Eng. *Sefowl*.

Stain, " stone," in the sense of firmness or hardness.

(*Biorn*, bear), O.N. Steinbiörn—Eng. *Stainburn*. (*Burg*, protection), O.G. Stemburg—Eng. *Steamburg*. (*Hard*), O.G. Stainhard—Stannard *Domesday*—Eng. *Stonard, Stoneheart*. (*Hari*, warrior), O.N. Steinhar—Eng. *Stainer, Stoner*. (*Wald*, rule), O.G. Stainold—Eng. *Stonhold*, and perhaps *Sternhold* as a corruption.

Tank, perhaps "thought."

(*Hard*), O.G. Tanchard—Eng. *Tankard*. (*Hari*, warrior), O.G. Thancheri—Eng. *Tankeray, Thackeray* (Scandinavian form). (*Rad*, counsel), O.G. Tancrad—Eng. *Tancred*.

Tad, supposed "father."

(*Hari*, warrior), O.G. Tether—Eng. *Tedder, Teather*. (*Man*, vir), A.S. Tatmonn—Eng. *Tadman*.[1] (*Wine*, friend), O.G. Daduin—Eng. *Tatwin*.

Thor, supposed from the name of the god, a stem specially Danish.

(*Biorn*, bear), O.N. Thorbiorn—Thurbern *Lib. Vit.*—Eng. *Thorburn*. (*Gaut*, Goth), O.N. Thorgautr—Turgod

---

[1] A corresponding name may be the Dutch Tadema, if *ma*, as is supposed, stands for *man*.

Lib. Vit.—Eng. *Thurgood, Thoroughgood.* (*Geir,* spear), O.N. Thorgeir—Eng. *Thorgur.* (*Fin,* nation), O.N. Thorfinnr—Thurfin *Lib. Vit.*—Eng. *Turpin.* (*Môd,* courage), O.N. Thormodr—Eng. *Thurmot.* (*Stein,* stone), O.N. Thorsteinn—Turstin *Lib. Vit.*—Eng. *Thurstan.* (*Wald* rule), O.N. Thorvaldr—Eng. *Thorold.* (*Vid,* wood), O.N. Thorvidr—Eng. *Thorowood.* (*Ketil* [1]) O.N. Thorketil— Eng. *Thirkettle.* (*Kel,* contraction of *ketel*), O.N. Thorkel —Turkillus *Lib. Vit.*—Eng. *Thurkle.* (Hence is borrowed as supposed the Gaelic Torquil.)

Ang.-Sax. *theod,* "people."

(*Bald,* fortis), A.S. Theodbald—Tidbald *Lib. Vit.*—Eng. *Theobald, Tidball.* (*Hari,* warrior), O.G. Theodahar, Tudhari—A.S. Theodhere—Eng. *Theodore, Tudor.* (*Ran,* raven), O.G. Teutran—Eng. *Teuthorn.* (*Man,* vir), O.G. Tiadman—Eng. *Tidman.* (*Mar,* famous), O.G. Thiudemer —A.S. Dydemer—Eng. *Tidemore.* (*Ric,* rule), A.S. Theodric—Eng. *Todrig, Doddridge.*

Wad, Wat, "to go," in the sense of activity?

(*Gis,* hostage), O.G. Watgis—Eng. *Watkiss.* (*Gar,* spear), O.G. Waddegar—Eng. *Waddicar.* (*Mar,* famous), O.G. Vadomar—Eng. *Wadmore.* (*New,* young), O.G. Wattnj— Eng. *Watney.*

Wald, signifying "power" or "rule."

(*Hari,* warrior), O.G. Waldhar—A.S. Wealdhere—Eng. *Walter.* (*Man*) O.G. Waldman—Eng. *Waldman.* (*Ran,* raven), O.G. Walderannus—Walteranus *Domesday*—Eng. *Waldron.*

[1] Probably from the mythological kettle of the Æsir.

Wal, "stranger " or " foreigner."

(*And,* life, spirit), O.G. Waland—Eng. *Waland.* (*Frid,* peace), O.G. Walahfrid—Eng. *Wallfree.* (*Hari,* warrior), O.G. Walaheri, Walher—Eng. *Wallower, Waller.* (*Had,* war), O.G. Wallod—Eng. *Wallet.* (*Raven*), Gothic Valer- auan—Walrafan *Lib. Vit.*—Eng. *Wallraven* (*Suffolk Sur- names*). *Rand,* shield), O.G. Walerand—Walerandus *Lib. Vit.*—Eng. *Walrond.*

War, perhaps signifying " defence." [1]

(*Bald,* bold), O.G. Warbalt—Eng. *Warbolt.* (*Burg,* pro- tection), O.G. Warburg—Eng. *Warbrick.* (*Gar,* spear), O.G. Weriger—Eng. *Warraker.* (*Goz,* Goth), O.G. Weri- goz—Eng. *Vergoose* (*Suffolk Surnames*). (*Hari,* warrior), O.G. Warher—Eng. *Warrior.* (*Laik,* play), O.G. War- laicus—Warloc *Hund. Rolls*—Eng. *Warlock.* (*Man*), O.G. Warman—A.-S. Wearman—Eng. *Warman.* (*Mar,* famous). O.G. Werimar—Eng. *Warmer.* (*Lind,* gentle), O.G. Wara- lind—Eng. *Warland.*

Wern, in the sense of " nationality."

(*Burg,* protection), O.G. Warinburg—Eng. *Warrenbury.* (*Frid,* peace), O.G. Warnefrid—Eng. *Warneford.* (*Hari,* warrior), O.G. Warenher, Warner—Eng. *Warrener, Warner.* (*Had,* war), O.G. Warnad—Eng. *Warnett.*

Wag, way, to "wave, brandish."

(*Hari,* warrior), O.G. Wagher—Eng. *Wager.* (*Bert,* famous), O.G. Wagpraht—Eng. *Weybret.*

---

[1] So many different words might be suggested in this case that the meaning must be left uncertain. It is most probable that there may be an admixture.

F

Wid, wit, of uncertain meaning.[1]

(*Brord,* sword), A.S. Wihtbrord, Wihtbrod—Witbred *Hund. Rolls*—Eng. *Whitbread.* (*Gar.* spear), O.G. Witker—A.S. Wihtgar—Eng. *Whittaker, Whitecar.* (*Hard*), O.G. Witart—Eng. *Whitehart.* (*Ron,* raven), O.G. Widrannus—Eng. *Witheron.* (*Hari,* warrior), O.G. Withar, Wither *Domesday*—Eng. *Wither, Whiter.* (*Ring,* armour), O.G. Witering—Eng. *Wittering.* (*Lag,* law), A.S. Wihtlæg, —Eng. *Whitelegg, Whitlaw.* (*Laic,* play), O.G. Widolaic, —A.S. Wihtlac—Eng. *Wedlake, Wedlock.* (*Man,* vir), O.G. Wideman, Witman—Eng. *Wideman, Whiteman.* (*Mar,* famous), Goth. Widiomar—Uitmer *Lib. Vit.*—Eng. *Whitmore.* (*Rad,* counsel), O.G. Widerad, Witerat—A.S. Wihtræd—Eng. *Withered, Whitethread, Whiterod.* (*Ric,* rule), Goth. Witirich—A.S. Wihtric—Eng. *Witherick, Whitridge.*

Will, in the sense of "resolution"?

(*Bern,* bear), O.G. Wilbernus—Eng. *Wilbourn.* (*Gom,* man), O.G. Willicomo—Uilcomæ *Lib. Vit.*—Eng. *Wilcomb, Welcome.* (*Frid,* peace), A.S. Wilfrid—Eng. *Wilford.* (*Gis,* hostage), A.S. Wilgis—Eng. *Willgoss.* (*Hard,* fortis), O.G. Willard—A.S. Willeard—Eng. *Willard.* (*Heit,* state, "hood") O.G. Williheit—Eng. *Willett.* (*Helm*), A.S. Wilhelm—Eng. *Williams.* (*Mar,* famous), O.G. Willemar —Eng. *Willmore.* (*Mot,* courage), O.G. Willimot—Eng. *Willmot.* (*Mund,* protection), A.S. Wilmund—Uilmund, *Lib. Vit.*—Eng. *Willament.*

Wind, Wend, supposed " from the people."

(*Hari,* warrior), O.G. Winidhar—Eng. *Winder.* (*Ram,* raven), O.G. Winidram—Eng. *Windram.* (*Rad,* counsel) —Eng. *Windred.*

[1] Three different words found in ancient names intermix so as to be hardly separable, viz., Anglo-Saxon *wiht,* strength or courage ; *wid,* wood ; and *wit,* wisdom.

- *Wine*, "friend."

(*Bald*, fortis), O.G. Winebald—Eng. *Winbolt.* (*Cof*, strenuous), A.S. Wincuf—Eng. *Wincup.* (*Gaud*, Goth), O.G. Winegaud—Eng. *Wingood.* (*Gar*, spear), O.G. Wineger, Vinegar—A.S. Winagar—Eng. *Winegar, Vinegar.* (*Hari*, warrior), A.S. Wyner—Eng. *Winer.* (*Laic*, play), O.G. Winleich—Uinlac *Lib. Vit.*—Eng. *Winlock.* (*Man*, vir), O.G. Winiman—A.S. Winemen—Eng. *Wineman, Winmen.* (*Stan*, stone), A.S. Wynstan—Eng. *Winston.*

Wig, Wick, "war."

(*Bert*, famous), O.G. Wigbert, Wibert—Eng. *Vibert.* (*Burg*, protection), O.G. Wigburg—Wiburch *Lib. Vit.*—Eng. *Wyberg, Wybrow.* (*Hard*, fortis), O.G. Wighard, Wiart—A.S. Wigheard—Uigheard *Lib. Vit.*—Eng. *Wyard.* (*Hari*, warrior), O.G. Wigheri, Wiccar, Wiher—Uigheri *Lib. Vit.*—Eng. *Wicker, Vicary, Wire.* (*Helm*), A.S. Wighelm—Uighelm *Lib. Vit.*—Eng. *Whigam.* (*Ram*, raven), O.G. Wigram—Eng. *Wigram.* (*Mar*, famous), O.G. Wigmar, Wimar—Wimar *Lib. Vit.*—Eng. *Wymer.*[1] (*Gern*, eager), O.G. Wicchern—A.S. Weogern—Eng. *Waghorn.* (*Had*, war), O.G. Wicod, Wihad—A.S. Wigod—Eng. *Wiggett, Wichett, Wyatt.* (*Man*, vir), O.G. Wigman—Eng. *Wigman, Wyman.* (*Ric*, rule), O.G. Wigirich—Eng. *Vickridge.*

Ang.-Sax. *wulf*, "wolf."

(*Bert*, famous) O.G. Wolfbert—Eng. *Woolbert.* (*Gar*, spear), A.S. Wulfgar—Eng. *Woolgar.* (*Gaud*, Goth), O.G. Wulfegaud—A.S. Wulfgeat—Eng. *Woolcot.* (*Hard*, fortis), A.S. Wulfheard—Eng. *Woollard.* (*Had*, war), O.G. Wolthad —Eng. *Woollat.* (*Helm*), A.S. Wulfhelm—Eng. *Woollams.* (*Heh*, high), A.S. Wulfheh—Eng. *Woolley.* (*Mar*, famous),

[1] The name of Wigmore Street seems to imply a man's name *Wigmore*, but I do not know of it at present.

A.S. Wulfmer—Eng. *Woolmer.* (*Noth,* bold), A.S. Wulf-
noth—Eng. *Woolnoth.* (*Ric,* rule), A.S. Wulfric—Eng.
Woolrych. (*Sig,* victory), A.S. Wulfsig—Eng. *Wolsey.*
(*Stan,* stone), A.S. Wulfstan—Eng. *Woolston.*

Ang.-Sax. *jû*, O.H.G. *êwa* "law." [1]

(*Hari,* warrior), O.G. Euhar—Eng. *Ewer.* (*Man,* vir),
O.G. Eoman—perhaps Iman and Iiman on Roman pottery
—Eng. *Yeoman, Yeaman.* (*Ric,* rule), O.G. Eoricus—Eng.
Yorick, (*Wald,* rule), O.G. Ewald—Eng. *Ewald.* (*Ward,*
guardian), O.G. Euvart—Eng. *Ewart, Yeoward.* (*Wolf*),
O.G. Eolf—Eng. *Yealfe.*

[1] Hence probably the name of the Eows, a tribe or family
mentioned in the "Traveller's Song." Also probably the name
Eawa, in the genealogy of the Mercian kings. The stem is
represented in our names by *Ewe, Yeo,* and *Yea,* and we have
also the patronymic *Ewing* (Euing in *Domesday*).

The foregoing is not put forward as by any means
an exhaustive list of the ancient compounds represented in our names, but only of the more common
and more important. And there are some ancient
stems well represented in other forms, such as those
referred to in Chapter II., from which I have not been
able to trace any compounds. It will be observed that
I have in two or three instances assigned a place to
an English name, without finding an ancient form to
correspond. This indeed I might have done to a
greater extent than I have done, for when we have such
a well-defined system, with the same forms of compounds regularly recurring, we may in many cases
assign a place to a name even though the ancient
equivalent may not yet have come to light.

CHAPTER IV.

THE researches of Mr. Kemble, supplemented by those of Mr. Taylor, in connection with the early Saxon settlements in England, have an important bearing upon the subject of our existing surnames. Mr. Kemble was the first to call attention to the fact that very many of the names of places in England, as disclosed by the forms in which these names appear in ancient charters, consist of a personal name in a patronymic form. Some of these names consist simply of a nominative plural in *ingas*, as Æscingas, the sons or descendants of Æsc, others of a genitive plural in *inga*, with *ton, ham*, &c., appended, as in Billingatun, the town of the Billings, *i.e.* sons or descendants of Billa. These he takes to denote tribal or family settlements, forming the Anglo-Saxon "mark," consisting of a certain area of cultivated land, surrounded by a belt of pasture land enjoyed by all the settlers in common, the whole inclosed by the forest.

Of these names he has made two lists, the one derived from the names found in ancient charters, and so perfectly trustworthy, the other inferred from

existing names of places which appear to be in the
same form. The latter list is of course subject to
considerable correction and deduction, inasmuch as it
depends entirely upon the ancient forms in which
these names would appear whether they would come
under this category or not. Thus, if a name were
anciently Billing*a*ham, it would be " the home of the
Billings," while if it were Billingham, it would simply
be the home of an individual man called Billing.
And in looking through this list, a few names will be
found, which a comparison with his own index of
place-names shows to be incorrectly assigned. Thus
he infers Impingas from Impington in Cambridgeshire,
and Tidmingas from Tidmington in Worcester,
whereas it appears from his index that the ancient
name of the one was Impintun, and of the other
Tidelminctun, both being thus from the name of an
individual and not of a tribe or family. Sempringham again in Lincolnshire, whence he derives
Sempringas, I find to have been Sempingaham, and
so used already for Sempingas. I also feel very great
doubt about names taken from places ending in *by*,
thorp, and *toft*, in Lincolnshire and the ancient
Denelaga, as being Scandinavian, and given at a
distinctly later period. Indeed I have a certain
amount of distrust of all names taken from the North
of England, in the absence, as far as I know, of any
distinct proof in any one case. Northumberland
would perhaps be the county to which, as containing
the greatest number of such forms, any such doubt
would the least strongly apply. Moreover, I do not
feel at all sure that *ing* is not in some cases simply a

form of the possessive, and that Dunningland, for instance, is not simply Dunn's land. This doubt is considerably strengthened when the name is that of a woman, as in Cyneburginctun (now Kemerton in Glouc). Cyneburg is certainly a woman's name, and as such could not, I should suppose—though the question is one for more experienced Anglo-Saxon scholars—form a patronymic, in which case Cyneburginctun can only be " Cyneburg's tun." And if it be so in one case, it may of course be so in others. Mr. Kemble's second list, then, requires to be used with a certain amount of caution, though in the main his deductions may be taken as trustworthy.

The corresponding forms in Germany have since been collected by Professor Foerstemann from ancient charters up to the eleventh century, and must all be considered therefore as trustworthy. His list contains upwards of a thousand different names, but inasmuch as many of these names are found in different parts of Germany, the total number of such names must amount to many thousands. These consist sometimes of a form in *ingas*, same as in England, and this obtains more particularly in Bavaria, sometimes of a form in *inga*, which he takes to be also a nominative plural, but most commonly of a dative plural, in *ingen*, as in Herlingen, "to the Harlings." This dative plural explains the origin of many existing names of places in Germany, as Göttingen, Dettingen, Tübingen, &c. A dative plural also occurs occasionally in England in the corresponding Anglo-Saxon form *ingum*, as in Godelmingum, now Godalming, Angemeringum, now Angmering, &c.

Meanwhile Mr. Taylor has instituted a detailed and very important comparison between the names contained in Mr. Kemble's two lists, and those of a corresponding kind in Germany, not indeed from ancient records, but from existing place-names. And he has further supplemented this by a list of similar orms disclosed by his own very interesting discovery of a Saxon area in France opposite to the shore of England, and which we can hardly doubt to be, as he considers it to be, the result of a Saxon emigration from England. He has, moreover, given some similar instances of German occupation in the north of Italy, and it can hardly be doubted that a more detailed examination would add to their number.

The question now to be considered is—what is the value of these various forms in *ingas, inga,* and *ingen,* in England and in Germany? In Anglo-Saxon and other Teutonic dialects *ing* is a patronymic, as in Bruning, son of Brûn. But it has also a wider sense implying any connection with a person or thing, and in certain of the names under consideration both in England and in Germany, it seems very clear that it is used simply in a geographical sense. Thus we cannot doubt that Madelungen and Lauringen, in Germany, signify, as Foerstemann suggests, the people of the Madel and of the Lauer, on which two rivers the places in question are respectively situated. Also that Salzungen signifies the people of the salt springs, in the neighbourhood of which the name is found.[1] So in England it seems clear that the Leamingas

---

[1] From a similar origin is the name of the Scandinavian Vikings, Vik-ing, from *vik*, a bay.

found in Leamington signifies the people of the Leam, on which river the place is situated. So also the Heretuningas, the Hohtuningas, and the Suthtuningas, must mean simply the people respectively of Heretun, of Hohtun, and of Suthtun, the Beorganstedingas the people of Beorgansted, the Eoforduningas the people of Eofordun, and the Teofuntingas, the people dwelling by the two fountains. But with these and perhaps one or two other exceptions, the word contained is simply a personal name, and the question is—in what connection is it used? Does Billingas mean the descendants of the man Bill or Billa, under whose leadership the settlement was made, or does it, as Mr. Kemble seems to think, refer to some older, perhaps mythical ancestor from whom the Billings claimed a traditional descent? Now, considering the great number of these names, amounting to more than a thousand in England alone, seeing the manner in which they are dispersed, not only over different counties of England, but as the annexed table will show, over the length and breadth of Germany, it seems to me utterly impossible to consider them as anything else than the every-day names of men common to the great German family. I am quite in accord then with the view taken by Sir J. Picton (Ethnology of Wiltshire).[1] "When the Saxons first invaded England, they came in tribes and families headed by their patriarchal leaders. Each tribe was called by its leader's name, with the termination *ing*, signifying family, and where they settled they gave their patriarchal name to the *mark* or central point

[1] *Archæological Journal.*

round which they clustered." This is also the view taken by Foerstemann with regard to the German names, and I cannot doubt that Mr. Kemble, if he had had the opportunity of extending his survey over this wider area, would have come to the same conclusion. I take it then that the name contained in these forms is simply that of the leader under whose guidance these little settlements were made, and that, inasmuch as members of the same family would generally keep together, it is in most cases that of the patriarch or head of the family. Each man would no doubt have his own individual name, but as a community exercising certain rights in common, from which outsiders were excluded, they would require some distinctive appellation, and what so natural as that of their leader.

I now come to consider some points of difference between the Anglo-Saxon settlements and the German. While all the settlements in England must be taken to have been made by a Low German race, a large proportion of those in Germany must be taken to have been made by a High German people. Thus when we find Bæbingas in England represented by Papinga in Austria, Bassingas by Pasingas, and Bædingas by Patinga in Bavaria, we have the distinction between High and Low German, which might naturally be expected. So when we find Eastringas represented by Austringa in Baden, we have again a High German form to compare with a Low German. But this distinction is by no means consistently maintained throughout, and we seem to have a considerable mixture of High and Low German forms. Thus we have both Bæcgingas and Pæccingas,

Dissingas and Tissingas, Gâringas and Coringas, Edingas and Odingas (representing as it seems the Anglo-Saxon *ead* or *ed*, and the High German *aud* or *od*). And even in some cases the rule seems to be reversed, and we have the High German in England, as in Eclingas against Egilinga in Bavaria, Hoppingas against Hobinga in Alsace, Ticcingas against Dichingen, &c. It would seem as if our settlements were made, at least in part, by a people who if not High German, had at any rate considerable High German affinities. To what extent the speech of the Angles which I suppose to have been the main element in the Northumbrian dialect, would answer these conditions, I would rather leave to our higher Anglo-Saxon scholars to decide. But it seems to me, so far as I may venture to give an opinion, that Lappenberg's theory, that the Saxons were accompanied by Franks, Frisians, and Lombards, would perhaps better than any other meet all the requirements of the case. Whence for instance could come such a form as Cwichelm for Wighelm, apparently a rather strongly marked Frankish form ? Or Cissa (Chissa) for, as I suppose, Gisa, which would be apparently in conformity with a Frisian form ? I have endeavoured to go into this subject more fully in a subsequent chapter, more particularly with regard to the Franks, and to show that there are a number of names in Anglo-Saxon times which might be of Frankish origin, and which perhaps it would be difficult to account for on any other theory. And it must be borne in mind that the earlier date now generally assigned for the first Teutonic settlements, naturally tends to give greater latitude to the inquiry as to the races by whom those settlements were made.

Another difference to be noted is that whereas all our settlements seem to have been made in heathen times, those of Germany extend into Christian times, as shown by such names as Johanningen, Jagobingen, and Steveningen, containing the scriptural names John, Jacob and Stephen. There is another and a curious name, Satanasinga, which, the place to which it is applied being a waste, seems to describe the people who lived in it, or around it, perhaps in reference to their forlorn condition, as " the children of Satan." The adoption of scriptural names seems to have taken place at a later period in England than either in Germany or in France. And we have not, as I believe, a single instance in our surnames of a scriptural name in an Anglo-Saxon patronymic form, as the Germans, judging from the above, might—possibly may—have.

Another point of difference between the Anglo-Saxon and the German settlements would seem to be this, that while the German list contains a considerable proportion of compound names, such as Willimundingas and Managoldingas, the Anglo-Saxon list consists almost exclusively of names formed of a single word, and the exceptions may almost be counted upon the fingers. With this I was at first considerably puzzled, but on looking more carefully into the lists, it seemed to me apparent that many of the names assumed by Mr. Kemble from names of places were in reality compound names in a disguised and contracted form. And as

Tidmington, whence he derives Tidmingas, was properly Tidhelmingtun, so I conceive that Osmingas derived from Osmington, ought properly to be Oshel-mingas, and Wylmingas, found in Wilmington, to be Wilhelmingas. So also I take it that Wearblingas, found in Warblington, ought to be Warboldingas, that Weomeringas, deduced from Wymering, ought to be Wigmeringas, and that Horblingas, found in Horbling, ought to be Horbaldingas. There are several other names, such as Scymplingas, Wramp-lingas, Wearmingas, Galmingas, &c., that seem as they stand, to be scarcely possible for names of men, and which may also contain compounds in a corrupted or contracted form. In addition to this, I note the following, found in ancient charters, which Mr· Kemble seems to have overlooked, Ægelbyrhtingas, found in Ægelbyrtingahyrst, No. 1041, Ceolredingas, found in Colredinga gemerc, 1149, and Godhelmingas found in Godelmingum, 314. If all these were taken into account, the difference, though it would still exist, might not be so great as to be unaccountable, considering that our settlements were made to a considerable extent at an earlier date, and by tribes more or less differing from those of Germany. It raises, moreover the question, dealt with in a very thorough manner by Stark, as to the extent to which these short and simple names may be contractions of compound names. I have referred to the subject in another place, and I will only observe at present that from the instances he cites the practice seems to have been rather specially common among the Frisians. Now it will be found on comparing the names of our ancient settlers with the Frisian names

past and present cited by Outzen and Wassenberg,
that there is a very strong family likeness between
them, though we need not take it to amount to more
than this, that the Frisian names may be taken
as a type of the kind of names prevalent among
the other neighbouring Low German tribes, until it
can be more distinctly shown that there were settlements made by the Frisians themselves. And
I have brought these names into the comparison
simply as being the nearest representatives that I
can find.

Notwithstanding the complete and valuable tables
drawn up by Mr. Taylor for the purpose of comparing the Anglo-Saxon settlements with those of
Germany, I have thought it useful to supplement
them by another confined exclusively to the names
drawn from ancient German records, and therefore,
so far as they go, entirely trustworthy. And I take
the opportunity to compare our existing surnames
with these ancient names thus shown to be common
to the great Teutonic family.

In the following table I have given then, first the
Anglo-Saxon names from Kemble's lists, then the
corresponding Old German from that of Foerstemann,
with the district in which it is found, and, wherever
identified, the existing name of the place, then names
corresponding from the *Liber Vitæ* or elsewhere to
show continued Anglo-Saxon use, with also Frisian
names as already mentioned, and finally, the existing
English surnames with which I compare them. It
will be seen that these surnames in not a few cases
retain an ancient vowel-ending in *a*, *i*, or *o*, as
explained in a preceding chapter.

THE EARLY SAXON SETTLEMENTS COMPARED WITH THOSE OF GERMANY.

Anglo-Saxon.	German.	Locality in Germany.	(L.V.), Liber Vitæ. (F.), Frisian.	English Surnames.
Aldingas Oldingas	Aldinge	{ Now Aldingen, in Würtemburg	Alda (L.V.), Alte (F.)	{ Allday, Allt, Old, Olding.
Æceringas¹	Aguringas	Now Egringen in Bavaria	Aker (L.V.)	Ager, Acres.
Ælingas	Allingen	Bavaria	Alli (L.V.), Alle (F.)	Alley, Allo.
Ælfingas Ælpingas	Albungen	Hesse Cassell	Alef (F.)	Aulph, Alpha, Elvy.
Æfeningas	Heveningare marca	Appenzell	Afun (L.V.)	Heaven ? Evening.
Antingas	Endinga	Now Endingen, in Baden	Anta (A.S.)	And, Andoe, Hand.
Æscingas	Esginga		Æsc (A.S.)	Ask, Ashe.
Ætingas	Adinga	Pruss. Saxony	Atta (A.S.), Atte (F.)	Hatt.
Bæbingas	Papinga	Now Pabing, in Austria	Babba (A.S.), Babe (F.)	Babb.
Baningas	Boninge		Beana (L.V.), Banne (F.)	Bann, Banning.
Bædingas Beadingas	Patinga	{ Now Beddingen, in Brunswick ; also Baden, Prussia, Austria	Bada, Betti (L.V.)	{ Batt, Batty, Betty, Batting.
Bassingas	Pasingas	Bavaria	Bass (A.S.)	Bass, Pass.
Bæcgingas	Bachingen	Würtenburg	Baga, Backa (L.V.)	{ Bagge, Back. Beck, Peck.
Beccingas Pæccingas	Beckinga	Rhenish Prussia		
Bensingas	Pinsinga	Bavaria	Benza (L.V.)	Bence.
Bircingas	Biricchingen			Birch.
Bebingas	Bebingun	Bavaria, Würtg.	Bebba (A.S.)	Bibb, Bibby, Beeby.
Billingas	Bilinga	Hess., Würt., Friesland		Bill, Billow, Billing.
Binningas	Binnungen	Now Bingen, on Rhine	Bynni (L.V.), Binne (F.)	Binney, Binning.

¹ The reader must bear in mind that Ang.-Sax. æ is pronounced as a in "aut."

THE EARLY SAXON SETTLEMENTS COMPARED WITH THOSE OF GERMANY.

Anglo-Saxon.	German.	Locality in Germany.	(L.V.), Liber Vitæ. (F.), Frisian.	English Surnames.
Bydelingas	Budilingen	Luxembg., Austria	Botel (F.)	Biddle
Briningas	......		Bryni (L.V.)	Brine, Brinney.
Beormingas	Pirninga	Würtemburg	Beorn (L.V.)	Burn, Burning.
Bondingas			Bonde (L.V., F.)	Bond.
Beormingahem	Bermingahem			Breem.
Brydingas	Breidinge	Hesse Cass., Pruss. Sax.		Bride, Bird.
Bridlingas	Britlingi	Now Brütlingen, in Hanr.		Bridle.
Blæcingas	......		Blaca (L.V.)	Black.
Bruningas	Brunninga	Austria	Brôn (L.V.), Bruyn (F.)	Brown, Browning.
Beorhtingas } Byrtingas	Perhtingen	Bavaria	Bercht (L.V.) Berti (F.)	{ Burt, Bright, Brighty, Brighting.
Brihtlingas	Bertelingas	Rhen. Prussia		Brightly, Brittell.
Buccingas	Puchinga		Bocco, Buco (F.)	Buck, Puck.
Bullingas	Bollinga	{ Bullingen, in Rh. Pruss. Also Tyrol and Westphal. }	Bolle (F.)	Bull, Bolley, Bulling.
Byttingas }	Buddinga	Baden, Würt., Friesland	Bota (L.V.)	Budd, Butt, Botting-
Potingas }	Potingin	Baden, Aust., Friesland	Botte (F.)	Pott, Potto.
Bobingas }	Bobinga	Bobingen, in Bav.	Bofa (L.V.), Poppe (F.)	Boby, Poppy.
Bofingas }				
Bosingas	Bosinga	Austria, Würt.	Bosa (L.V.)	Boss, Bossey.
Buselingas	Buselingen	Büssling, by Schaffhausen		Bussell.
Burringas	Buringen	Würtemburg.	Burra (L.V.), Bore (F.)	Burr.
Cægingas	Cachinga		Kay, Key (F.)	Kay, Key (see p. 10).
Callingas	Callinge	Holland	Kalle (F.)	Call, Callow.
Ceaningas	Conninge	Würtemburg	Canio (L.V.) Keno (F.)	Cann, Canning.
Cearlingas	Chirlingen	Kierling, in Austria	Karl (L.V.), Carl (F.)	Charly, Charles.

EARLY SAXON SETTLEMENTS COMPARED WITH THOSE OF GERMANY.

Anglo-Saxon.	German	Locality in Germany.	(L.V.); Liber Vitæ. (F.) Frisian.	English Surnames.
Cifingas	Cheffingin	Würtemburg	Cecfi (L.V.)	Chaff, Chaffey.
Ceopingas	Chuppinga	Würtemburg		Chope, Chubb.
Copingas	Cofunga	Hesse Cassel	Cufa, Coiti (Ang.-Sax.)	Coffey, Cuff, Cuffey.
Codingas	Cuttingas	Near Metz	Goda, (L.V.) } Gode (F.) }	Goad, Codd, Coale, Godding.
Cotingas }	Gotinga	Bavaria		
Colingas	Cholinga	....	Ceolla (L.V.)	Coll, Collie, Colling.
Cocingas	Gukkingin	Gugging, in Austria		Cock.
Cressingas	Chresinga	Würtemberg		Cressy.
Cnottingas	Knutingen	....	Cnut (L.V.)	Knott.
Cnudlingas	Cnutlinga	Baden		Nuttall.
Cenesingas¹ {	Kenzinga	Kenzingen, in Baden	....	Chance ?
	Gensingen	Gensungen, Hess. Cass.		
Centingas	Gandingen	Friesland	Kaenta (L.V.)	Cant, Gant, Gandy.
Culingas	....	....	....	Cull, Cooling.
Denningas	Daningen	Baden	Dene (L.V.)	Dane, Dana, Denn, Denning.
Dillingas	Dilinga	Dillengen, in Bav.	Tilli (L.V.), Tiio (F.)	Dill, Till, Tilly.
Deorlingas } Teorlingas }	Darlingin	Brunswick		Darrell, Darling.
Dissingas } Tissingas }	Tisinga	.Bavaria	Tisa, Disa (F.)	Dyce, Dicey, Tisoe.
Ticcangas	Dichingen	Friesland, Bav.	Tycca (A.S.)	Dick.
Dyclingas	Tuchilingen	Now Tuchling		Dickle, Tickle.
Doccingas	Dockinga	Friesland	Tocki (L.V.), Tocke (F.)	Dock, Togue, Docking.
Dodingas	....	....	Doda (F.)	Dodd, Todd.

¹ I take the word contained herein to be "ganz," an ancient stem in names.

G

EARLY SAXON SETTLEMENTS COMPARED WITH THOSE OF GERMANY.

Anglo-Saxon.	German.	Locality in Germany.	(L.V.), Liber Vitæ. (F.), Frisian.	English Surnames.
Dunningas	Tuningas	......	Duna (L.V.)	Dunn, Dunning.
Eastringas	Austringa	Oestringen, in Baden	......	Easter.
Edlingas {	Edinga	Holland, Baden, Bav.	Ede (L.V.), Edle (F.)	Eddy.
Oddingas }	Odinga	·Westphal., Bav.	Oda (L.V.), Odde (F.)	Oddy.
Elcingas		......		Elk, Elcy, Elgee
Ecgingas	Eginga	Schaffhausen, Bav.	Ecga (L.V.), Egga (F.)	Egg.
Eclingas	Egilinga	Bavaria	Ecgel (A.S.)	Edgell, Egle.
Elsingas	Elisingun	Hesse	Elsi (L.V.), Ealse (F.)	Else, Elsey, Elliss.
Eppingas }	Ebinga	Baden, Austria	Ebbi (L.V.)	Epps.
Ippingas }	Ippinga	Ippingen, on Danube	Eppe (F.)	Hipp.
Everingas }	Eburingen	Pruss. Silesia	......	Ever, Every, Heber.
Eoforingas }				
Eorpingas	Arpingi	......	......	Harp, Earp.
Fearingas	Faringa	Upper Bav. & L. Constance	Earbe (L.V.), Arpe (F.)	Farre, Farrow.
Fearningas	......	......	......	Fearn.
Finningas	Finninga	......	Forne (L.V.)	Finn, Finney.
Fincingas	......	......	Finn (A.S.)	Finch.
Folcingas	Fulchingen	......	Finc (A.S.), surname	Fulke.
Frodingas	......	......	Folco (L.V.)	Froude.
			Frode (L.V.)	
Garingas } / Coringas }	Geringen	Würtemberg	......	Gore, Cory.
Gestingas	......	Austria	......	Guest, Gasting.
Geofuningas	Gebeningen	......	......	Giffen.
Gisilingas } / Gillingas }	Gisilinga	Bavaria	Gisle, Gille (L.V.)	Gill.
Gealdingas } / Goldingas }	Geltingen	Gelting, in Bav.	Golde (A.S.), Giolt (F.)	Gola Galt Golding.

EARLY SAXON SETTLEMENTS COMPARED WITH THOSE OF GERMANY.

Anglo-Saxon.	German	Locality in Germany.	(L.V.), Liber V.tæ. (F.), Frisian.	English Surnames.
Hallingas	Halinge	Bavaria	Halle (L.V.)	Hall, Halling.
Hæglingas	Hegelinge	Bavaria	Hagel (A.S.)	Hail, Hailing.
Hanesingas	Anzinga	Bavaria		Hance.
Heardingas	Hardinghen	Pas de Calais	Hart (F.)	Hard, Hardy.
Heartingas	Hertingen	Bavaria		Hart, Harding.
Hæslingas / Æslingas	Hasalinge	Near Bremen	Esel (L.V.), Hessel (F.)	Hasell.
Hanningas / Heningas / Anningas	Heninge		Anna (L.V.). Hanne, Enno (F.)	Hann, Hanning, Henn, Anning, Anne.
Hillingas / Illingas	Illingun	Illingen, in Baden	Ylla (L.V.), Hille (F.)	Hill
Honingas	Oningas	Oeningen, on L. Constance	Ona (L.V.), Onno (F.)	Hone.
Horningas		Austria	Horn (A.S.)	Horne, Horning.
Herelingas	Herlingun	Near Metz	Harrol (F.)	Harle, Harley, Harling.
Hoppingas	Hobinga	Haching. near Munich	Cbbe, Hobbe (F.)	Hopp, Hoby, Hopping.
Hæcingas	Hahhinga	Rhen. Pruss.	Hacci (L.V.), Acke (F.)	Hack, Hacking.
Hafocingas	Hauechingas	Near Cologne and Zurich	Hauc (L.V.)	Hawke.
Hocingas	Hobingun	Friesland	Hoso (F.)	Hockey.
Hucingas	Huchingen			Hook.
Huningas	Huninga	Hüningen, near Basle	Una (L.V.), Hunne (F.)	Hunn, Honey.
Huntingas	Huntingun	Baden		Hunt, Hunting.
Ifingas			Ivo (L.V.)	Ive, Ivy.
Immingas	Eminga	Enningen, in Würt.	Imma (L.V.), Eno, Imme (F.)	Eames, Yems, Ilime.
Læferingas	Livaringa	Near Salzburg		Laver.

EARLY SAXON SETTLEMENTS COMPARED WITH THOSE OF GERMANY.

Anglo-Saxon.	German.	Locality in Germany.	(L.V.), Liber Vitæ. (F.), Frisian.	English Surnames.
Lullingas	Lolinga	Lullingen, in Rh. Pruss.	Lolle (F.)	Lull, Lully.
Luddingas	Liutingen	Baden	Lioda (L.V.), Ludde (F.)	Lyde, Lutto.
Lofingas	Luppinge	......	Lufe (L.V.), Lubbe (F.)	Love, Loving.
Lidelingas	Lutilinga	Würtemburg	......	Liddle.
Locingas		......	Locchi (L.V.)	Lock, Lockie.
Leasingas	Lasingi	......	Leising (L.V.)	Lees, Lessy.
Manningas	Meningen	......	Man (L.V.), Manno (F.)	Mann, Manning.
Massingas	Masingi	......	Maessa (A.S.)	Massey, Messing.
Madingas	Madungen	Sax-Weimar		Maddey.
Mægdlingas [1]		......	Mædle (L.V.)	Madle.
Mæccingas	Maginga	{ Maching, in Bavaria / Mechingen, by L. Constance	Mecga (A.S.) / Mekke (F.)	} Mœggy, May.
Mycgingas		......	......	Mico, Michie.
Merlingas	Marlingen	Bavaria		Merrill, Marl, Marlung.
Mundlingas	Mundilinga	Bavaria		Mundell.
Marringas	Maringen	Baden, Würt.	Mar (A.S.)	Marr.
Meringas	Meringa	Hanover		Merry.
Millingas	Milinga	Bav., Rhen. Pruss.	Milo (L.V.)	Millie, Milo, Millinge.
Myrcingas [2]	Mirchingen	Lower Austria	Murk (F.)	Murch, Murchie.
Nydingas } Neddingas }	Nidinga	Neidingen, in Rh. Pruss.	Nytta (L.V.), Nette (F.)	Need, Neate.
Nottingas	Notingen	Upper Bavaria	Noedt, (F.)	Nott, Nutting.
Ossingas	Ossingen	Rh. Bavaria	Hosa (L.V.)	Hose.
Palingas		......	Paelli (L.V.)	Palev, Paling.

1 Properly, I think, " Mædlings," as it has nothing to do with Ang.-Sax. " mæʒd," " maid."
2 The same, I take it, as the " Myrgingas " in the *Traveller's Tale*.

EARLY SAXON SETTLEMENTS COMPARED WITH THOSE OF GERMANY.

Anglo-Saxon.	German.	Locality in Germany.	(L.V.), Liber Vitæ. (F.), Frisian.	English Surnames.
Pegingas	Biginga	Westphalia	Pega (L.V.)	Pegg, Bigg.
Penningas	Penningin	North Germany	Benna (A.S.)	Penn, Benn
Puningas	Buninga		Buna (A.S.)	Bunn.
Pitingas	Pidinga	Austria		Pitt.
Poclingas	Puchilinga	Pückling, on Danube		Puckle, Buckle.
Piperingas				Piper.
Readingas	Radinga	Reding, in Luxembg.	Reid (F.)	Read.
Riccingas			Riki (F.)	Rich, Richey.
Ridingas	Ridingin	Rieding, in Upp. Bav.		Riddy, Rita, Ridding.
Riclingas	Richilinga	Reichling, on Rhine	Rykle (F.)	Regal, Wrigley.
Riplingas	Rupilinga	Upper Bavaria		Ripley.
Rollingas	Roldingen	Rolingen, in Luxembg.	Rolle (F.)	Rolle.
Racfningas	Ravininge	Bavaria	Reuen (L.V.)	Raven.
Rodingas	Hrotthingun	Rh. Pruss., Bav.	Rudda L.V.), Rode (F.)	Rodd, Rudd, Rudding.
Rossingas	Rossunga		Russe (F.)	Ross.
Ruscingas			Rosce (L.V.)	Rush.
Rocingas	Roggingun	Bavaria	Rogge, Rocche (F.)	Rock.
Rucingas			Rouke (F.)	Rugg, Ruck.
Sandringas	Sinderingum	Würtemburg	Sander (F.)	Sander.
Swaningas	Swaningun	Schwanningen, near Schaff-hausen / Sittling, in Bav.	Suan (L.V.)	Swan.
Syclingas	Sikilingin			Sickle, Sickling.
Seaxlingas	Saxlinga			Satchell?
Sceardingas	Scardinga	Bavaria	Scyta (A.S.)	Scard, Scarth.
Scytingas	Scithingi			Skitt, Skeat, Shute.
Surlingas			Serlo (L.V.)	Sarle, Scarle.

EARLY SAXON SETTLEMENTS COMPARED WITH THOSE OF GERMANY.

Anglo-Saxon.	German.	Locality in Germany.	(L.V.), Liber Vitæ. (F.) Frisian.	English Surnames.
Scyrlingas	Skirilinga	Schierling, in Bav.	....	Shirley.
Sælingas	....	....	Salla (L.V.)	Sule, Sala.
Sceafingas	Sceuinge	....	....	Sheaf.
Scealingas	Scelinga	....	Sceal (L.V.)	Scally, Scales.
Snoringas	Snoringer marca	Rh. Bav.	Snearri (L.V.)	Snare.
Snotingas	Snudinga	....	Snod (A.S.)	Snoad.
Sealfingas	Selvingen	....	Stuf (A.S.)	Self, Selvey.
Stubingas	Staubingen	Staubing, in Bavaria	Sigga (L.V.)	Stubbs, Stubbing.
Seccingas	Siggingahem	Belgium	Spech (Domesday)	Siggs, Sick.
Specingas	Speichingas	Spaichengen, in Westph.		Speck.
Sceaflingas	Schuffelinga	Schiflingen, in Luxembg.		Shovel.
Stæningas	....	....	Stean (L.V.), Steen (F.)	Stone, Stenning.
Sinningas	Siningas	....	Sinne (F.)	Siney, Shinn.
Stellingas	....	....		Stell.
Tædingas	Tattingas	Dettingen, in Bav.	Tade (F.)	Tadd, Taddy.
Tælingas	Telingen	Bavaria	Tella (L.V.), Tiele (F.)	Tall, Telling.
Dorringas	Torringun	Töring, in Austria	Tori (L.V.)	Torr.
Tutlingas	Tutlingun	Dutling, in Bav.		Tuttle.
Trumpingas[1]	....	....		Trump, Trumpy.
Thorningas	Thurninga	Dürningen, in Alsace		Thorne, Thorning.
Terringas	....	....	Terri (L.V.)	Terry.
Tucingas	Tuginga	Switzerland	Tuk (A.S.), Duce (L.V.)	Tuck, Duck.
Duringas	Turinga	Würtemburg		Turr, Durre, Turing.
Uffingas	Uffingen	Oeffingen, in Würtemburg	Offa (L.V.)	Ough, Hough, Huff.

1 Properly, I take it, "Trumingas," Ang-Sax. "trum" firm, strong.

EARLY SAXON SETTLEMENTS COMPARED WITH THOSE OF GERMANY.

Anglo-Saxon.	German.	Locality in Germany.	(L.V.), Liber Vitæ. (F.), Frislan.	English Surnames.
Wearningas	Warningas	.....	Warin (L.V.)	Warren, Warne.
Waceringas	Wacheringa	.....		Waker.
Wealdringas	Waltringen	Friesland and Bav.	Wealdere (A.S.)	Walder, Walter
Wasingas	Wasunga	Würtg., Sax. Mein.	Wasso (A.S.)	Wass.
Wippingas		.....		Whipp.
Wittingas	Wittungen	Pruss. Sax.	Uitta (L.V.), Witte (F.)	Whit.
Willingas	Willinga	Bavaria	Wille (F.)	Will, Willow, Willing.
Winingas	Winninge	Winningen, on Rhine	Wynna, Uini (L.V.)	Wine, Winn, Winning.
Wealdingas	Waltingun	Austria	Wald (A.S.), Walte (F.)	Waldie, Waldo.
Wælsingas	Walasingas	.....		Walsh.
Watingas	Waddinga	Weddingen, in Rh. Pruss.	Uada (L.V.), Uatto (F.)	Watt, Waddy.
Wellingas	Wellingen	Baden		Well.
Wigingas } Wiccingas }	Wikinka	Bavaria	{ Uicga (L.V.), Wigge, Wicco (F.) }	Wigg, Wicking.
Wylfingas	Vulfinga	.....	Wulf (A.S.)	Wolf.
Wrihtingas	Wirtingen	Austria	.....	Wright.
Watringas	Wateringas	Wettringen, in Westph.	.....	Water.
Wendlingas	Wenilinga	Near Strasburg	Windel (A.S.)	Windle, Wintle.
Wrihtlingas	Riutilinga	Reutlingen, in Würtg.	.....	Riddle.
Wealcingas	.....	.....	Walch (L.V.), Walke (F.)	{ Walk, Walkey, Walking.
Wealcringas	.....	.....	Wealcere (A.S.)	Walker.
Wealingas	Walanger marca } { Waplinga }	On the Lahn	Walle (F.)	Wall.
Waplingas		.....		Waple.
Wræningas		.....		Wren, Rennie.
Wilrincgas	Williheringa	Willcring, on Danube	Wyler (A.S.)	Willer.

I may observe with regard to the Anglo-Saxon names in the above lists that there is occasionally a little corruption in their forms. The English trouble with the letter *h* seems to have been present even at this early day. We have Allingas and Hallingas, Anningas and Hanningas, Eslingas and Haslingas, Illingas and Hillingas, in all of which cases the analogy of Old German names would show the *h* to be in all probability an intruder. And the same applies to the Hanesingas, the Honingas, and the Hoppingas. There is also an occasional intrusion of *b* or *p*, thus the Trumpingas, whence the name of Trumpington, should be properly, I take it, Trumingas, A.-S. *trum*, firm, strong. Stark suggests a Celtic word, *drumb*, but the intrusion of *p* is so easy that I think any other explanation hardly necessary. The Sempingas, found in Sempingaham, now Sempringham, should also, I take it, be Semingas, which would be in accordance with Teutonic names, whereas *semp* is a scarcely possible form. Basingstoke, the original of which was Embasingastoc, owes its name to a similar mistake. It would be properly I think Emasingastoc, which would correspond with a Teutonic name-stem. A similar intrusion of *t* occurs in the case of Glæstingabyrig (now Glastonbury), which should I think be Glæssingabyrig ; this again would correspond with an ancient name-stem, which in its present form it does not. So also I take it that Distingas, found in Distington in Cumberland, is only a phonetic corruption of Dissingas, if indeed, (which I very strongly doubt) Distington is from a tribe-name at all. Both of these intrusions are natural from a phonetic point of view, tending as they do to give a little more backbone to a word, and they frequently occur, as I shall have elsewhere occasion to note, in the range of English names.

My object in the present chapter has been more especially to show the intimate connection between our early Saxon names, and those of the general Teutonic system. But now I come to a possible point of difference. All the names of Germany would tend to come to England, but if Anglo-Saxon England made any names on her own account, they would not go back to Germany. For the tide of men flows ever west-ward, and there was no return current in those days. Now there do seem to be certain name-stems peculiar to Anglo-Saxon England, and one of these is *peht* or *pect*, which may be taken to represent Pict. The Teutonic peoples were in the habit of introducing into their nomenclature the names of neighbouring nations even when aliens or enemies. Thus the Hun and the Fin were so introduced, the latter more particularly by the Scandinavians who were their nearest neighbours. There is a tendency among men to invest an enemy upon their borders, of whom they may be in constant dread, with unusual personal characteristics of ferocity or of giant stature. Thus the word *Hun*, as Grimm observes, seems to have become a synonym of giant, and Ohfrid, a metrical writer of the ninth century, describes the giant Polyphemus as the " grosse hun." Something similar I have noted (in a succeeding chapter on the names of women, *in voce* Emma) as possibly subsisting between the Saxons and their Celtic neighbours. The Fins again, who as a peculiarly small people could not possibly be magnified into giants, were invested with magical and unearthly characteristics, and the word became almost, if not quite, synonymous with magician. This then seems to represent something of the general principle, upon which such names have found their way into the Teutonic system of nomenclature.

While then England received all the names formed from peoples throughout the Teutonic area, the Goth, the Vandal, the Bavarian, the Hun, and the Fin, in the names of men, there was one such stem which she had and which the rest of Germany had not, for she alone was neighbour to the Pict. Perhaps I should qualify this statement so far as the Old Saxons of the seaboard are concerned, for they were also neighbours, though as far as we know, the Pict did not figure in their names of men. From the stem *pect* the Anglo-Saxons had a number of names, as Pecthun or Pehtun, Pecthath, Pectgils, Pecthelm, Pectwald, Pectwulf, all formed in accordance with the regular Teutonic system, but none of them found elsewhere than in Anglo-Saxon England. Of these names we may have one, Pecthun, in our surname *Picton*, perhaps also the other form Pehtun in *Peyton* or *Paton*. The Anglo-Saxons no doubt aspirated the *h* in Pehtun, but we seem in such cases either to drop it altogether, or else to represent it by a hard *c*, according perhaps as it might have been more or less strongly aspirated. Indeed the Anglo-Saxons themselves would seem to have sometimes dropped it altogether, if the name Piott, in a will of Archbishop

Wulfred, A.D. 825, is the same word (which another name Piahtred about the same period would rather seem to indicate). And this suggests that our name *Peat* may be one of its present representatives. We have again a name *Picture*, which might represent an Anglo-Saxon Pecther (*heri*, warrior) not yet turned up, but a probable name, the compound being a very common one.

I do not think it necessary to go into the case of any other name-stem which I do not find except among the Anglo-Saxons, inasmuch as, there being in their case no such reason for the restriction as in that to which I have been referring, it may only be that they have not as yet been disinterred.

CHAPTER V.

WE have seen in a preceding chapter that the earliest Saxon place-names in England are derived from a personal name, and that the idea contained is that of a modified form of common right. We shall find that a very large proportion of the later Anglo-Saxon place-names are also derived from the name of a man, but that the idea contained is now that of individual ownership or occupation. The extent to which English place-names are derived from ancient names of men is, in my judgment, very much greater than is generally supposed. And indeed, when we come to consider it, what can be so naturally associated with a *ham* as the name of the man who lived in that home, of a *weorth* as that of the man to whom that property belonged, of a Saxon *tun* or a Danish *by* or *thorp* as that of the man to whom the place owed its existence ? If we turn to Kemble's list of Anglo-Saxon names of places as derived from ancient charters, in the days when the individual owner had succeeded to the community, we cannot fail to remark to how large an extent this obtains, and how many of

these names are in the possessive case. Now, it must
be observed that there are in Anglo-Saxon two forms
of the possessive, and that when a man's name had
the vowel ending in *a*, as noted at p. 24, it formed
its possessive in *an*, while otherwise it formed its
possessive in *es*. Thus we have Baddan byrig,
"Badda's borough," Bennan beorh, "Benna's barrow"
or grave, and in the other form we have Abbodes
byrig, "Abbod's borough," Bluntes ham, "Blunt's
home," and Sylces wyrth, "Silk's worth" or property.
And as compound names did not take a vowel ending,
such names invariably form their possessive in *es*, as
in Haywardes ham, "Hayward's home," Cynewardes
gemæro, "Cyneward's boundary," &c. I am not at all
sure that *ing* also has not, in certain cases, the force of
a possessive, and that Ælfredincgtun, for instance,
may not mean simply "Alfred's town" and not
Alfreding's town. But I do not think that this is
at any rate the general rule, and it seems scarcely
possible to draw the line. From the possessive in
an I take to be most probably our present place-
names Puttenham, Tottenham, and Sydenham, (respecting the last of which there has been a good
deal of discussion of late in *Notes and Queries*), containing the Anglo-Saxon names *Putta*, *Totta*, and
Sida. With regard to the last I have not fallen in
with the name *Sida* itself. But I deduce such a name
from Sydanham, C.D. 379, apparently a place in
Wilts, also perhaps from Sidebirig, now Sidbury, in
Devon; and there is, moreover, a corresponding O.G.
Sido, the origin being probably A.S. *sidu*, manners,
morals. Further traces of such a stem are found in

Sidel deduced from Sidelesham, now Sidlesham, in Sussex, and also from the name *Sydemann* in a charter of Edgar, these names implying a pre-existing stem *sid* upon which they have been formed.

As well as with the *ham* or the *byrig* in which he resided, a man's name is often found among the Anglo-Saxons, connected with the boundary—whatever that might be—of his property, as in Abbudes mearc, Abbud's mark or boundary, and Baldrices gemæro, Baldrick's boundary. Sometimes that boundary might be a hedge, as in Leoferes haga and Danehardes hegeræw, "Leofer's hedge," and "Danehard's hedge-row" Sometimes it might be a stone, as in Sweordes stân, sometimes a ridge, as in Eppan hrycg, "Eppa's ridge," sometimes a ditch or dyke, as in Tilgares dic and Colomores sîc (North. Eng. syke, wet ditch). A tree was naturally a common boundary mark, as in Potteles treôw, Alebeardes âc (oak), Bulemæres thorn, Huttes æsc (ash), Tatmonnes apoldre (apple-tree). Sometimes, again, a man's name is found associated with the road or way that led to his abode, as in Wealdenes weg (way), Sigbrihtes anstige (stig, a foot-path) Dunnes stigele (stile). Another word which seems to have something of the meaning of "stile" is *hlip*, found in Freobearnes hlyp and in Herewines hlipgat. In Anglo-Saxon, *hlypa* signified a stirrup, and a "hlipgat" must, I imagine, have been a gate furnished with some contrivance for mounting over it. Of a similar nature might be Alcherdes ford, and Brochardes ford, and also Geahes ofer, Byrhtes ora, and Æscmann's yre (*ofer*, contr. *ore*, shore or landing-place). Something more of the rights of water may be contained in Fealamares brôc (brook), Hykemeres strêm (stream), and Brihtwoldes wêre (weir); the two latter probably referring to water-power for a mill. The sense of property only seems to be that which is found in Cybles weorthig, Æscmere's weorth (land or property), Tilluces leah (lea), Rumboldes den (*dene* or valley), Bogeles pearruc (paddock), Ticnes feld (field). Also in Grottes grâf (grove), Sweors holt (grove), Pippenes pen (pen or fold), Willeardes hyrst (grove), Leofsiges geat (gate), Ealdermannes hæc (hatch), and Winagares stapol (stall, market, perhaps a place for the sale or interchange of produce). The site of a deserted dwelling served sometimes for a mark, as in Sceolles eald cotan (Sceolles old cot), and Dearmodes ald tun (Deormoda's old town, or inclosure, dwelling and appurtenances ?).

But it is with a man's last resting-place that his name will be found in Anglo-Saxon times to be most especially associated. The principal words used to denote a grave are *beorh* (barrow), *byrgels*, and *hlæw* (low), in all of which the idea seems to be that of a mound raised over the spot. We have Weardes beorh, " Weard's barrow," also Lulles, Cartes, Hornes, Lidgeardes, and many others. We have Scottan byrgels, "Scotta's barrow," also Hôces, Wures, and Strenges. And we have Lortan hlæw, "Lorta's low," also Ceorles, Wintres, Hwittuces, and others. There is another word *hô*, which seems to be the same as the O.N. *haugr*, North. Eng, *how*, a grave-mound. It is found in Healdenes hô, Piccedes hô, Scotehô Tilmundes hô, Cægeshô, and Fingringahô. It would hardly seem, from the location of four of them, Worcester, Essex, Beds, Sussex, that they can be of Scandinavian origin. Can the two words, *haugr* and *hlau* (*how*, and *hlow*), be from the same origin, the one assuming, or the other dropping an *l*?

I take the names of persons thus to be deduced from Anglo-Saxon place-names, and which are in general correspondence with the earlier names in the preceding chapter, though containing some new forms and a greater number of compound names, to give as faithful a representation as we can have of the every-day names of Anglo-Saxons. And as I have before compared the names of those primitive settlers with our existing surnames, so now I propose to extend the comparison to the names of more settled Anglo-Saxon times.

Anglo-Saxon Men's Names.	Place-Names.	English Surnames.
Abbod	Abbodesbyrig	} *Abbott*
Abbud	Abbudesmearc	
Æcemann	Æcemannes ceaster	*Ackman, Aikman*
Acen	Acenes feld	*Aikin*
Ægelweard	Ægelweardes mearc	*Aylward*
Alberht	Alberhtes treow	*Albert*
Alcherd	Alcherdes ford	*Allcard*
Alder	Aldrestub	*Alder*
Ælfgar	Ælfgares gemæro	*Algar*
Ælfred	Ælfredes beorh	*Alfred, Allfrey*
Ælfher, or Ælfheri	} Ælfheres stapol	*Alvary*
Æscmer	Æscmeres weorth	*Ashmore*
Æscmann	Æscmannes yre	*Ashman*
Alebeard	Alebeardes âc	*Halbard*
Amber	Ambresbyrig	*Amber*
Æthelstan	Æthelstanes tûn	*Ethelston*

Anglo-Saxon Men's Names.	Place-Names.	English Surnames.
Babel	Babeles beorh	*Bable*
Badherd	Badherdes sled	*Beddard*
Baldher	Baldheresberg	*Balder*
Baldric	Baldrices gemæro	*Baldridge*
Baldwin	Baldwines heath	*Baldwin*
Beored, or Beoret	Beoredes treôw	*Berrette*
Beornheard	Beornheardes lond	*Bernard*
Beornwold	Beornwoldes sætan	*Bernold*
Blunt	Bluntesham	*Blunt*
Bogel	Bogeles pearruc	*Bogle*
Bohmer	Bohmeres stigele	*Bowmer*
Bregen	Bregnesford	*Brain*
Brochard	Brochardes ford	*Brocard*
Buga	Buganstôc	} *Bugg*
Bugga	Bugganbrôc	
Bulemær	Bulemæres thorn	*Bulmer*
Buntel .	Bunteles pyt	*Bundle*
Bunting	Buntingedîc	*Bunting*
Burhgeard	Burhgeardeswerthig	*Burchard*
Carda	Cardan hlæw	*Card, Cart*
Ceapa	Ceapan hlæw	*Cheape*
Ceawa	Ceawan hlæw	*Chew*
Cerda	Cerdan hlæw	*Chard*
Cissa	Cissan anstige	*Cheese*
Chetol (Danish)	Chetoles beorh	*Kettle*
Creoda	Creodan âc	} *Creed*
Cridd	Criddes hô	
Cumen	Cumenes ora	*Cummin*
Ceatewe	Ceatewesleah	*Chattoway*
Ceada	Ceadanford	*Chad*
Catt	Cattes stoke	*Cat, Catty*
Cæstæl	Cæstælesham	*Castle*
Cludd	Cludesleah	*Cloud*
Coten	Cotenesfeld	*Cotton*
Cruda	Crudan sceat	*Crowd*
Colomor	Colomores sîc	*Colmer*

Anglo-Saxon Men's Names.	Place-Names.	English Surnames.
Cydd	Cyddesige	*Kidd*
Cyble	Cybles weorthig	*Keble*
Celc	Celces ora	*Kelk*
Cylman	Cylmanstun	*Killman*
Cynlaf	Cynlafes stan	*Cunliffe*
Cynric	Cynrices gemæro	*Kenrick*
Cyneward	Cynewardes gemæro	*Kenward*
Cyppa	Cyppanham	*Chipp*
Dægel, or	Dæglesford	} *Dale*
Deil	Deilsford	
Dearnagel	Dearnagles ford	*Darnell*
Dæneheard	Dæneheardes hegerawe	*Denhard*
Deorlaf	Deorlafestun	*Dearlove*
Deormod [1]	Deormodes ald tun	*Dermott*
Dodd	Doddesthorp	} *Dodd*
Dodda	Doddan hlæw	
Dolemann	Dolemannes beorh	*Dollman*
Duceman	Ducemannestun	*Duckman*
Ducling	Duclingtun	*Duckling*
Dunn	Dunnes stigele	*Dunn*
Dogod	Dogodeswel	*Doggett, Dugood*
Dydimer	Dydimertun	*Tidemore*
Ealder	Ealderscumb	*Alder*
Ealdmann	Ealdmannes wyrth	*Altman*
Ealdermann [2]	Ealdermannes hæc	*Alderman*
Ealmund	Ealmundes treow	*Almond*
Eanulf	Eanulfestun	*Enough*
Earn	Earnesbeorh	*Earney*

---

[1] Cf. also Diormod, moneyer on Anglo-Saxon coins, minted at Canterbury. There is, however, an Irish Diarmaid which might in certain cases intermix, and whence we must take *McDermott.*

[2] I take Ealdermann to be, as elsewhere noted, a corruption of Ealdmann.

Anglo-Saxon Men's Names.	Place-Names.	English Surnames.
Eastmond	Eastmondestun	*Esmond*
Ecgell	Ecgeles stiel	*Edgell, Eagle*
Fealamar	Fealamares brôc	{ *Fillmore* { *Phillimore*
Flegg	Flegges garan	*Flew*
Focga	Focgancrundel	*Fogg, Foggo*
Freobearn	Freobearnes hlyp	*Freeborn*
Frigedæg	Frigedæges treôw	*Friday*
Fuhgel	Fuhgeles beorh	*Fuggle, Fowl*
Gandar	Gandrandun	*Gander*
Gæcg	Gæcges stapol	{ *Gay*
Geah	Geahes ofer	{
Gatehlinc	Gatehlinces heafod	*Gatling*
Geleca	Gelecancamp	*Jellicoe*
Geyn	Geynes thorn	*Gain*
Giselher	Gislhereswurth	*Giller*
Godincg	Godincges gemæro	*Godding*
Godmund	Godmundesleah	*Godmund*
Godwin	Godwines gemæro	*Godwin*
Grobb	Grobbes den	*Grove, Grubb*
Grott	Grottes grâf	*Grote*
Gund	Gundestige	*Gunn, Gundey*
Hærred	Hærredesleah	*Herod*
Heafoc	Heafoceshamme	*Hawk*
Hassuc	Hassuces môr	*Haskey*
Hering	Heringesleah	*Herring*
Hnibba	Hnibbanleah	*Knibb, Knipe*
Hayward	Haywardes ham	*Hayward*
Healda	Healdan grâf	*Hald*
Healden	Healdenes hô	*Haldan*
Helm	Helmes treow	*Helme*
Helfær	Helfæres gemæro	*Helper*
Help	Helpestonne	*Helps*
Herebritt	Herebrittes comb	*Herbert*
Herewin	Herewines hlipgat	*Irwine*

Anglo-Saxon Men's Names.	Place-Names.	English Surnames.
Hiccemann	Hiccemannes stân	*Hickman*
Humbald	Humbalding grâf	*Humble*
Hycemer, or Higemar	} Hycemeres strêm	*Highmore*
Hnæf	Hnæfes scylf	*Knapp*
Hocg	Hocgestun	*Hogg, Hodge*
Horn	Hornes beorh	*Horne*
Hringwold	Hringwoldes beorh	*Ringold*
Hwittuc	Hwittuces leah	*Whittock*
Hutt	Huttes æsc	*Hutt*
Hygelac [1]	Hygelaces git	*Hillock*
Kyld	Kyldesby	*Kilt*
Leofer	Leoferes haga	*Lover*
Laferca	Lafercanbeorh	*Laverick*
Leofmann	Leofmannes gemæro	*Loveman*
Leommann	Leommannes grâf	*Lemon*
Leofsig	Leofsiges geat	*Lovesy*
Leofric	Leofrices gemæro	*Loveridge*
Lidgeard	Lidgeardes beorh	*Ledgard*
Lipperd	Lipperdes gemæro	*Leopard*
Lower	Lowereslege	*Lower*
Locer	Loceresweg	*Locker*
Lorta	Lortanberwe	*Lord*
Lorting	Lortinges bourne	*Lording*
Luder	Luderston	*Luther*
Ludmann	Ludmannes put	*Lutman*
Lull	Lulles beorh	*Lull, Lully*
Myceld	Myceldefer	*Muckell*
Mûl	Muleshlæw	*Moule*

[1] Mr. Kemble, in default of finding Hygelac as a man's name in Anglo-Saxon times, has taken the above place-name to be from the legendary hero of that name. The fact is, however, that Hygelac occurs no fewer than four times as an early man's-name in the *Liber Vitæ*, so that there does not seem to be any reason whatever for looking upon it as anything else than the every-day name of an Anglo-Saxon.

Anglo-Saxon Men's Names.	Place-Names.	English Surnames.
Negle	Neglesleah	*Nagle*
Næl	Nælesbrôc	*Nail*
Nybba	Nybban beorh	*Nibbs*
Oslac	Oslaces lea	*Hasluck*
Ogged	Oggedestun	*Hodgett, Howitt*
Oswald	Oswaldes mere	*Oswald*
Orlaf	Orlafestun	*Orlop*
Owun	Owunes hild	*Owen*
Pehtun	Pehtuns treow	*Peyton*
Pender	Penderes clif	*Pender*
Picced	Piccedes hô	*Pickett*
Pinnel	Pinnelesfeld	*Pennell*
Pippen	Pippenes fen	*Pippin*
Pyttel	Pittelesford	*Piddel*
Pitterich	Piterichesham	*Betteridge*
Pottel	Potteles treow	*Pottle*
Potten	Pottenestreow	*Potten*
Punt	Puntes stân	*Punt*
Puntel	Punteles treow	*Bundle'*
Prentsa	Prentsan hlaw	*Prentiss*
Redwin	Redwines thorn	*Readwin*
Rahulf	Rahulfes furlong	*Ralph*
Rugebeorg	Rugebeorges gemæro	*Rubery*
Rumbold	Rumboldes den	*Rumbold*
Sceaft	Sceaftesbirig	*Shaft, Shafto*
Sceoll	Sceolles ealdcotan	*Sholl*
Scytta	Scyttandun	*Skeat, Shute*
Scyter [1],	Scyteres flôd	*Shuter*
Scealc	Scealces hom	*Shawkey, Chalk ?*
Scyld	Scyldes treow	*Shield*

[1] From a similar origin is probably Shooter's Hill, near London.

Anglo-Saxon Men's Names.	Place-Names.	English Surnames.
Simær	Simæres ford	Seymour
Secmær	Secmæres ora	Sycamore
Sigbriht	Sigbrihtes anstige	Sibert
Sibriht	Sibrihtesweald	Seabright [1]
Siger	Sigeres âc	Segar
Snell	Snellesham	Snell
Snod	Snodes hyl	Snoad
Streng	Strenges hô	Strong
Stut	Stutes hyl	Stout, Stott
Stutard	Stutardes cumb	Stothard, Studeard
Sucga	Sucgangrâf	Sugg
Sumer	Sumeresham	Summer
Sumerled (Danish)	Sumerledetun	Sommerlat
Sunemann	Sunemannes wyrthig	Sunman
Sweor	Sweores holt	Swire, Swears
Sweord	Sweordes stân	Sword
Tæcel	Tæcelesbrôc	Tackle
Tatmonn	Tatmonnes apoldre	Tadman
Tatel	Tatlestrop	Tattle
Thuner	Thunresfeld	Thunder
Thurgar (Danish)	Thurgartun	Thurgur
Thrista	Thristan den	Trist
Theodhcr	Theoderpoth	Theodore
Thurold (Danish)	Thuroldes gemæro	Thorold
Toma	Tomanworthig	Tomey
Ticcen	Ticnesfeld	Dickin
Tilgar	Tilgares dîc	Dilger
Tilluc	Tilluces lcah	Tillick, Dilke
Tilmann	Tilmannes den	Tilman
Titferth	Titferthes gcat	Titford
Upicen	Upicenes hlyw	Hopkin
Wahgen	Wahgenes gemæro	Wain
Wealden	Wealdenes weg	Walden

---

[1] There is also an A. S. Sæbriht, from *sæ*, sea, whence *Seabright* might be derived.

Anglo-Saxon Men's Names.	Place-Names.	English Surnames.
Wealder	Wealderes weg	*Walter*
Westan	Westanes treow	*Weston*
Wigheard	Wigheardes stapol	*Wyard*
Wighelm	Wighelmes land	*Whigam*
Wihtlac	Wihtlaces ford	*Whitelock*
Wihtric	Wihtricesham	*Whitridge*
Wilmund	Wilmundes leah	*Williment*
Willher	Willheres triow	*Willer*
Wicg	Wicgestan	*Wigg*
Uuigga	Wuiggangeat	
Winagar	Winagares stapul	*Winegar*
Wileard	Wileardes hyrste	*Willard*
Wistan for Wigstan ?	} Wistanes gemæro	*Whiston*
Wulfsig	Wulfsiges croft	*Wolsey*
Wulfgar	Wulfgares gemæro	*Woolgar*
Wulfmer	Wulfmeres myln	*Woolmer*
Wulfric	Wulfrices gemæro	*Woolrych*
Wyner	Wyneres stig	*Winer*
Waring	Wæring wîc	*Waring*
Wifel	Wifelesham	*Whipple*
Woden [1]	Wodnesbeorg	*Woodin ?*
Wydda	Wyddanbeorh	*Widow*

The above names are deduced entirely from the names of places found by Mr. Kemble in ancient charters. The list is not by any means an exhaustive one, as I have not included a number of names taken into account in Chap. IV., and as also the same personal name enters frequently into several place-names. With very few exceptions these names may be gathered

[1] Upon the whole I am inclined to think that Woden is here an Anglo-Saxon man's name, though the traces of it in such use are but slight. There is a Richard Wodan in the *Lib. Vit.* about the 15th century. And Wotan occurs once as a man's name in the *Altdeutsches Namenbuch.*

to the roll of Teutonic name-stems, notwithstanding a little disguise in some of their forms, and a great, sometimes a rather confusing, diversity of spelling. I take names such as the above to be the representatives of the every-day names of men in Anglo-Saxon times, rather than the names which come before us in history and in historical documents. For it seems to me that a kind of fashion prevailed, and that while a set of names of a longer and more dignified character were in favour among the great, the mass of the people still, to a great extent, adhered to the shorter and more simple names which their fathers had borne before them. Thus, when we find an Æthelwold who was also called Mol, an Æthelmer who was also called Dodda, and a Queen Hrothwaru who was also called Bucge, I am disposed to take the simple names, which are such as the earlier settlers brought over with them, to have been the original names, and superseded by names more in accordance with the prevailing fashion. Valuable then as is the *Liber Vitæ* of Durham, as a continuous record of English names for many centuries, yet I am inclined to think that inasmuch as that the persons who come before us as benefactors to the shrine of St. Cuthbert may be taken to be as a general rule of the upper ranks of life, they do not afford so faithful a representation of the every-day names of Anglo-Saxons as do the little freeholders who lived and died in their country homes. And, moreover, these are, as it will be seen, more especially the kind of names which have been handed down from Anglo-Saxon times to the present day.

In connection with this subject, it may be of interest to present a list of existing names of places formed from an Anglo-Saxon personal name, as derived from the same ancient charters dealt with in the previous list. And in so doing I confine myself exclusively to the places of which the present names have been positively identified by Mr. Kemble. And in the first place I will take the place-names which consist simply of the name of a tribe or family unqualified by any local term whatever.

Name in Anglo-Saxon Charters.	Present Name.	
Æfeningas	Avening	Gloucestershire
Angemeringum	Angmering	Sussex
Ascengas	Eashing	Surrey
Banesingas	Bensington	Oxfordshire
Bærlingas	Barling	Kent
Beadingum	Beden	Gloucestershire
Berecingas	Barking	Essex
Brahcingum	Braughin	Herts.
Byrhtlingas	Brightling	Sussex
Cerringes	Charing	Kent
Ciwingum	Chewing	Herts.
Culingas	Cooling	Kent
Cytringas	Kettering	Northampton
Diccelingas	Ditchling	Sussex
Geddingas	Yeading	Middlesex
Godelmingum	Godalming	Surrey
Hallingas	Halling	Kent
Herlinge	Harling	Norfolk
Horningga	Horning	Norfolk
Meallingas	Malling	Kent
Pæccingas	Patching	Sussex
Puningas	Poynings	Surrey
Readingan	Reading	Berkshire
Rodinges	Roothing	Essex

Name in Anglo-Saxon Charters.	Present Name.	
Stæningas	Steyning	Sussex
Swyrdhlincas (Swyrdlingas)	Swarling	Kent
Terringes	Tarring	Sussex
Terlinges	Terling	Essex
Totingas	Tooting	Surrey
Wellingum	Wellwyn	Herts.
Werhornas	Warehorne	Kent
Wihttringas	Wittering	Surrey
Uoccingas	Woking	Surrey
Wyrtingas	Worting	Hants.

I will now take the places which in a later and more settled time have been derived from the name of a single man, as representing his dwelling, his domain, or in not a few cases his grave.

Anglo-Saxon Man's Name.	Place-Name.		Present Name.
Abba	Abbandun	Abingdon	Berks.
Ægel	Ægelesbyrig	Aylesbury	Bucks.
	Æglesford	Aylesford	Kent
	Ægeleswurth	Aylesworth	Nthmptn.
Agmod	Agmodesham	Agmondesham	Bucks.
Æsc	Æscesbyrig	Ashbury	Berks.
Æscmer	Æscmeres weorth	Ashmansworth	Hants.
Amber	Ambresbyrig	Amesbury	Wilts.
	Ambresleah	Ombersley	Worc.
Ælfreding	Ælfredincgtun	Alfreton	Derby.
Badda	Baddanby	Badby	Nthmptn.
Badhelming	Badimyncgtun	Badminton	Glouc.
Baldher	Baldheresberg	Baltonsborough	Somerset.
Becca	Beccanleah	Beckley	Sussex.
Beda	Bedanford	Bedford¹	Beds.
Benna	Bennanham	Beenham	Berks.
Benning	Benningwurth	Bengworth	Worc.

Anglo-Saxon Man's Name.	Place-Name.	Present Name.	
Bledda	Bleddanhlæw	Bledlow	Bucks.
Blunt	Bluntesham	Bluntisham	Hunts.
Bodeca	Bodecanleah	Butleigh	Somerset.
Bodek	Bodekesham	Bottisham	Camb.
Bocga	Bocganora	Bognor	Sussex
Bordel	Bordelestun	Burleston	Dorset.
Brand	Brandesburh	Bransbury	Hants.
Bregen	Bregnesford	Bransford	Worc.
Cada	Cadandun	Chadlington	Oxford.
Cæg	Cægeshô	Keysoe	Beds.
Calmund	Calmundes den	Calmsden	Glouc.
Ceadela	Ceadelanwurth	Chaddleworth	Berks.
Ceadel	Ceadeleshunt	Chadshunt	Warw.
Ceader	Ceadresleah	Chaseley	Worc.
Cendel	Cendeles funta	Chalfont	Bucks.
Celta	Celtenhom	Cheltenham	Glouc.
Ceol	Ceolesig	Cholsey	Berks.
Cippa	Cippenham	Chippenham	Wilts.
Ceolbalding	Ceolbaldinctun	Chilbolton	Hants.
Ceort	Ceortesege	Chertsey	Surrey
Cinhild (woman)	Cinildewyrth	Kenilworth	Warw.
Cissa	Cissanceaster	Chichester	Sussex
Coda	Codanford	Codford	Wilts.
Codda	Coddanhrycg	Cotheridge	Worc.
Coling	Colingham	Collingham	Notts.
Crym	Crymesham	Crimsham	Sussex
Croppa	Croppanthorn	Cropthorn	Worc.
Cumen	Cumenora	Cumnor	Berks.
Cungar	Cungaresbyrig	Congressbury	Somerset
Cwichelm	Cwichelmes hlæw	Cuckamslow hill	Berks.
Cyneburging [1]	Cyneburgincton	Kemerton	Glouc.
Cynlaf	Kynleveden	Kelvedon	Essex
Ketel (Danish)	Kitlebig	Kettleby	Linc.

[1] Or Cyneburg ; see p. 71.

Anglo-Saxon Man's Name.	Place-Name.	Present Name,
Dæcca, or Dægga	} Daccanhaam	Dagenham	Essex
Dægel	Dæglesford	Daylesford	Worc.
Deôrlaf	Deorlafestun	Darlaston	Staffs.
Dodda	Doddanford	Dodford	Nthmptn.
Dodd	Doddesthorp	Dogsthorp	Nthmptn.
Dogod	Dogodeswel	Dowdswell	Glouc.
Domec	Domecesige	Dauntsey	Wilts.
Duceling	Duceling dun	Ducklington	Oxford.
Dunning	Dunnincland	Donyland	Essex
Dideling	Didelingtun	Didlington	Dorset.
Eadric	Eadricestun	Edstone	Warw.
Eccing	Eccingtun	Eckington	Worc.
Eccle, or Egil	Eccleshale	Exhall	Warw.
Effing	Effingeham	Effingham	Surrey
Erping	Erpingham	. Erpingham	Norfolk
Eof, or Eofa	Eofesham	Evesham	Worc.
Fecca	Feccanhom	Feckenham	Worc.
Flæda	Flædanburg	Fladbury	Worc.
Folc	Folcesstan	Folkstone	Kent
Gidding	Gjddincford	Gidding	Suffolk
Gyseling	Gyselingham	Gislingham	Suffolk
Godmer	Godmeresham	Godmersham	Kent
Grim	Grimaston	Grimstone	Norfolk
Gun or Gund	Gunthorpe	Gunthorp	Nthmptn.
Gyp	Gypeswich	Ipswich	Suffolk
Hauek	Hauekestun	Hauxton	Camb.
Hæfar	Hæfaresham	Haversham	Bucks.
Hamela	Hamelendûn	Hambledon	Hants.
Hærigeard	Hærigeardesham	Harrietsham	Kent
Haling	Halington	Hallington	Linc.
Hanekyn	Hanekynton	Hankerton	Wilts.
Hanning	, Hanningtun	Hannington	Hants.
Hæda	Hædanham	Haddenham	Camb.

Anglo-Saxon Man's Name.	Place-Name.	Present Name.	
Helming	Helmyngton	Hemington	Nthmptn
Help	Helpestonne	Helpstone	Nthmptn.
Hemming	Hemmingford	{ Hemingford Abbots	} Hunts.
Hengest	{ Hengesteshricg Hengestesige	Henstridge Hinksey	Somerset. Berks.
Hild	Hildesdûn	Hillersdon	Bucks.
Heorulf	Heorelfestun	Harleston	Staff.
Heorting	Heortingtun	Hardington	Somerset.
Honekyn	Honekynton	Hankerton	Wilts.
Honing	Honingtun	Honington	Linc.
Horning	{ Horningeseie Horningges hæth	Horningsea Horningsheath	Camb. Suffolk
Hôd	Hôdesâc	Hodsoak	Worc.
Hunewald	Hunewaldesham	Windlesham	Surrey
Hunta	Huntandun	Huntingdon	Hants.
Hwiting	Hwitingtun	Whittington	Worc.
Kyld	Kyldesby	Kilsby	Nthmptn.
Laua	Lauanham	Lavenham	Suffolk
Lauing	Lauingtun	Barlavington	Sussex
Lamb (Danish?)	Lambehith	Lambeth	
Lott	Lottisham	Lottisham	Somerset.
Mealdhelm	Mealdumesburg	Malmsbury	Wilts.
Myceld	Myceldefer	Mitcheldover	Hants.
Mûl	{ Mûleseige Mûlesham ·	Moulsey Moulsham	Surrey Essex
Munda	Mundanham	Mundham	Sussex
Neteling	Netelingtun	Nettleton	Wilts.
Offa	Offanleah	Offley	Herts.
Orlaf	Orlafestun	Orleston	Derby.
Orm (Danish)	Ormisby	Ormsby	Norfolk
Osgot	Osgotbi	Osgodby	Linc.
Oshelming	Osmingtun	Osmington	Dorset
Oswald	Oswaldeshlaw	Oswaldslow	· Worc.

Anglo-Saxon Man's Name.	Place-Name.	Present Name.	
Pading	Padingtun	Paddington	
Parting	Partingtun	Patrington	Yorks.
Peda	Pedanhrycg	Petridge	Surrey
Peada	Peadanwurth	Padworth	Berks.
Peatting	Peattingtun	Pattingham	Salop
Pecga	Pecganham	Pagham	Sussex
Peden	Pednesham	Pensham	Worc.
Piterich	Piterichesham	Petersham	Worc.
Port	Portesham	Portisham	Dorset.
Raculf	Raculfcestre	Reculver	Kent
Remn [1] for Raven	Remnesdun	Ramsden	Sussex
Rydemær, or Redmer	Rydemæreleah	Redmarley	Worc.
Riking	Rikinghal	Rickinghall	Suffolk
Ring	Ringestede	Ringstead	Norfolk
Rodda	Roddanbeorg	Rodborough	Glouc.
Rolf, for	Rolfestun	Rolleston	Staffs.
Rodulf	Rollesby	Rollesby	Norfolk
Sidel	Sidelesham	Sidlesham	Sussex
Sceaft	Sceaftesbirig	Shaftesbury	Dorset.
Secg	Secgesbearue	Sedgeberrow	Worc.
Snodd	Snoddesbyrig	Upton Snodsbury	Worc.
Snoding	Snodingland	Snodland	Worc.
Sumer	Sumeresham	Somersham	Hunts.
Sumerled(Danish)	Sumerledetun	Somerleyton	Suffolk
Sunna	Sunnandun	Sundon	Beds.
Swythbriht	Swythbrihtesweald	Sibbertswold	Kent
Swithreding	Swithrædingden	Surrenden	Kent
Sylc	Sylceswyrth	Silksworth	Durham
Tadmær	Tadmærtun	Tadmarton	Oxford.

---

[1] It seems clear from the names collated by German writers that *ramn, remn,* and *ram* in ancient names are contractions of raven. Compare the names of the ports, Soderhamn, Nyhamn, and Sandhamn, for, no doubt, Soderhaven, Nyhaven, and Sandhaven.

Anglo-Saxon Man's Name.	Place-Name.		Present Name.	
Tæfing	Tæfingstoc		Tavistock	Devon.
Teotting	Teottingtun		Teddington	Wor .
Taling	Talingtun		Tallington	Linc.
Toda	Todanhom		Toddenham	Glouc.
Toma	Tomanworthig		Tamworth	Warw.
Theogen	Theogendethorp		Theddlethorp	Linc.
Thunar	Thunresfeld		Thundersfield	Surrey
Ticen	Ticnesfeld		Tichfield	Hants.
Tidhelming	Tidelminctun		Tidmington	Worc.
Tilling	Tillingham		Tillingham	Essex
Tocca	Toccanham		Tockenham	Wilts.
Toting	Totingtun		Tottington	Norfolk
Treding	{	Tredingtun	Tredington	Glouc.
	{	Tredinctun	Tredington	Worc.
Trosting	Trostingtun		Troston	Suffolk
Tuding	Tudingtun		Teddington	Middlsx.
Tunweald	Tunwealdes stân		Tunstone	Glouc.
Turca	Turcanden		Turkdean	Glouc.
Twica	Tuicanham		Twickenham	Middlsx.
Thurgar (Danish)	Thurgartun		Thurgarton	Norfolk
Ufing	Ufinctun		Ovington	- Hants.
Wacen	Uacenesfeld		Watchfield	Berks.
Watling	Uætlinctun		Watlington	Oxford.
Wassing	Wassingburg		Washingborough	Linc.
Wald	Waldeswel		Woldswell	Glouc.
Weard	Weardesbeorh		Warborough	Oxford.
Wifel	{	Wifeles cumb	Wiveliscomb	Somerset.
	{	Wifelesford	Wilsford	Wilts.
Wilburg (Woman)	{	Wilburgeham	Wilbraham	Camb.
	{	Wilburhtun	Wilburton	Camb.
Willer	Willerseia		Willersey	Glouc.
Weogern	Weogernacester		Worcester	Worc.
Wine	{	Uines hlau	Winslow	Bucks.
	{	Wines hyl	Winshill	Derby.
Wrening	Wreningham		Wreningham	Norfolk

Anglo-Saxon Man's Name.	Place-Name.	Present Name.	
Werot	Uurotaham	Wrotham	Kent
Wulfwarding	Wulfweardigleâ	Wolverley	Worc.
Wendel, or Windel	Wendlesora, or Windlesora	Windsor	Berks.

The last name, Windsor, is an amusing instance of the older attempts at local etymology. First it was supposed, as being an exposed spot, to have taken its name from the "wind is sore;" then it was presumed that it must have been a ferry, and that the name arose from the constant cry of "wind us o'er" from those waiting to be ferried across. It was a great step in advance when the next etymologist referred to the ancient name and found it to be Windelsora, from *ora*, shore, (a contraction of *ofer?*) Still, the etymon he deduced therefrom of "winding shore" is one that could not be adopted without doing great violence to the word; whereas, without the change of a letter, we have Windels ore, " Windel's shore," most probably in the sense of landing-place. The name Windel forms several other place-names; it was common in ancient times, and it has been taken to mean Vandal. I refer to this more especially to illustrate the importance of taking men's names into account in considering the origin of a place-name.

The above names are confined entirely, as I have before mentioned, to the places that have been positively identified by Mr. Kemble. And as these constitute but a small proportion of the whole number, the comparison will serve to give an idea of the very great extent to which place-names are formed from men's names.

CHAPTER VI.

CORRUPTIONS may be divided broadly into two kinds, those which proceed from a desire to improve the sound of a name, and those which proceed from a desire to make some kind of sense out of it. The former, which we may call phonetic, generally consists in the introduction of a letter, either to give more of what we may call "backbone" to a word, or else to make it run more smoothly. For the former purpose *b* or *p* is often used—thus we have, even in Anglo-Saxon times, *trum* made into *trump*, *sem* into *semp*, and *emas* into *embas*. So among our names we have *Dumplin*, no doubt for Dumlin (O.G. Domlin), *Gamble* for Gamel, and *Ambler* for Ameler, though in these names something of both the two principles may apply. In a similar manner we have *glas* made into *glast* in Glæstingabyrig, now Glastonbury (p. 88). So *d* seems sometimes to be brought in to strengthen the end of a word, and this, it appears to me, may be the origin of our names *Field*, *Fielding, Fielder.* The forms seem to show an ancient stem, but as the word stands, it is difficult to make anything out of it, whereas, as Fiell, Fielling, &c.,

I

the names would fall in with a regular stem, as at
p. 50). So also our name *Hind* may perhaps be
the same, assuming a final *d*, as another name, *Hine*,
which, presuming the *h* not to be organic, may be
from the unexplained stem *in* or *ine*, as in the name
of Ina, King of Wessex. In which case *Hyndman*
might be the same name as *Inman*. Upon the same
principle it may be that we have the name *Nield*
formed upon the Celtic Niel. So also *f* appears to be
sometimes changed for a similar purpose into *p*, as
in *Asprey* and *Lamprey* for Asfrid (or Osfrid) and
Landfrid. The ending *frid* commonly becomes *frey*
(as in Godfrey, Humphrey, Geoffrey), and when we
have got Asfrey and Lanfrey (and we have Lanfrei
in the *Liber Vitæ*), the rest is easy.

The most common phonetic intrusion is that of *r*,
and one of the ways in which it most frequently
occurs is exhibited in the following group of names:
Pendgast, Pendegast, Prendergast, Prendergrass.
Pendgast is, I take it, an ancient compound, from
the stem *bend* (p. 44), with *gast*, hospes. It first
takes a medial vowel between the two words of the
compound, and becomes Pend-e-gast. Then *e*
naturally becomes *er*, passing the very slight barrier
which English pronunciation affords, and the name,
having become Pendergast, finds the need of a second
r to balance the first, and becomes Prendergast. In
the last name, Prendergrass, the other principle comes
in, and a slight effort is made to give a shade of
meaning to the word.[1] One of the features in men's

---

[1] There is another name *Snodgrass*, which may be a similar
corruption of Snodgast, from the stem *snod*, A.S. *snot*, wise.

names, it will be seen, is that as they have (differently to what is the case with regard to the words of the language) become crystallised in all stages, one is sometimes permitted to see the various steps of a process.

Now it is in such a way as that described above that the Anglo-Saxon name Ealdermann (whence our name *Alderman*) has, according to my opinion, been formed. There is another Anglo-Saxon name, Ealdmann, an ancient compound. Now if you, as in the previous case, introduce a medial vowel, and make it Eald-e-mann, there is virtually nothing left between that and Ealdermann. Such a name, as derived from the office, would be impossible as a regular Anglo-Saxon name. The only other alternative would be that he had been so called as a *sobriquet* by his office till it had superseded his regular name. And there does appear to have been such a case, viz., that of a man called Preost who *was* a priest, but the way which I have suggested seems to me to account more easily for the name. From a similar origin I take to be our name *Ackerman*, and the present German *Ackermann*. There is an Anglo-Saxon Æçemann (p. 96), from which, on the principle described above, they might be derived. So also *Sigournay* may be formed in a similar manner from an old German name Siginiu (*niu*, "new," perhaps in the sense of "young"), and *Alderdice* from an old Frankish Aldadeus (*deus*, servant).

I have taken Prendergast for Pendgast as an illustration of the intrusion of *r*, and there is even in Anglo-Saxon times an example of the very same

I 2

word as so treated. This is the name Prentsa (p. 101),
(whence our *Prentiss*), and which I take to be properly
Pentsa. This would bring it in as a regular Anglo-
Saxon stem (*cf.* Penda, Pender, Penduald, Pendwine),
whereas otherwise it is difficult to know what to make
of it. Among English surnames thus treated we have
Bellringer for Bellinger, *Sternhold* for Stonhold (p. 63),
Proudfoot for *Puddefoot* (*bud,* messenger), and possibly
Cardwell for the Anglo-Saxon Cadweal.[1]   On the
same principle I think that *Wordsworth,* a name of
local origin, may be, with an intrusive *r*, the same as
Wodsworth or Wadsworth (Wad's property or estate).
There is certainly a stem *wurd* (supposed to mean
fate, destiny), in ancient names, but it is of rare
occurrence, and I do not know of it in English names,
though we have *Orde,* which I take to be from the
Scandinavian form of it.   On the other hand we have
an instance in Anglo-Saxon times of the reverse
process, viz., the elision of *r*, in the case of Wihtbrord, Minister of Edward the Elder, who, though
he spells his names both ways, spells it more
frequently Wihtbrod, the other being no doubt
etymologically the correct form (*brord,* sword), though
euphony is certainly promoted by the elision. This
may probably be the origin of our name *Whitbread,*
with the variation *Wheatbread.*

The intrusion of *d* has had the effect of changing
a man's name into a woman's in two cases, *Mildred*

---

1 This however is by no means certain, inasmuch as there is
a stem *card* or *gard* from which it might be formed, though the
corresponding ancient name has not turned up.   On the other
hand it is to be observed that *wealh* is not one of the more
common endings.

and *Kindred.* The former should be properly Milred, answering to an Anglo-Saxon Milred, and the latter should be Kenred, answering to the German Conrad ; Mildryd and Cynedryd were, and could only be, Anglo-Saxon women's names.

On the other hand, the loss of an *r* has had such a disastrous effect in the case of an American *Bedbug* as to compel him to apply, like his English name-sake, for a change of name. For while, in America, all insects of the beetle tribe are called by the name of "bug," the "bedbug" is that particular insect which is a "terror by night," so that the name was pointedly disagreeable. It ought properly to be, I doubt not, Bedburg, a name of local origin, and the same as Bedborough.

Before going on to deal with the corruptions which originate in the desire to make some kind of sense out of a name, I propose to refer briefly to some of the changes and contractions which are more strictly in accordance with regular phonetic principles. I have referred at p. 9 to a final *g* as opposed to the English ear, and to two different ways in which it is got rid of, viz., by changing it into *dg*, and by dropping it altogether. There is yet a third way, that of changing it into *f*, as in Anglo-Saxon *genug*, English *enough*. And we can show examples of all these in the same name, from the ancient stem *wag*, probably signifying to wave, brandish, as in the name Wagbrand ("wave-sword"), in the genealogy of the Northumbrian kings. For we have the name in all four forms, *Wagg*, *Way*, *Wadge*, *Waugh* (Waff). The common ending in Teutonic names of *wig*, war;

often, anciently even, softened into *wi*, most commonly in such case becomes in our names *way*. Thus we have *Alloway* from an ancient Alewih, *Chattoway* from Ceatewe, *Dalloway* from Daliweh, *Galloway* from Geilwih, *Garroway* from Gerwi, *Hathaway* from Hathuwi, *Kennaway* from Kenewi, *Lanoway* from Lantwih, *Reddoway* from Redwi, and *Ridgway* from Ricwi. I cite this as a case in which a number of coincidences prove a principle, which the reader, if he confined his attention to one particular case, might be disposed to question. We also generally drop the *g* in the middle of a word in such names as *Payne*, from A.S. Pagen,[1] *Wain* from A.S. Wahgen, *Gain* from A.S. Gagen, *Nail* from A.S. Negle. So also in *Sibbald* for Sigebald, *Sibert* for Sigebert, *Seymore* for Sigimar, *Wyatt* for Wighad, &c. There is also a frequent dropping of *d*, though I think that in this case the names have more frequently come down to us from ancient times in such contracted form, the practice being more specially common among the Franks, from whom I think that most of the names in question have been derived. Thus we have *Cobbold* for Codbald or Godbold, *Cobbett* for Godbet or Codbet, *Lucas* (Lucas, *Lib. Vit.*), from a Frankish Liucoz for Liudgoz, *Boggis* from a Boggis for Bodgis, *Lewis* for Leodgis, *Rabbit* for Radbod, *Chabot* for Chadbod, So also *Ralph* and *Rolfe* for Radulf and Hrodulf (though also for Ragulf and Hrogulf), *Roland* for Rodland, *Roman* for Rodman, &c. So *f* is often

---

[1] Pagan occurs as an A.S. name, (Thorpe, p. 648), and may probably be referred to *bagan*, to contend. *Cf.* also Pagingas among the early settlers.

dropped when it is followed by *m* or *n*, as in A.S. Leomman for Leofmann, whence our *Lemon.* It is probable that our *Limmer* is a similar contraction of A.S. Leofmer.

As a case of transposition I may note *Falstaff* from, as supposed, the O.G. name Fastulf. It may be a question whether this is not an Old Frankish name come to us through the Normans, for at Gambetta's funeral the French Bar was represented by M. *Falsteuf.*

I now come to corruptions which arise from the attempt to give to a name something of an apparent meaning in English. Let me observe that, almost as an invariable rule, corruptions are made towards a meaning and not away from it; the ancient name Irminger might be corrupted into Ironmonger, but Ironmonger could not be corrupted into Irminger. It is natural to men to try to get some semblance of meaning out of a name, and all the more that it approaches to something which has a familiar sound to their ears. Thus H.M. ship, the *Bellerophon,* was called by the sailors the "Billy Ruffian," and a vessel owned by a fore-elder of mine, and which he christened the *Agomemnon,* invariably went among the sailors by the name of the "Mahogany Tom." Thus the Anglo-Saxon Trumbald has first become *Trumbull* and then *Tremble,* and as suggested by Mr. Charnock, *Turnbull.* So we have the Old Norse name Thorgautr (Turgot, *Domesday*) variously made into *Target* and into *Thoroughgood.*[1] In some cases a very slight change suffices to give a new complexion

---

[1] According, no doubt, as the ancient name appeared as Thorgaut or Thorgaud.

to the name, thus the Old Frankish Godenulf, (*ulf*, wolf), through a Norman Godeneuf, is scarcely changed in our *Goodenough*. Similarly we might have had Badenough (O.G. Badanulf), and Richenough (A.S. Ricnulf). We have *Birchenough* (reminding us of Dr. Busby) no doubt from a name of similar formation not yet turned up. Then we have several names as *Garment, Rayment, Argument, Element, Merriment, Monument*, from ancient names ending in *mund* or *munt*, supposed to mean protection, with only the change of a letter. I have referred in an earlier part of this chapter to the name Pendgast, and to the phonetic corruptions to which it has been subjected. But it seems also to have been subjected to a corruption of the other kind, for I take it that our name *Pentecost* is properly Pentecast, as another or High German form of Pendegast. Another case of a corruption easily made is that of our name *White-thread* which seems obviously the Anglo-Saxon name Wihtræd, of which also we have another obvious corruption in *Whiterod*. So also the Anglo-Saxon name Weogern, p. 111 (more properly Wiggern, *wig*, war, and *gern*, eager), by an easy transition becomes *Waghorn*. And in this way also the paradoxical-looking name *Fairfoul*, by a slight change of spelling, may be explained as Farefowl, "wandering bird," as a name probably given by the Saxon or Danish sea-rovers.

Let us take a name of a different kind, *Starbuck*, no doubt of local origin, from the place called Starbeck in Yorkshire. Now beck is a Northern word signifying brook; it is probably of Danish origin, inasmuch as its use precisely corresponds with the limits of the Danish occupation. So long then as Starbeck lived in the north among his own people, to whom *beck* is a familiar word, there would be no fear of his name being corrupted. But when he migrated to a part of England where *beck* has no meaning, then by and by the natural craving for some kind of a meaning would assert itself, and, as the best it could do, change *beck* into *buck*. But the name of the place itself affords an illustration of the same principle. For *star* is in all probability the same word as *stour*, so common as a river-name (Arm. *ster*, water, river), made into *star* in the craving for some kind of a meaning.

Let us take another name with the same ending, *Clutterbuck*, also, I doubt not, a name of local origin, though I am unable in this case to identify the place. But *clutter* seems evidently to be from the Anglo-Saxon, *hluttor*, clear, pure, limpid, and the word must have been *hluttorbeck*, " clear brook," so that this is another case of a similar corruption. The Anglo-Saxons, no doubt, strongly aspirated the initial *h*, so that the name has become Clutterbuck.

Another name which may be taken to be of the same kind is· *Honeybun*, no doubt a corruption of another name *Honeyburn*, from *burn*, a brook, *honey* being apparently used by the Anglo-Saxons as an epithet to describe sweet waters. But to the modern ear Honey*bun* is a much more natural association than Honey*burn*, particularly since the Anglo-Saxon *burn* for *brook* has passed out of use in England.

Among the Germans, corruptions towards a meaning

are also common, as in such names as *Guttwein* for Godwine or Gotwine, *Warmbadt* for Warinbod, *Leutenant* for Liutnand (*liud*, people, *nant*, daring). There is a curious-looking and seemingly profane name *Heiliggheist*, as if from the third person of the Trinity, which may, however, be a corruption of an ancient name, perhaps of the name Haldegast.

The odd-looking names *Oyster* and *Oysterman* in *Suffolk Surnames* are probably the German names Oster and Ostermann (*oster*, orientalis) in an anglicised form, the marvellous power of assimilation possessed by the great Republic evincing itself, among other things, in the way in which it anglicises foreign names. Thus the name *Crumpecker*, placed by Bowditch among names from birds, is, we can hardly doubt, a corruption of a German Krumbacher, *i.e.* "a native of Krumbach," of which name there are several places in Germany. So also the ending *thaler* in German names, from *thal*, valley, is changed into "dollar" as its supposed equivalent. Hence the Americans have *Milldolar, Barndollar,* and *Cashdollar*, corruptions of some such German names as Mühlthaler, Bernthaler, and Käsenthaler, signifying an inhabitant respectively of Mühlthal, of Bernthal, and of Käsenthal. It would seem as if a man coming to this new-world, where everything around him is changed—presumably for the better—accepts it as, among other things, a part of the new dispensation, that whereas his name has hitherto been, say Käsenthaler, he shall henceforth answer to the name—perhaps not an inauspicious one —of Cashdollar.

CHAPTER VII.

To any one who takes note of the large proportion of French Christian names which are of German origin, the question, one would think, might naturally suggest itself—If such be the case with Christian names, may it not also be the case with regard to surnames? The Christian names *Albert, Adolphe, Alfonse, Charles, Claude, Edouard, Edmonde, Ferdinand, Gerard, Henri, Louis, Philibert, Robert, Richarde, Rudolfe, Guillaume,* and the women's *Adèle, Clotilde, Louise, Mathilde, Héloïse,* and many others, serve to remind us that the French have come of the Franks. That the same holds good also of French surnames I have in a previous work endeavoured to prove in considerable detail, and I will not go over the ground again further than at the end of this chapter to present as an illustration of my views upon the subject one or two stems complete with their branches.

The Franks being a branch of a High German, and the Saxons of a Low German stock, it follows that French names, as compared with English, should, in names of Teutonic origin, exhibit High German forms in comparison with our Low German. One of these differences is, for instance, *au* for *ea*, as in German *auge*, Anglo-Saxon, *eage*, English, *eye*. Thus the Anglo-Saxon *ead*, happiness, prosperity, so common in men's names, is in Frankish represented by *aud*, or *od*—hence the name of the Norman bishop Odo is the counterpart of an Anglo-Saxon Eada or Eda, and the name of the Lombard king Audoin (Audwin), is the counterpart of the Anglo-Saxon Eadwin. It will be seen then that the French Christian name *Edouard* is not a true Frankish form—the proper form is shown in two French surnames, *Audouard* and *Audevard*. I cannot account for the particular case of this Christian name on any other ground than that simply of euphony. The corresponding Italian Christian name, *Odoardo*, come to them through the Franks or the Lombards, represents, it will be seen, the proper High German form. The High German forms, then, that appear in English names may be taken to a great extent to represent Old Frankish names that have come to us through the Normans. But the number of such names appears to be greater than could reasonably be thus accounted for, and moreover we seem, as I have noted at p. 75, to have had such forms even in Anglo-Saxon times, *e.g.* both the forms *ead* or *ed*, and *aud* or *od*, in the names of our early settlers. And it appears to me therefore that Lappenberg's theory that Franks, Lombards, and Frisians were among the early settlers, is one that deserves most careful consideration. And I propose at present to deal with the subject, so far as the Franks are concerned, and to trace out to the best of my ability, the Frankish forms that seem to present themselves in Anglo-Saxon times, and also in our existing surnames. In so doing, I wish to disclaim any assumption of philological knowledge such as might be implied by dealing with the niceties of ancient dialects. All that I proceed upon is this—I find from German writers that certain forms prevailed in Frankish names, and I compare them with certain forms apparently of the same kind which I find in Anglo-Saxon times.

Now the ancient Frankish speech, along with the ordinary characteristics of a High German dialect, had some special peculiarities of its own, and it is through these that we have the best chance of obtaining satisfactory indications. Of these there are three forms in particular, with each of which I propose to deal in turn, placing at the head the group of surnames which I take to owe their origin to this source. And as assisting to throw light upon the subject I have in some cases introduced the present French names corresponding.

CHAD, CHATTO, CHATTING, CHADDOCK, CHABOT, CHADBORN, CHADMAN, CHADWICK, CHATTOWAY, CHATWIN, CHATWOOD, CHARD, CHART, CHARTER, CHAIN, CHANEY, CHILDAR, CHILDREN, CHILL, CHILLMAN, CHILLMAID, CHUBB, CHUBBACK, CHOPPIN.

One of the peculiarities of the Frankish dialect especially during the Merovingian period, was the prefix of *c* before names beginning with *h*, as in Childebert and Childeric for Hildebert and Hilderic. Of this there seem to be considerable traces in

Anglo-Saxon times, as will be seen from the following :—

Chad for *had*, war.

A.S. Chad, bishop of Lichfield—Ceada, found in Ceadanford—Cedda, found in Ceddanleah—Frankish, Chaddo. Eng. Chad, Chatto.

Diminutive.

Frnk. Chadichus. Eng. Chaddock.

Patronymic.

Eng. Chatting.

Compounds.

(*Bad*, war), Frnk. Chadbedo, Chabedo—Eng. Chabot.[1] (*Wine*, friend), Frnk. Chaduin—Eng. Chadwin, Chatwin. (Wig, war), A.S. Chatewe (*wi* for wig) found in Ceatewesleah—Eng. Chadwick, Chattoway.

(We have also the other form Hathaway, O.G. Hathuwi, to compare with Chattaway.)

Then we have a stem *chard, chart*, which it seems to me may be a similar Frankish form of *hard* or *hart*, durus, fortis, a very common stem for men's names.

Chard for *hard*.

A.S. Cerda (Cherda) found in Cerdanhlæw. Ceorta, found in Ceortan stapol. Ceort, found in Ceortesege, now Chertsey. Eng. Chard, Chart.

Diminutive.

A.S. Cerdic, king of Wessex. Also Ceardic, found in Ceardices beorh.

Compound.

(*Har*, warrior), Frnk. Charterius—Eng. Charter.

In the next group, *child* for *hild*, war, the Anglo-Saxon names seem rather uncertain, and though the

---

[1] This name may be, not improbably, one of those that were brought over after the Revocation of the Edict of Nantes.

Franks had many names from it, I only find one to compare in that form.

Child for *hild*, war.

A.S. Cild, found in Cildeswic—Cilta found in Ciltancumb, now Chilcomb in Hants—Frnk. Childi, Cheldio, Chillo—Eng. Child, Chill.

Compounds.

(*Hari.* warrior), O.G. Hilder—Eng. Childar. (*Man*, vir), O.G. Hildman—Childman, *Hund. Rolls*—Eng. Chillman, French, Chilman. (*Mod*, courage), O.G. Hildemod—Eng. Chillmaid. (*Ran*, raven), Frnk. Childerannus—Eng. Children.

We have a number of other names beginning with *ch*, which might with more or less certainty be brought in here, as Chaine comparing with an A.S. Chen, found in Chenestun, and with a Frankish Chaino for Chagno (Hagen-spinosus). Also Chubb and Choppin comparing with the Ceopingas (Chopingas) in Kemble's list. He has also Hoppingas and Upingas, different forms I take it, of the same name, and upon these might be formed by the prefix in question, the form Ceopingas. Compare also the present French names, Choupe, Chopin, Chopard.

CLAUDE, CLOADE, CLODD, CLOUD, CLOUT, CLUCAS, CLOUDMAN, CLOUTMAN, CLOTHIER. CROAD, CROWD, CROWDY, CRUTE, CROTTY, CRUDEN, CROWDER, CROGER. CROKE, CROCK, CROOKE, CROTCH, CRUTCH, CROKER. CREED, CREEDY, CRIDDLE.

Another peculiarity of the Frankish dialect was the change of *hl* at the beginning of a name into *cl* or *chl*, and *hr* into *cr* or *chr.* Hence the names of the Frankish kings Clothar, Chlodomir, and Clodowich, for Hlothar, Hlodomir, and Hlodowich. Of this form there appear to be considerable traces in Anglo-Saxon times ; there are three names in Kemble's list of early settlers which may find a place here, the Crangas, the Cramlingas, and the Crucgingas. The name Crangas, as it stands, is difficult to deal with, and I should suppose it to be properly either Cringas or Craningas —in the former case from *hring*, circle, perhaps in the sense of shield — in the latter from *chrann*, as a Frankish form of *raban* or raven, Cf. Chrannus in the genealogy of the Merovingian kings. Cramlingas, again compares with a Frankish name Chramlin from the same stem, while Crucgingas seems to be a Frankish form of Rucingas, also on Kemble's list.

The first group of names, Claude, Cloud, &c., are referred to O.H.G. *laut*, loud, in the supposed sense of famous.

Clod for *hlod*, fame.

A.S. Clodd (found in Cloddes heal), Clott (found in Clottismôr), Clud (found in Cludesleah)[1]—Frnk. Chlodio, Cludio, 5th cent.—Eng. Claude, Cloade, Clodd, Cloud, Clout.

Compounds.

• (*Gis* or *kis*, hostage), O.G. Hludokis—Eng. Clukas (for Cludkis?). (*Hari*, warrior), Frnk. Clothar, Chluthar— Eng. Clothier, Clutter. (*Man*, vir), Eng. Cloudman, Cloutman (for which no ancient equivalents as yet turn up.)

---

[1] We also find the other form, Hlud, in Hludes beorh, Hlud's barrow, or grave.

The next group, Croad, Crowd, &c., may be referred to *hrod*, glory, the stem from which are formed Robert, Roland, Roger, &c.

Crod for *hrod.*

A.S. Cruda, found in Crudan sceat—Frnk. Chrodo, Crodio—Eng. Croad, Crowd, Crowdy, Croot, Crout.

Ending in *en*, p. 27.

Frnk. Chrodin—Eng. Cruden.

Compounds.

(*Har*, warrior), Frnk. Chrodohar—Eng. Crowder. (*Gar*, spear), Frnk. Crodeger—Eng. Croger (=Roger). (*Mar*, famous), A.S. Cruddemor, found in Cruddemores lacu— Frnk. Chrodmar—Eng. Cromar.

The next group, Croke, Crock, &c.; are from a stem *hroc*, the root-meaning of which seems to be the same as Eng. *croak*, and the idea of which, as in some other stems (see *im* in voce Emma), may probably be that of strength, fierceness, or huge stature, derived from a harsh and gruff voice. Cf. O.N. *hrokr*, vir fortis et grandis.

Crock for *hroc.*

A.S. Crucga, found in Crucgingas; Croch, found in Crochestun, now Croxton in Norf.—Frnk. Crocus, Cruccus —Eng. Croke, Crock, Crooke, Crotch, Crutch.

Compounds.

(*Her*, *heri*, warrior), O.G. Roacheri—Eng. Croker, Crocker. Eng. Crockett might represent a Frankish Crochad or Crochat (*had*, war), not turned up.

Perhaps from a similar origin may be the name of Crida or Creoda, king of Mercia, as representing a stem, *hrad*, or *hred* (O.H.G. *hradi*, celer), whence

K

probably the Hræda in the Traveller's Song. Kemble has two tribe-names, Creotingas and Cridlingas (the latter, derived from a place in Yorkshire, being perhaps doubtful so far as regards the tribe, though a man's name all the same).

Crad for *hrad.*

A.S. Creoda, found in Creodan âc, Creodan hyl, Creodan treow—Cridda, found in Criddan wyl—Cridd, found in Criddes hô—Creota, found in Creotingas—Cretta, *lib. vit.*— Eng. Creed, Creedy.

Ending in *el.*

A.S. Cridel, found in Cridlingas—Eng. Criddle.

Perhaps the most characteristic peculiarity of the Frankish dialect is the prefix of *g*, or its sharper form *c*, before names beginning with *w*.[1] Hence it is that the French have such a word as guerre (= gwerre) which is *g* prefixed to a German *wer* or *war*. And such names as Guillaume, Gualtier, and Guiscard, which are from *g* prefixed to Wilhelm, Walter, and Wiscard (our Wishart). Hence, also, such a place-name as Quillebœuf in Normandy, being, with a ʾc prefixed, the same, I take it, as an English Willaby (*bœuf*, as Mr. Taylor has shown, representing the Danish *by*). I have referred, p. 75, to the name Cwichelm for Wighelm or Wichelm as a strongly-marked Frankish form, but I cannot say that I find such forms generally prevalent in Anglo-Saxon times. Kemble has three tribe-names in this form, Cwædr-ingas, Cwæringas, and Queningas. The Cwædringas answer to the Wætringas, and the Wedringas, both

---

[1] Some further remarks on this Frankish prefix will be found in the succeeding chapter on Italian names.

also on Kemble's list, and both, I take it, different forms of the same name; the Cwæringas to the Wæringas and the Werringas, also different forms of the same name; the Queningas to the Weningas or the Winingas. One or two of our names beginning with *gw*, as Gwilliams, Gwatkin, and perhaps Gwalter, are probably due to the Welsh, of which this prefix is also a characteristic. As representing the Frankish form, we have more names in the sharper form *cw*, which is represented by *q*. Under the present head comes the name of the highest lady in the land, *Guelph* (further referred to in next chapter), being a Frankish form of Welf (O. H.G. *hwelf;* Eng. *whelp*). The names *Welp, Whelps,* and *Guelpa,* appear in *Suff. Surn.,* but whether English or not does not appear.

QUARE, QUARY, QUARRY, QUEAR, QUERY, QUAR-RIER, QUARMAN. QUIDDY, QUITMAN, QUIT-TACUS. QUIG, QUICK, QUY, QUIGGLE, GWYER, QUIER, QUIRE. GUILLE, GUILY, QUILL, QUILKE, GWILLAM, QUILLMAN, QUILLINAN. GUINEY, QUIN, QUEEN, QUEENEY, GUINAN, QUINAN, QUEENAN, QUINER. QUAIL, QUALEY, QUINT. QUAINT, QUANTOCK. GWILT, QUILT, QUILTY, QUILTER, QUAKER, QUASII.

The meaning of the stem *war* is very uncertain; Foerstemann proposes five different words, without including O.H.G. *werra,* Eng. *war,* and it seems very probable that there may be a mixture of different words.

Gwar, cwar, for war.

A.S. Cwara, found in Cwæringas—Frnk. Guario—Eng. Quare, Quary, Quarry, Quear, Query—French Querrey.

Compounds.

(*Hari,* warrior), O.G. Warher—Eng. Quarrier. (*Man,* vir), O.G. Warman—Eng. Quarman—French Guermain.

The stem *wid,* on which is formed *guid* and *cwid,* may perhaps be referred to O.H.G. *wid,* wood, in the sense of weapon (see next chapter *in voce* Guido), though in this case also there may probably be a mixture of words.

Gwid, cwid, for *wid.*

Frnk. Guid, Guido, Quido—Eng. Quiddy—French, Guidé.

Compounds.

(*Man,* vir), O.G. Witman—Eng. Quitman. (*Gis,* hostage), O.G. Witichis—Eng. Quittacus (*Suff. Surn*).

The stem *wig* or *wic,* on which are formed *gwig* and *cwic,* may be taken to be from *wig,* war.

Gwig, cwic, for *wig, wic.*

Frnk. Gwigo—Eng. Quig, Quick, Quy—Fr. Guiche, Quyo.

Ending in el.

O.G. Wigilo—Eng. Quiggle.

Compound.

O G. Wigger, Wiher—Eng. Gwyer, Quier, Quire.

The stem *will,* on which are formed *guill* and *cwill,* may be referred to Goth. *wilya,* will, perhaps, in the sense of resolution.

Guil, cwil, for *will.*

Frnk. Guila—Eng. Guille, Guily, Quill — Fr. Guille, Quille.

Diminutive

O.G. Willic—Eng. Quilke—Fr. Quillac.

Compounds.

(*Helm*, helmet), Frnk. Guilhelm—Eng. Gwillam—Fr. Guillaume. (*Man*, vir), O.G. Wilman—Eng. Quillman—Fr. Guillemain. (*Nand*, daring), O.G. Willinand—Eng. Quillinan.

I am inclined, from the way in which the names run into each other, to take *cwen* and *cwin* to be one and the same stem, and to refer them to A.S. *wine*, friend.

Gwin, cwin, cwen, for *win.*

A.S. Cwena, found in Cweningas ; Quena, found in Quenanden—Frnk. Guuine, Quino—Eng. Guiney, Quin, Queen, Queeney—Fr. Gueneau, Quenay, Quineau.

Ending in *en*, p. 27.

A.S. Cwenen, found in Cwenenabrôc—Eng. Guinan, Quinan, Queenan—Fr. Guenin.

Compounds.

(*Hari*, warrior), O.G. Winiheri — Eng. Quiner— Fr. Guinier, Guinery, Quinier. (*Bert*, famous), Frnk. Quinabert —Eng. Guinibert.

From the Ang-Sax. *wealh*, stranger, foreigner, may be the following stem :

Gual, cwal, for *wal.*

Frnk. Gualo, Guala—Eng. Quail, Qualey—Fr. Guala.

· Then there are some other stems not sufficiently represented to make it worth while to put them into a tabular form, as Quint, a Frankish form of Wind (the stem being supposed to mean Wend), with the present French, Quinty. Also Quaint and Quantock, representing Old German names, Wando and Wendico, the stem being perhaps as in the previous case. And

Gwilt, Quilt, Quilty, and Quilter, which seem to be formed similarly on Wild (ferus) and Wilder. Also Quart for Ward or Wart, and perhaps Quaker for Waker and Quash for Wass (as in Washington from Wassingation).

With regard to this last Frankish peculiarity, which I conceive not to be of such ancient date as the preceding ónes, I am inclined to suppose that the greater part of the English names in which it appears have come to us through the Normans. And with regard to the others I would venture the general remark that inasmuch as the Anglo-Saxons in all probability more or less aspirated an initial *h*, it would perhaps be going too far to conclude that, in all cases where it has been hardened into a *c,* Frankish influence is necessarily to be presumed. Still, I think that the general result of the comparison which I have instituted, more especially considering the comparatively limited area from which the Anglo-Saxon examples have been drawn, is such as to give considerable support to the theory that Franks were among the early settlers.

Besides the names of Old Frankish, *i.e.* German origin, which have come to us through the Normans, we have also received from them some names, mostly of a religious character, from the Latin, and from the Hebrew. I have even ventured to suggest, in the next chapter, that it is to the Franks that the Italians are indebted for the name of Dante (Durante) from Lat. *durans.* More certainly it is from them that the corresponding name *Durand* has come to us. The early Frankish Christians adopted several such names, some from the Latin, as Stabilis, Clarus, Celsus, Electus (perhaps in some cases from the names of Roman saints), some from the Hebrew, not only scriptural names of men and women, but also such words as Pasc (passover), Seraphim, Osanna, &c., and these they often mixed up with the Old German words to which they had been accustomed, the names of the Apostles Peter and Paul being so dealt with, and even the name of Christ himself. This probably arose from the desire of parents to connect the names of their children with their own, as seems clearly shown in the case of a woman called Electa, who gives to her two children the same name with a German addition, calling one Electard, and the other Electrudis. From one of these hybrid Frankish names, Clarembald, come our *Claringbold* and *Claring-bull* and the French *Clérambault*. From the above word, *pasc*, we have *Pascoe, Paske,* and *Pash,* and the French have *Pasquin,* corresponding with a Frankish Pascoin (Pascwin). There is one Richard Osannas, a witness to an acquittance in the later Anglo-Saxon times, the name being probably from the Frankish Osanna, which seems, however, to have been originally a woman's name. In the same charter occurs also Jordan, another of these old Frankish names, taken presumably from the river—whence I take to be our *Jordan,* and the French *Jordan, Jourdan,* and *Jourdain,* probably also the name of the Dutch painter *Jordaens.* The name Crist, which seems most probably from this origin (Cristeus in the *Pol. Irm.*) is not very uncommon in France ; it occurs also in Germany, and though I have not met with it in England, yet

Bowditch gives it as the name of a member of the New York legislature, where it may, however, possibly be German. It is rather amusing to see how the learned Germans are occasionally a little mystified by these Old Frankish Scriptural names. Stark, for instance, sets down Elisaba (Elischeba, the Hebrew form, I take it, of Elisabeth) as Celtic, and Foerstemann, excusably perhaps, is posed with Erispa (Rispah, the daughter of Aiah ?), though I think he might have guessed Osanna.

Before concluding this chapter I may refer to the *Roll of Battle Abbey*, containing the names of the principal Normans who came over with the Conqueror. This has been severely impugned by some excellent antiquaries on the ground that some of the names are, on the face of them, regular English names, and such as could not reasonably be supposed to have been borne by Normans. And hence it has been supposed that interpolations must have been made to gratify the vanity of certain families who wished their names to appear in the Roll. This in itself does not seem an improbable suspicion, and I do not desire to go into the question further than to express the opinion that so far as the names themselves are concerned, there is not one that might not be a genuine Norman name. Indeed, the undisguised English form of some of them is to me rather a proof of the honesty of the scribe, for it would have been so easy to have given them a thin Norman disguise. The suspicious-seeming names are of two kinds, names which appear to be from English place-names, as Argentoune, Chaworth, Newborough

Sanford, Valingford, Harewell; and names which seem to be from English surnames of occupation, or description, as Hayward, Archere, Loveday. The former did present a genuine difficulty, and did justify suspicion till now that Mr. Taylor's discovery of an area in the north of France full of regular Anglo-Saxon place-names, and no doubt settled by Anglo-Saxons, has disclosed the source from which they could be derived. I opine then that the English scribe has done nothing more in the case of such names than restore them to the original form from which they had been more or less corrupted. Nor indeed has he done it to as great an extent as he might have done, for I find several others which may be brought back to an Anglo-Saxon form, and it may be of some little interest to take a few of these Norman surnames derived from place-names of the kind discovered by Mr. Taylor, and compare them with corresponding Anglo-Saxon place-names in England. I will take the names ending in *uil*, "well," of which the scribe has Anglicised one (Harewell), and show how many more there might have been. We have Bereneuile and Boranuile, corresponding with A.S. Bernewell (now Barnwell, in Northamptonshire), from A.S. *brune*, brook, of which the well might be the source. Then we have Rinuuill, corresponding with an A.S. Runawel (now, Runwell in Essex), *i.e.* a running or flowing well, Berteuilay corresponding with A.S. Beorhtanwyl (now Brightwell, in Oxfordshire), and Vauuruile with an A.S. Werewell (now Wherwell, in Hants), an inclosed well; from A.S. *wær*, inclosure. Then we have Beteruile comparing with an A.S. Buterwyel (Butterwell, butter and honey being used apparently to describe sweet waters), Greneuile (Greenwell), and Glateuile, probably from A.S. *glade*, brook, and so same as Bernewell.

With respect to the second class of suspected names, such as Hayward, Archere, and Loveday, these are all Old Frankish names, and the resemblance to anything English is only an accident. Hayward represents an ancient Agward or Egward, and would be more properly Ayward, though we find it as Hayward (see p. 99) even in Anglo-Saxon times. So also Archere (see p. 42) and Loveday (p. 57) fall into their places as ancient Frankish names. Such names again as Brown and Gray, though a little Anglicised in spelling, are names common to the whole Teutonic system, and, as far as we are concerned, both came in with the Saxons, being found in Kemble's list of original settlers.

I do not think it necessary to go more at length into the ancient Frankish names contained in that Roll, but before leaving the subject I would call attention to some of the names derived from the Danish place-names of Normandy. There are four names, Dabitott, Leuetot, Lovetot, and Tibtote (our name *Tiptoft*), from the ending *tot*, which, as Mr. Taylor has shown, represents the Scandinavian *toft*. And two names, Duilby and Linnebey, representing the Danish *by ;* house, habitation, village, so common in Yorkshire and Lincolnshire ; also two more, Braibuf and Olibef, with the ending *buf* or *bœuf*, which, as Mr. Taylor has shown, also represents the Danish *by*, Olibef being, perhaps, Olafby, from the Danish name Olaf.

Seeing this to be the case, I venture to hint a
suspicion as to the redoubtable name Front-de-bœuf,
and to suggest that it may after all be properly
nothing more than one of these Norman place-names
ending in *bœuf.* Such a name as, for instance,
Frodebœuf, from a Danish man's name, Frodi, might
give it. On the other hand, the plebeian-looking
name *Chassebœuf,* which Volney is said to have
changed rather than have it supposed that any one of
his ancestors had been a cow-boy, is, I doubt not,
from a similar origin. Such a name as Shaftsby (from
the Anglo-Saxon man's name Shaft) would, when *by*
became corrupted into *bœuf,* naturally be made into
Chasse-bœuf. I take, however, the name *Lebœuf* to
be from a different origin, viz. from a Frankish Libolf
or Liubolf. There is yet one more name, Lascales (our
Lascelles), which I think may be also from a Danish
place-name, the word *scale* (O.N. *skali,* a wooden hut)
being common, particularly in the Lake District—in
Cumberland and Westmoreland.

I purpose to conclude this chapter with a few
stems illustrative of the common Teutonic element
in French, English, and German names, including
such Italian names as I have been able to fall in
with. The first stem, from A.S. *til,* bonus, præstans,
seems to have been more common among the Saxons
than among the Franks, and there are, consequently,
more names corresponding in English than in French.

Dill, till, bonus.

A.S. Dilla, Tilla, in Dillingas and Tillingas—O.G. Dilli,
Tilli, Thilo ; Tilli, *Lib. Vit.* ; Dill, Tilly, Tillé, *Hund. Rolls—*
Eng. *Dill, Dilley, Dillow, Till, Tilley*—Germ. *Dill, Till,
Tilo*—Fr. *Dilly, Dillé, Tilly, Tillé*—Ital. *Tilli.*

Ending in *ec*, probably diminutive.

A.S.Tilluc—Eng. *Dillick, Dilke, Tillick, Tilke*—Fr. *Dilhac.*

Patronymic.

Eng. *Tilling*—Germ. *Dilling.*

Ending in *en*, p. 27.

Tilne, *Lib. Vit.*—Eng. *Dillon*—Germ. *Dillen*—Fr. *Dillon, Tillon.*

Compounds.

(*Fred*, peace), Tilfred, *Lib. Vit.*—Eng. *Tilford.* (*Gar*, spear), A.S. Tilgar—Dilker, *Hund. Rolls*—Eng. *Dilger, Dillicar.* (*Had*, war), Tilhaed, *Lib. Vit.*—Eng. *Tillott*—Fr. *Dillet, Tillot.* (*Man*, vir), A.S. Tillman—Tilmon, *Lib. Vit.*—Tileman, *Hund. Rolls*—Eng. *Dillman, Tillman, Tileman*—Germ. *Dillemann, Tilmann*—Dutch. *Tillemans*—Fr. *Tilman.* (*Mar*, famous), O.G. Tilemir—Eng. *Dillimore.* (*Mund*, protection), A.S. Tilmund—Fr. *Tilmant.* (*Wine*, friend), Tiluini, *Lib. Vit.*—Eng. *Dillwyn.* (*Her, heri*, warrior), A.S. Tilhere (Bishop of Worcester)—Eng. *Diller, Tiller, Tillier*—Fr. *Dillery, Tillier.*

The following stem may be taken to be from A. S. *hyge ;* O.H.G. *hugu*, mind, thought; A.S. *hogian*, to study, meditate. The form *hig*, which seems to be more particularly Saxon, intermixes considerably in the English names.

Hig, hog, hug, *thought, study.*

A.S. Hig, Hicca, Hocg—O.G. Hugo, Hug, Huc, Hughi, Hogo—Eng. *Hugo, Hug, Hugh, Huie, Huck, Hogg, Hodge, Hoe, Hick, Hickie*—Germ. *Huge, Hugo, Hucke, Hoge*—Fr. *Hugo, Hugé, Hug, Huc, Hue, Hua*—Ital. *Ugo.*

Ending in *el*, probably diminutive.

A.S. Hicel—O.G. Hugila, Huckili—Eng. *Hugall, Huckell, Whewell, Hickley*—Germ. *Hügel*—Fr. *Hugla, Huel*—Ital. *Ughelli.*

Ending in *lin*, probably diminutive.

A.S. Hugelin (Chamberlain to Edward the Confessor)—
Hugelinus, *Domesday*—Hueline, *Lib. Vit.*—Eng. *Huelin*,
Hicklin—Fr. *Huguelin, Higlin*—Ital. *Ugolino.*

Ending in *et*, probably diminutive.

A.S. Hocget—O.G. Huetus, thirteenth century—Hueta,
Domesday—Eng. *Huggett, Howitt, Hewitt*—Fr. *Hugot,
Huet*—Ital. *Ughetti.*

Ending in *es*, probably diminutive.

O.G. Hugizo—Eng. *Hughes, Hewish, Hodges*—Fr.
Hugues.

Kin, diminutive.

Hogcin, *Lib. Vit.*—Eng. *Hodgkin.*

Ending in *en*, p. 27.

A.S. Hyeken—Hygine, *Lib. Vit.*—Eng. *Hoggin, Hucken,
Higgen*—Fr. *Hugan, Hogan, Huan, Hoin, Hienne.*

Compounds.

(*Bald*, fortis), A.S. Higbald (Bishop of Lindisfarne),
Hibald—O.G. Hugibald, Hubald—Eng. *Hibble, Hubble*—
Fr. *Hubault*—Ital. *Ubaldo, Ubald(ini).* (*Bert*, famous),
A.S. Higbert (Bishop of Worcester)—O.G. Hugubert,
Hubert—Eng. *Hibbert, Hubbard*—Germ. *Hubert*—Fr.
Hubert. (*Hard*, fortis), O.G. Hugihart, Hugard—Eng.
Huggard, Heward—Fr. *Hugard, Huard, Huart.* (*Laic*,
play), A.S. Hygelac—O.G. Hugilaih—O.N. Hugleikr—Eng.
Hillock, Hullock—Fr. *Hulek.* (*Lat*, terrible, ?), Hugolot,
Lib. Vit.—Eng. *Hewlet, Higlet.* (*Lind*, mild), O.G.
Hugilind—Eng. *Hewland.* (*Man*, vir), A.S. Hiccemann—
Eng. *Hugman, Hughman, Human, Higman, Hickman*—
Germ. *Hieckmann*—Fr. *Humann.* (*Mot*, courage), O.G.
Hugimot—Eng. *Hickmot.* (*Mar*, famous), A.S. Hykemer
—O.G. Hugimar—Eng. *Hogmire, Homer, Highmore.* (*Wald*,

power), O.G. Hugold—Fr. *Huault.* Perhaps also, from
noth, bold, though I do not find an ancient name to
correspond—Eng. *Hignett,* and Fr. *Hugnot, Hognet.*

I will take for the last example the stem *magin,
main ;* A.S. *mægin,* strength, force ; Eng. *main,*
which is rather better represented in French names
than in English. There are names, Maianus and
Meinus on Roman pottery, which might, however, be
either German or Celtic.

O.G. Magan, Main—Main, *Lib. Vit.*—Eng. ˙ *Magnay,
Mayne*—Germ. *Mehne*—Fr. *Magné, Magney*—Ital. *Magini.*

Compounds.

(*Bald,* fortis), O.G. Meginbold—Fr. *Magnabal.* (*Burg,*
protection), O.G. Meginburg—Fr. *Mainbourg.* (*Frid,*
peace), O.G. Maginfrid—Fr. *Mainfroy.* (*Gald,* value),
O.G. Megingald—Fr. *Maingault.* (*Ger,* spear), O.G.
Meginger—Eng. *Manger.* (*Gaud,* Goth), O.G. Megingaud
Fr. *Maingot.* (*Had,* war), O.G. Magenad—Fr. *Maginot*—
(*Hard,* fortis), O.G. Maginhard, Mainard—Eng. *Maynard*
—Germ. *Meinert*—Fr. *Magnard, Maynard*—Ital. *Mainardi*
—(*Hari,* warrior), O.G. Maganhar, Mayner—Germ. *Meiner*
—Fr. *Magnier, Maynier*—Ital. *Maineri.*

Perhaps also to this stem (with *nant,* daring) we may put
Magnentius, the name of a German who usurped the
imperial purple and was slain A.D. 353, also the Fr. *Magnan*
and *Maignan.*

These three stems, in one of which the Anglo-
Saxon predominates, and in another the Frankish or
High German, while in a third there are two parallel
forms, Anglo-Saxon and Frankish, running side by
side, may be taken as fairly representative of the
system upon which Teutonic names are formed.

CHAPTER VIII.

THE GERMAN ORIGIN OF GREAT ITALIANS AS EVIDENCED IN THEIR NAMES.

THE successive waves of German invasion that swept over Italy, leaving their record in the name of one of its fairest provinces, while they added a few German words to the language, left a much larger number of German patronymics in the names of its families. The Christian names borne by well-known Italians, such as *Alberto, Arnolfo, Bernardo,. Carlo, Enrico, Federigo* (Frederic), *Francesco, Leonardo, Luigi, Ludovico, Mainardo, Odoardo* (Edward), *Ridolphi, Sinibaldo, Ugo* (Hugo or Hugh), *Onofrio* (Humphrey), all of German origin, sufficiently attest this to have been the case. And I think we shall be warranted in assuming, as in the case of France, that if this be the case with Christian names, it cannot be essentially different with regard to surnames.

But inasmuch as I have not had the same opportunity of collating and examining the mass of Italian surnames that I have had in the case of those of France, I propose to shape the comparison into a rather different form, and, without departing from its etymological

purpose, to endeavour to give it something of an
ethnical interest as well.   This admixture of German
blood could not fail to have an influence—and, we
can hardly doubt, an invigorating influence—upon the
character of the softer and more receptive Italian
race.   It may not then be without interest—though
we need not attach more importance to the result
than it deserves—to endeavour to trace the result of
that admixture in the names of illustrious Italians.
For it is somewhat remarkable how many of the
men most distinguished in the council and in the field,
in science, literature, and in art, bear names which
testify to a German origin.   And we are even able,
in certain cases, to indicate with a fair amount of
probability the particular race of Germans from
whom these names may be taken to be derived.
The rule laid down by Max Müller (*Science of
Language*) that words in Italian beginning with *gua,
gue, gui*, may be taken to be pretty certainly of
German origin, holds good also of Italian names.
Now this form of *gua, gue, gui* represents the prefix of *g* before *w*, which was a special characteristic
of the Franks, as it is still of their descendants,
the French, in such names as Guillaume (=Gwill-
aume) for Wilhelm or William.   In some cases,
though more rarely, this prefix of *g*, in accordance
with a High German tendency, becomes a hard *c*
and is represented by *q*, as in *Queringi* and perhaps
Quirini.   Such names then as *Gualdo, Guardi, Guido,
Guicciardini, Guarnerius*, may be taken as certainly
of German, and I think, more especially of Frankish
origin.

To begin with the names of warriors, the list may well be headed by that of the old hero, *Garibaldi.* Garibald (*gar*, spear, and *bald*, bold) was a well-known Old German name, being borne, among others, by a Duke in Bavaria in the sixth century, by six bishops in the three centuries following, and, what is more to the purpose, by two Lombard kings in Italy. We ourselves have the name in its Saxon form (*gor* for *gar*) as *Gorbold* and *Corbould* (O.G. Kerbald), and the French have it as *Gerbault.* "Blind old *Dandalo*" may also be claimed as German; Dandalo, corresponding with an O.G. Dantulo, being formed as a diminutive from the Old German name Dando. I have elsewhere made the suggestion, which I venture here to reproduce, that *Bonaparte* may also be a name of German origin, slightly changed to give it a seeming meaning in Italian. The case stands thus. Bonibert and Bonipert are found as Old Frankish names, respectively of the seventh and the ninth centuries. In that part of Italy which was overrun by the Franks, namely at Turin, is to be found the present Italian name *Boniperti*, which we can hardly doubt to be derived from the Old Frankish Bonipert. Now from this part of Italy came originally also the Bonapartes, and the question is simply this, May not the name · *Bonaparte* originate in an attempt to give something of an Italian meaning to this other name *Boniperti*, which would convey no sense to an Italian ear ? The French still have the Old Frankish name as *Bompart* (changing *n* before a labial into *m*, as they do in Edimbourg for Edinburgh) ; there was a vice-

L

admiral of that name who proved his courage by
engaging, though unsuccessfully, an English frigate
of superior force.   And we—or at any rate the Americans—have it in a Saxon form as *Bonbright (Suffolk
Surnames).*   And very appropriate, if we were to trans-
late it, would be the meaning—*bona,* a slayer, and
bert or *pert,* illustrious.

The two distinguished families of the *Adimari* at
Florence and of the *Grimaldi* at Genoa both give
evidence of German descent in their names (O.G.
Adimar and Grimwald) ; as regards the latter indeed it
is to be traced historically, though the position of the
present representative, as ruler of the principality of
Monaco and recipient of its doubtful gains, is perhaps
hardly in accordance with the higher traditions of
his family.   The name, *Alphonso,* of a Duke of
Ferrara in the middle ages, was one given also by
the Germans to a still more illustrious lineage in
Spain.   Alphonso is a contraction of the O.G.
Adalfuns *(adal,* noble, *funs,* eager).   The Saxon form
of *funs* being *fus,* it seems to me that our name
Adolphus may be properly Adel-fus, and not a latin-
ization of Adolph.   German also are the names of
the two great rival factions of the *Guelphs* and the
Ghibellines, Guelph being a Frankish form of Welf or
Welp, Eng. whelp, and the Ghibellines deriving from
an. Old German name Gibilin, traced by Mone
to a Burgundian origin.   Thus the Guelphs, given
originally by Germany to Italy, were afterwards
transplanted again to Germany, and thence to England, to rule far above all factions.   And again, we
find the Bonaparte, whose ancestor was expelled from

Italy as a Ghibelline, come forward to pursue on a grander scale his hereditary feud with the Guelphs.

In the names of scholars and men of science the German element is very strongly represented. We find *Accolti* (O.G. Achiolt for Agiovald[1]), *Alamanni* (O.G. Alaman), *Algarotti* (O.G. Algar for Adelgar), *Ansaldi* (O.G. Ansald for Ansovald), *Audifredi* (O.G. Audifred), *Bertrandi* (O.G. Bertrand), *Gualdo* (O.G. Waldo), *Giraldi* (O.G. Girald), *Gosselini* (O.G. Gosselin), *Guicciardini* (O.G. Wichard), *Lanzi* (O.G. Lanzi), *Lamberti* (O.G. Lambert for Landbert), *Manfredi* (O.G. Manfred), *Maraldi* (O.G. Marald), *Odevico* (O.G. Ottwic for Audewic), *Orlandi* (O.G. Arland for Hariland), *Raimondi* (O.G. Raimund), *Rolandini* O.G. Roland for Rodland), *Roberti* (O.G. Robert for Rodbert), *Sacchi* (O.G. Sacco), *Quirini* (O.G. Guerin, Werin). We may add to the list the name of the historian *Sismondi* (Sigismund), who, though born at Geneva, must, I apprehend, have been of Italian origin. The name in its uncontracted form, *Sigismondi*, is also found in Italy.

Among the names of distinguished explorers and discoverers, we have *Americus* (O.G. Emrich), who gave his name to America, and *Belzoni* (O.G. Belzo). German are also the names of the Pope *Aldobrandini* (O.G. Aldebrand), and of the philanthropist *Odeschalchi* (O.G. Odalschalch), whose name, if translated, would be the appropriate one of "Servant of his country."

[1] When there are two Old German names, the former is that which is found in a form most nearly corresponding with the Italian, the latter is that which may be taken to be the most correct form.

L 2

The painters are not quite so strongly represented as the men of letters and science, the two principal names being those of *Lionardo* (O.G. Leonhard) and of *Guido*. Guido is one of the Frankish forms to which I have before alluded, and is formed by the prefix of *g* to the name Wido or Wito,—it was not an uncommon name among the Old Franks, and is found at present among the French as *Videau, Viteau,* and *Guidé*. The ill-omened name of the assassin *Guiteau* I take to be from the same origin, and to be of French extraction. So also may be our own name *Widow,* which corresponds with a Wido of about the twelfth or thirteenth century in the *Liber Vitæ*. There is another Italian name, *Guidubaldi,* that of a Duke of Urbino, in the middle ages, formed on the same stem with the addition of *bald,* bold, and corresponding with a Frankish Guidobald. The word concerned seems to be most probably Goth. *vidus,* O.H.G. *witu,* wood, used in a poetical sense for weapon.[1]

Other names of painters are *Baldi* (O.G. Baldo), *Baldovin (etti)* (O.G. Baldwin), *Anselmi* (O.G. Anshelm), *Ansuini* (O.G. Answin), *Aldighiero* (O.G. Aldegar), *Algardi* (O.G. Alagart), *Alberti* (O.G. Albert for Adalbert), *Alloisi* (O.G. Alois = Alwis), *Ghiberti* (O.G. Gibert), *Gherardini* (O.G. Gerard), *Gennari* (O.G. Genear), *Ghirlandaio* (O.G. Gerland), *Tibaldi* (O.G. Tiebald for Theudobald). Also *Guardi,* another of

---

[1] Names of a similar kind are the O.G. Gervid, our *Garwood,* signifying " spear-wood." Also the O.G. Asquid, whence the Ascuit in *Domesday,* and our present names *Asqwith* and *Ashwith,* signifying " ash-wood," of which spears used to be made.

the Frankish forms before referred to, representing an O.G. Wardi, and the same name as Eng. *Ward*, for which we find a corresponding A.S. Weard.

Of those eminent in the sister art of music, we have *Castoldi* (O.G. Castald for Castwald), and *Frescobaldi*. This last name does not figure in Foerstemann's list, but we can hardly doubt its German origin, *bald* being a typical German ending, while Fresc, as a Teutonic name, is found in the Fresc(ingas), early Saxon settlers in England, another instance of the common tie which binds all Teutonic names together. We may add to the list, as the name of a living composer, *Guglielmo* = Wilhelm or William. Among those who were accessory to music as instrument-makers, we have *Stradivarius* and *Guarnerius* (O.G. Guarner for Warinhar) corresponding with our own names *Warriner* and *Warner*, and present French names *Ouarnier* and *Guernier*. It will not be out of keeping with what we should expect if we find the German element develop itself in the conception rather than in the execution of music, and in the combination of science and patience which led to the success of the old instrument-makers.

But it is in the names of immortal singers that we find the German element most conspicuously represented. Dante himself bears a name which, though not in itself German, may yet have been given to Italy by the Germans, while as to his second title, *Alighieri*, there seems hardly any doubt of its German origin.[1] Dante is a contraction of *Durante*, which

[1] Diez takes it to be a contraction of Adalgar.

seems to be derived most naturally from Latin *durans*, and it might seem something of a paradox to suppose a Latin race to be indebted to the Germans for a Latin name. And yet I think that there are some grounds for supposing it to be a name adopted by the early Frankish converts to Christianity, and by them transmitted to the Italians. For we find Durant, Durand, and Durann as not uncommon German names, apparently Frankish, in the eighth and the ninth centuries. And we find the word moreover made up into a German compound as Durandomar (*mar*, famous). The French have moreover at present, derived we may presume from their Frankish ancestors, another name, *Durandard*, similarly formed (*hard*, fortis). Now this is precisely the same principle as that on which the early Frankish converts, as we find from the *Pol. Irm.* and the *Pol. Rem.*, used to form many of their names, taking a word of Christian import from the Latin or otherwise, and mixing it up with the Old German compounds to which they had been accustomed. Thus, for an example, we find that a woman called Electa, which we can hardly doubt means "elect," gives to her son the name of Electard, a similar compound to Durandard. There seems then, on the whole, a fair amount of probability for this suggestion, which would moreover sufficiently account for the manner in which the name is common to France, Italy, Germany, and England. The French have it as *Durand, Durant,* and *Durandeau* (besides *Durandard* already noted); the Italians as *Durante, Duranto,* and *Durandi;* the Germans as *Durand* and *Dorand;* and we ourselves as *Durand*

and *Durant.* Our names came to us no doubt
through the Normans,—there is a Durand in the *Roll
of Battle Abbey*, and it is not till after this period
that we find it as an English name.

For the German origin of *Tasso* a rather stronger
case can be made out, Tasso and Taso being found
as ancient German names, and the latter in particular
being a Lombard leader in Italy. But there was another
Lombard called Taso, who, as a man of remarkable
sanctity of life, and as the founder of a monastery at
Volterra, was eminently likely to leave a name
behind him in Italy. *Tasso* is still a current name
in that country, and our surname *Tassie*, along
with the French *Tassy*, may be taken to be the same
name. Both we and the French have also *Tassell*,
formed from it and corresponding with Tassilo, the
name of a Bavarian king of the sixth century. The
meaning of the word has not been satisfactorily explained, and this may be one of the cases in which
the original word has either greatly changed in
meaning, or else has perished out of the language.

Another name which we may take pretty certainly
to be of German origin is *Leopardi*, corresponding with
the O.G. Leopard, for Liubhard (*liub*, love, and *hard*,
fortis). There was a Lombard named Leopard who
was abbot of Nonantola in Italy in the tenth century.
Then we have *Amalungi*, from the O.G. Amalung,
fifth century, a patronymic form, "son of Amal or
Amala," the (perhaps mythical) forerunner of the
Goths. The French have the name, *Hamel* and
Ameling, and we have *Hammill*, *Hamling*, and *Hamb-
ling*. This is another of the cases in which a name

has outlived its etymon; we know that *amal* was a word of honourable meaning, but as to its origin even the patient research of the Germans has failed to find a clue. The name *Amalthius* may also be taken as certainly German, from *amal* as above, and the common Old German ending *thius, dio,* or *tio,* servant, though we do not find a name to correspond in the *Altdeutsches Namenbuch.* There was also a painter *Amalteo,* whose name is a variation of the same. Another name which I take to be German, without finding the ancient name to correspond, is *Boiardo, boi* (supposed by the Germans to mean Bavarian) being a common prefix in Old German names, and *hard* one of the most common endings. The French have, among other names derived from their Frankish ancestors, the corresponding names *Boyard* and *Poyard,* and we ourselves have *Byard,* which I take to be from the same origin. Then we have *Berni* (O.G. Berno), *Bernini* (O.G. Bernin), and *Beroaldus* (O.G. Berowald).

There remain yet two distinguished names, *Alfieri* and *Guarini.* The former may be from the O.G. Alfheri, *alf,* elf, and *heri,* warrior, the sense contained in the former word being perhaps that of occult wisdom. Hence it would correspond with our surnames *Albery* and *Aubery,* Alfheri and Albheri being convertible Old German names. *Guarini* may, with somewhat more of certainty, be taken to be from the Old Frankish name Guarin, formed on the principle already referred to on other Old German names, Warin and Warno. Hence our names *Warren* and *Warne,* and the French *Guérin.* The Wearningas, " sons or descendants of Wearn," are among the early

Saxon settlers referred to in Chapter IV., and Warin is found as an early name in the *Liber Vitæ.* There are some other names which may very possibly be of German origin, but the form of which is not sufficiently distinct to make the connection generally intelligible.

I conclude this chapter with a suggestion as to the possibly German origin of one who but of late occupied a considerable place in European politics, viz. *Gambetta.* This name is of Italian origin, and I venture to think may be one of those given to Italy by the Germans, and perhaps most probably by the Lombards. There was a Gambad who ruled over Ticino in the ancient duchy of Milan, and was subsequently driven out by· Pertharit, who thereupon became the ruler of the whole of Lombardy. Gambad seems to be probably a Lombard form of Ganbad (*gan*, magic, or fascination, and *bad*, war), or it might be of Gandbad (*gand*, wolf), both ancient German stems. This name Gambad would in French take the form of Gambette,[1] and in Italian of Gambetta. It would be curious if this name were one left behind by the Lombards (or possibly even the Franks) in their invasion of Italy, and restored to France to rouse her to a gallant though unavailing attempt to stem the tide of another German invasion. And very suitable too would be the name, in the sense of magic or fascination, to one whose energy and eloquence acted as such a potent spell to revive the drooping courage of his countrymen.

[1] As in the French names *Gerbet* and *Herbette*, representing the Old Frankish names Gerbad and Herbad.

CHAPTER IX.

IN the present chapter I propose to include a few stems which were not taken into account in my previous work, or respecting which I may have something more to say.

I have referred, at page 75, to Lappenberg's theory, that · Franks, Lombards, and Frisians were associated with the Saxons in the early invasions of England. His theory seems to be based only upon the general relations which subsisted between these different tribes, and the various other occasions on which they are found to have been acting in concert. I have, in a previous chapter, referred to the subject so far as the Franks are concerned, and endeavoured to show that there were in Anglo-Saxon times, and that there are in our names at present, certain peculiarities which are in accordance with Frankish forms, and so far favour the theory that Franks were among the early settlers.

There is another peculiarity which seems to be found in some of the names of Anglo-Saxon times, the form *ch* for (as I suppose) *g*, as in such a name as Cissa (Chissa) and Cippa (Chippa). Cissa I should suppose to be the same name as Gisa, that of a bishop in the time of Edward the Confessor, and Cippa the same as Gyp in Gypeswich. May not this be a Frisian form? Chippo comes before us as a name apparently Frisian.

CHIPP, CHIPPING, CHIPMAN, CHEESE, CHESSON, CHESMAN, CHESNUT, CHURN, CHIRNIE, CHITTY.

If the above be, correct, Chipp, corresponding with an Anglo-Saxon Cippa found in Cippenham, a Ceapa found in Ceapan hlæw, and Cypa in Cypingas, also with a Chippo probably Frisian, would be another form of Gibb or Gipp, *geban*, to give. And Cheese, which appears as Chese in the *Hundred Rolls*, may represent Cissa as another form of Gisa (*gis*, hostage). There is a present Friesic name Tsjisse, which, though it looks more like an attempt to represent a sneeze than anything else, I take to have the sound of Chissa. Chesson may be taken to be from the ending in *en*, p. 27, and Chesnut might be from the ending *noth*, bold, frequent in Anglo-Saxon names. Churn and Chirney, corresponding with an O.G. Chirno, and perhaps with the Cearningas among the early settlers, might come in here as another form of *gern*, eager. And Chitty, perhaps the same name as that found in the Cidingas, may possibly be, on the same principle, another form of Giddy, Kiddy, or Kitty (stem *gid*, hilaris).

MUMM, MUMMY, MUMMERY.

There are a few Old German names, mostly of women, in Mam and Mum. And there are also two

Old Frankish women's names, Mamma and Momma (apparently overlooked by Foerstemann), in the *Pol. Irm.* It seems difficult to take these names as from anything else than the widely-spread word signifying mother. In an age when names sat much more lightly than they do now, one might fancy such a word superseding a woman's original name. I can even conceive the possibility of such a name, its origin having somewhat passed out of sight, being given in a masculine form to a son. We have several instances in the *Pol. Irm.* of such a custom ; .for instance, where, the mother being called Genesia, the son is called Genesius, and the mother being called Deodata, the son is called Deodatus. However, this cannot be taken for anything more than a somewhat speculative suggestion. As in present use, the French name Mumm is well known in connection with dry champagne ; the Germans have Muhm, and though I am not quite certain of Mumm as an English name, I think we may count upon Mummy (ending in *i*, p. 24). Mummery might be a compound (*hari*, warrior), but from the facility with which *n* passes into *m*, I should be more disposed to take it to be a corruption of Munnery, corresponding with an O.G. Munihari, Goth. *munan*, to think.

BODY, FREEBODY, GOODBODY, LIGHTBODY, PEABODY, HANDSOMEBODY.

Body I take to be from O.N. *bodi*, envoy or messenger. It is found as an ending in many ancient names, particularly among the Saxons. And in our surnames it appears sometimes as representing ancient names, and sometimes more probably as a sobriquet of a later period. In the "Household Expences" of Eleanor, Countess of Montford, A.D. 1265, the names of her three messengers are given as Treubodi, Gobithesty, and Slingaway. These are all sobriquets,—Treubody is "trusty messenger," Gobithesty is from A.S. *sti*, a footpath, hence the name may be equivalent to "short-cut," and the last explains itself. Our name Handsomebody has clearly been a sobriquet of the same kind, and, referring to the older sense of "handsome," means a handy or useful messenger. Peabody, which I think may have been originally Pipbody, from *pipr*, swift, active, may also have been a sobriquet. So may Goodbody and Lightbody, but it is by no means certain. We might take our Lightfoot to have been a sobriquet, but we find a corresponding name, Lytafus (*fus*, foot) on Roman pottery. Freebody probably represents the O.G. Frithubodo, compounded with *frith*, peace.

BRAGG, BRACKIE, BRAY, PRAY, BRAGAN, BRACKEN, BRAIN, BRACKING, BRACKETT, BRAYMAN, BRAKE-MAN, BREWIN.

There are two different origins from which this stem might be derived, A.S. *brego*, king, ruler, and A.S. *bracan*, to break, subdue, crush, the former being perhaps preferable upon the whole. There are but very few names in Old German, and Foerstemann does not make any suggestion as to the origin.

A.S. Brӕg (found in Brӕgeshale), Bracca (found in Braccanheal). O.G. Brachio, Thuringian, sixth century. Eng. Bragg, Brackie, Bray, Pray.

Ending in *en*, p. 27.

A.S. Bregen (found in Bregnesford). Eng. Bragan, Bracken, Brain.

Ending in *el*, prob. diminutive.

A.S. Brakel (fonnd in Brakelesham).   Eng. Breakell.

Patronymic.

Eng. Bracking.

Compounds.

(*Had*, war?), A.S. Breged (found in Bregedeswere)— Eng. Brackett. (*Man*, vir), Eng. Brakeman, Brayman (Mod. G. Brackmann, French Braquemin). (*Wine*, friend), A.S. Bregowin (Archbishop of Canterbury)—Eng. Brewin.

LORD, LORDING.

We may take the above to be the same as an A.S. Lorta and Lorting, p. 100. And whatever may be the origin, it is certainly not A.S. *hlaford*, Eng. " lord." There are two isolated names in the *Altdeutsches Namenbuch*, Laurad and Lorad, both seventh century, of which the Anglo-Saxon name seems not improbably to be a contraction. The word concerned might be A.S. *lår*, lore, learning, Old North. *lærdr* (larad?), learned. Stark however seems to take Laurad and Lorad to be Celtic. But in the genealogy of the sons of Woden in the *Edda* of Snorro occurs the name Loride, which, though Snorro's names are not always trustworthy, seems to point to the existence of an ancient Teutonic name corresponding with those in the *Altdeutsches Namenbuch*, and so far to favour the derivation which I have suggested.

STUDD, STOTT, STOUT, STUTTER, STODDART, STUD-EARD. STITT, STEED, STADD, STIDOLPH.

We find Anglo-Saxon names to account for all the names of the former of these two groups, viz., Stut, Stuter (*her*, warrior), and Stutard (*hard*, fortis). The word concerned does not seem to have anything to do with Eng. "stout," which seems to have lost an *l*, and to have been originally *stolt*. The group is no doubt parallel with the second group, which is more distinctly represented in Old German names, and which may be referred to O.N. *stedia*, firmare, *staddr*, constitutus, A.S. *stide*, *stith*, firm, steadfast ; our Stidolph corresponding with an O.G. Stadolf, and a Stithuulf in the *Liber Vitæ*.

FOGG, FOGGO, FUDGE, FEW.

There are Old German names Focco and Fucco, for which Foerstemann proposes O.N. *fok*, flight. And there is a Fuca, rather probably a corresponding name, on Roman pottery. Among the Anglo-Saxons we have Focingas, early settlers in Kent. Also Focga and Fucg, deduced from place-names, p. 99. Foerstemann seems to take this as the stem on which is formed *fugal*, fowl, bird.

FLAGG, FLACK, FLECK, FLUCK, FLY, FLEA, FLEW.

The Fleccingas are among the early settlers inferred by Mr. Kemble. And there are also Anglo-Saxon names Flegg, Flecg, and Flogg, deduced from place-names, p. 99. The name Flôki, of a Northman in the *Landnamabôk*, also comes in here. There is also another Northman called Flugu-Grimr, "Fly or Flyer Grim," a kind of. inverted surname. The origin may be taken to be A.S. *fleogan*, O.N. *fliuga*, to fly. And this group may be taken to be fundamentally parallel with the last.

CLEAN, CLINE, KLYNE.

There is a Clen in the genealogy of the Merovingian kings, and there is perhaps an A.S. Clena to be deduced from the place-names Clenanford, Clenancrundel, &c. It may probably be from A.S. *clêne*, clean, pure. "The original sense seems to have been bright."—*Skeat.* This may probably be the sense in names.

SWEARS, SWEARING, SWIRE, SQUIRE, SQUARE, SQUAREY, SQUIRRELL.

The stem *swar*, *swer*, in O.G. names, is referred by Foerstemann to O.H.G. *suari*, weighty, important, Goth. *swers*, honourable. There is an A.S. Sweor found in a place-name, p. 102, and there is an O.G. Suaring corresponding with our Swearing. Also a Suara on Roman pottery, which I take to be German, and to represent the stem of which Suaring is a patronymic. I take Squire and Square to be phonetic corruptions of Swire and Swear, and Squirrell to be properly Swirrell, a diminutive.

LUMB, LUMP, LUMPKIN.

Lumbe is also a present German name, and seems to be the same as an O.G. Lumpe, which Stark takes to be a contraction of some compound name, perhaps

Lundbert. Lump and the diminutive Lumpkin are from *Suffolk Surnames*, and may. be German and not English.

KNELL, NELLY, NILL, KNELLER.

Of the Cnyllingas, settled in Northamptonshire, I find no further trace in Anglo-Saxon times, nor anything to correspond in Old German names. The name is also a very uncommon one at present, the above Knell, Nelly, and Nill being all taken from *Suffolk Surnames*, though Knell at all events was an English name. Kneller, as the name of the painter, is of Dutch origin ; it seems to be a compound from this stem (*hari*, warrior). The origin may perhaps be found in O.N. *hnalla*, to beat.

KNAPP, KNAPPING, KNIBB, KNIPE, KNIPPING, NAF NAPP, NAPKIN, KNIFE, KNYVETT.

One of the oldest Low German names on record is Hnaf, mentioned in the "Traveller's Song," written, as supposed, about the fifth century. There is a corresponding O.G. Hnabi, eighth century, the origin being, no doubt, A.S. *cnapa*, *cnafa*, son, boy. To this may be placed our names Knapp, Napp, and the patronymic Knapping. (The name Naf, in *Suffolk Surnames*, may possibly not be English.) I also take the A.S. Cnebba [1] to come in here, also Hnibba, found in Hnibbanleah (Hnibba's lea), and Nybba, found in Nybbanbeorh (Nybba's barrow), and so connect also our names Knibb, Knipe, and Knipping. Stark also brings in here the name Cniva, of a Gothic king of the third

[1] Kemble explains Cnebba as "he that hath a beak," which would seem to make it a sobriquet. But it certainly seems more reasonable to bring it into an established stem.

M

century, and Cnivida, also the name of a Goth, placed
by Foerstemann to A.S. *cnif*, knife. If this be correct,
our name Knife might also come in here, parallel with
Knipe, and also Knyvet as probably a diminutive.
Also Napkin, another diminutive = Germ. *knabchen*.

PIM, PYM.

The father of the Lombard king Rachis was called
Pimo. There is also a Pymma about the tenth
century in the *Liber Vitæ*. As to the origin of the
name, I am unable to offer any suggestion. It may
be, as Stark opines, a contraction of some compound
name.

WAMBEY, WAMPEN.

Wamba was the name of a West-Gothic king in
the seventh century, and there was also a deacon of
the same name a few years earlier. I do not know of
it as an Anglo-Saxon name, but I suppose Scott must
have had some authority for introducing it as the name
of the jester in *Ivanhoe*. The only derivation that
can be suggested is from the Goth. *wamba*, belly,
giving it the meaning of "paunchey." But it was
not a nickname in the case of the Gothic king, for he
bore it upon his coins, and it is difficult, as Stark
observes, to suppose such a name for a king. Finding,
however, on certain of his coins the variation Wanba,
Stark is inclined to think that it may be a contraction
of some name such as Wanbert. Was it by literary
intuition that Scott pitched upon such a name for the
jester, or did he know of its supposed meaning of
"paunchey"?

The name may be represented in our Wambey,

though it is perhaps quite as likely to be from some
Danish place-name in *by*, such as Wanby or Wandby.
Wampen, however, if there is such a stem, might be
placed to it.

STRANG, STRONG, STRANK, STRANGWARD, STRANG-
WICK, STRINGLE, STRINGFELLOW.

There are two A.S. forms, *strang* and *streng*,
represented in the above. The only Anglo-Saxon
names that I can find are a Stranglic dux in a charter
of Ina, and a Streng, found in Strengeshô, " Streng's
grave-mound." Stranglic is the A.S. *stranglic*,
strong, and looks like a sobriquet which had superseded his original name. Streng might be the same
as far as it is itself concerned, but there is an O.G.
· Strangulf (*ulf*, wolf) which, along with our own names
Strangward and Strangwick, strongly suggests an
ancient baptismal name, and a formation in accordance
with the Teutonic system. The last name, Stringfellow,
must have been a sobriquet,—it probably represents a
mediæval Strengfelaw, and has been rather curiously
corrupted, owing to the meaning of *streng* not being
recognised.

STRAY,   STRAW,   STRETCH,   STREEK,   STRAIN,
STRICKETT, STRAIGHT.

Closely allied to *strang* and *streng* are A.S. *strac*
and *strec*, violent, powerful, brave, whence I take the
above. The only ancient names to correspond are an
O.G. Strago, ninth century, and Strocgo, eighth century.
Strain and Straight represent respectively the forms
Stragin and Stragget, formed with the endings in *en*
and in *et* referred to in Chapter II.

M 2

Stark, Starkie, Starr, Starch, Sturge, Sturgin, Sturgeon, Stericker.

From the A.S. *stearc, sterc,* O.H.G. *starah, starh,* stiff, strong, I take the above. This form *starc* seems formed by metathesis from the above *strac,*—indeed, all the three forms, *strang, strack,* and *stark,* are etymologically very closely allied. This stem enters distinctly into the Teutonic system, but besides the simple form Stark, corresponding with O.G. Starco and Staracho, we have only Stericker, corresponding with an O.G. Starcher (*her,* warrior).

Eavestaff, Langstaff, Wagstaff, Hackstaff, Shakestaff, Costiff.

These names ending in *staff* might naturally be taken to have been sobriquets, to be classed along with Shakespear, Breakspear, and other names of the same kind. But as regards two of them at least, Hackstaff and Shakestaff, there may be something more to be said. There is an ending *staf* in Teutonic names, for which Grimm, referring to Gustaf, thinks of O.H.G. *stab,* A.S. *staf,* staff,—in the sense, as I should suppose, of baton, or staff of office. There are only discovered as yet two Old German names with this ending, Chustaff and Sigestab. The former, which seems to be from *cunst* or *cust,* science, learning, may be the original of the Swedish Gustaf, and possibly of Costiff, one of the curious names gathered by Mr. Lower. Corresponding with the O.G. Sigestab, we find an A.S. Sigistef, a moneyer of Coenwulf. And there is also a Hehstaf, witness to a charter (*Thorpe,* p. 69). Shakestaff, then, might be a not very difficult corruption of Sigestef (which in the form of Sicestaf would approach still nearer). And Hackstaff might represent the A.S. Hehstaf, in which the second *h* was no doubt strongly aspirated, and might be more like a hard *c*. I, however, only bring this forward as a possible explanation ; there is quite as much to be said for the other view, unless other ancient names turn up.

NAGLE, NAIL, HARTNOLL, DARNELL, TUFFNELL, HORSENAIL, HOOFNAIL, ISNELL, BRAZNELL, COPPERNOLL.

There is in my view no more curious or puzzling set of names than those which, as above, are derived from *nagel* or nail, clavis. It appears to me, though the line is difficult to draw, that they may be divided into two groups, one of which is the representative of ancient baptismal names, and the other of sur-names of a later, perhaps a mediæval, date.

Connected with the former we have Nagle and Nail, corresponding with an O.G. Nagal, ninth century, and an A.S. Negle and Næle, found in place-names, p. 101. Then there are two Old German compounds, Hartnagal (hard nail) and Swarnagal (heavy nail), respectively of the eighth and ninth centuries. The former of these two names we have as Hartnoll, and the Germans have it as Härtnagel. Then I find two more examples among the Anglo-Saxons, Spernægle in a charter of manumission at Exeter, and Dear-nagle in a place-name, p. 98. Spernægle is "spear-nail," and Dearnagle is probably the same, from O.N. *dörr*, spear. The latter of these two names we seem to have as Darnell, and the Germans as Thürnagel. Then we have Tuffnell, which, as Mr.

Lower mentions, was in the seventeenth century spelt Tufnaile, and might be taken to mean "tough-nail," but for this we find no corresponding ancient name. There is a Celtic Dufnal, to which, as being a name adopted from them by the Northmen, and so having an increased chance of being represented, it might perhaps be placed. But if this be the case (which I rather doubt), it would have nothing to do with the present group. The sense in these ancient names may be taken to be a warlike one, as in the case of other names having the meaning of point or edge, acies. We find Nægling as the name given by an Anglo-Saxon to his sword, in accordance with the ancient custom, prevalent both among the Celts and the Saxons, of giving names to weapons, and this assists to point the meaning as that of edge, acies. And it seems to me hardly necessary to assume, with Mone (*Heldensage*), any connection with the mythological smith, Weland.

Then there is another set of names of which we have a considerable number, and the Germans still more, which appear to have been given at a later period, and to be perhaps, at least in some cases, derived from trade. Such are Horsnail, and the corresponding German Rosnagel; Hoofnail, and the German Hufnagel; while there are others, such as Isnell (iron nail), Coppernoll (and Germ. Kupfernagel), about which I hardly know what to think.

HONE, HEAN, HEANEY, ONKEN, ENNOR, HONNER, HENFREY, ENRIGHT, ONWHYN, ENOUGH.

A very common stem in A.S. names is *ean*, the meaning of which remains yet unexplained. We seem to have received it both in the Low German form *ean* and the High German form *aun* or *on*. The Honingas (Oningas) among the early settlers must, I think, be placed to it. It is very apt to intermix with another stem *an*, to which I formerly placed a few names which I think should come in here.

Stem *ean, en, aun, on.*

A.S. Eana, Enna (found in Ennanbeorh), Hean (found in Heanspôl, &c). Also Onna (found in Onnandun). Hona, found in Honingas. Ona, *Lib. Vit.* O.G. Ono, Oni. Eng. Hean, Heaney, Hone. Fries. Onno.

Diminutive.

A.S. Honekyn (found in Honekyntûn, now Hankerton). Eng. Onken.

Compounds.

(*Frid*, peace), A.S. Eanfrith—O.G. Aunefrit, Onfred— Eng. Henfrey.[1] (*Hari*, warrior), O.G. Onheri—O.N. Onar —Eng. Honnor, Ennor. (*Rad, Red*, counsel), A.S. Eanred —O.G. Onrada—Eng. Enright (= Enrat?). (*Wine*, friend), A.S. Eanwini, Inwine (found in Inwines burg) — Eng. Onwhyn. (*Wulf*, wolf), A.S. Eanulf—O.G. Aunulf brother of Odoaker, fifth century—Eng. Enough. (*Ward* guardian), Eng. Onword.

IMPEY, EMPEY, HEMP, HAMP, HAMPER, HEMPER.

Mr. Kemble finds Impingas in Impington, in Cambridgeshire, though it would seem incorrectly, as far as the tribe or family is concerned, the name being only that of a man, Impin. The name Impa

---

[1] This name might also be deduced from another stem.

is found also in Ympanleage, in Worcestershire. A sufficient meaning may perhaps be found in A.S. *impan*, to plant, engraft. To this stem I place Impey, Hemp, and probably Hamp, while Hamper and Hemper may be compounds (*hari*, warrior). There is a stem *umb* in Old German names, which may perhaps claim relationship.

CAUNCE, CHANCE, CHANCEY, CHANCELL, CANSICK, KENSAL, KENSETT.

The Cenesingas, found by Kemble in Kensington, would, if the Anglo-Saxons had possessed the requisite letters, have been better represented by Kenzingas, being, as I take it, from a stem *ganz*, *genz*, *kenz*, referred by Foerstemann to *ganz*, integer. I am inclined to take our names Chance, Chancey, &c., to represent the form *kanz* in a softened form, come to us through the Normans. The forms of the name in the *Roll of Battle Abbey*, Kancey, Cauncy, and Chauncy, and the present French names, Cance, Chanceau, and Chanzy, seem to be in conformity with this view. The French seem to have some other names from the same stem, as Cançalon (O.G. Gansalin) and Gantzère (O.G. Gentsar). The forms Cansick, Kensal (both diminutives, and the latter answering to Chancel), and Kensett, may be taken to represent the native form of the stem as found in Kenzingas.

SNOAD, SNODIN, SNOWDEN (?), SNODGRASS.

Of the Snotingas, who gave the name to Snotingaham, now Nottingham, we have not many traces, either in Anglo-Saxon times or at present. There are three Anglo-Saxon names, Snode, Snodd, and Snoding, derived from place-names, p. 102. In Old German names it only occurs as the ending of two or three names of women. The meaning is to be found in A.S. *snot*, prudent, sagacious. The name Snodgrass may be a compound from this stem as a corruption of Snodgast, though no ancient correspondent has turned up, — compare Prendergrass, p. 114.

THRALE.

This is a very uncommon name; I never knew of an instance other than that of the brewer who is handed down to posterity as the friend of Johnson. So also in ancient times there is only one name on record, Thralo, for which Foerstemann proposes Old Friesic, *thrall*, swift, nimble.

EARWAKER, EDDIKER.

The curious-looking name Earwaker is no doubt the same as an Eueruacer (Everwacer), in *Domesday*, from *evor*, boar, and *wacar*, watchful, and it is of interest as supplying a missing link in the study of Old German names. For the Old German name corresponding to this appears as Eburacer, and while some other German writers have taken the ending to be *acer* (Eng. *acre*), Foerstemann has, rightly as it is proved, suggested that it is a contraction of *wacer*. Similarly the ancient name Odoacer, of the king of the Heruli, is proved by corresponding Anglo-Saxon names, Edwaker in a charter of manumission at Exeter, and Edwacer on coins minted at Norwich (A.S. *ed* = O.H.G. *od*), to be properly Odwacer. From this A.S. Edwaker may be our name Eddiker; and some others of our names, as *Goodacre* and *Hardacre*, may represent ancient names not yet turned up.[1] The second part of the compound, *wacer* (whence our *Waker*), is itself a very ancient stem, being found on the one hand in the Wacer(ingas), among the early Saxon settlers, and on the other in the name Vacir, probably Frankish, on Roman pottery.

SHAWKEY, CHALKEY, CHALK, CAULK, KELK, CHALKLEN, CALKING, CHALKER, CHAUCER.

We may take it that our name Shawkey (Shalkey) is the same as an A.S. Scealc, p. 101, and as an O.G. Scalco, from *scalc*, servant. And the question is, whether our names Caulk, Chalk, and Chalkey, corresponding with an A.S. Cealca (found apparently in Cealcan gemero), and our name Kelk, corresponding with an A.S. Celc, p. 98, may not be forms of the same name without the initial *s*. Or whether they may be, as I before suggested, from the tribe-name of the Chauci or Cauci, one of the peoples included in the Frankish confederation. Of such a stem, however, there is not any trace in the *Altdeutsches Namenbuch*, which one might rather expect to be the case, seeing how fully Old Frankish names are therein represented. However, I am not able to come to any definite conclusion respecting this stem, which the forms above cited show to be an ancient one. The French names Chaussy, Chaussée, Cauche, Cauchy, seem to be in correspondence, as also Chaussier, comparing with Chaucer, which, as a softened form, I think may have come through the Normans.

[1] Unless, as seems possible, Goodacre may represent the Old German name Gundachar.

CHAPTER X

IT follows inevitably that, among the multitude of names such as are included within the scope of this work, there must be many which, though being of ancient origin, accidentally coincide with other words of modern meaning. And thus there are several which might be taken to be from names of women, such as the following :—

ANNE, NANNY, BETTY, SALL, MOLL, PEGG, BABB, MAGG, MEGGY, MAY, MAYO, NELLY, LUCY, KITTY, HANNAH, MAUDE.

These are all English surnames, and have sometimes been accounted for on the supposition of illegitimacy. Now, I am very much inclined to doubt the existence, at least in England, of any names derived from women, inasmuch as in the whole range of our surnames I do not know of one that is *unmistakably* so derived. There is certainly a case, referred to at p. 57, of a surname ending in *trud*, a specially female ending, but, as I have there remarked, it does not necessarily follow that the word is the same as that used in women's names. There is, moreover, another name which a little puzzles me, *Goodeve*, which looks as if it were from the A.S. Godgefa, later Godiva. This is from a special female ending, and I know of no corresponding masculine. But this might be an exceptional case, for I doubt not that many a child in England, and possibly even boys, with an unwonted masculine ending, might be called after the noble woman who freed her people from the tax—

"And made herself an everlasting name."

However, whether this might be so or not, the case seems scarcely sufficient of itself to establish the principle. And with regard to names such as those of which I am now treating, the resemblance is only apparent, and, as I shall proceed to show, these are all in reality ancient names of men. Anna, for instance, was a king of the East Angles, and Moll the name of a king of Northumbria. Anna, Betti, Salla, Moll, Pega, are early men's names in the *Liber Vitæ*, and all of the above are to be found in some kindred form ƒin the *Altdeutsches Namenbuch*. And some of these names still bear their ancient meaning on their front, thus Pegg is the " pegger," and Moll (or Maule, the more proper form) is the " mauler," the stem being referred to Goth. *mauljan*, to maul.

To take, then, these names in order, Anne, which corresponds with many ancient names besides that of the king of the East Angles, among others with that of an Anna, Archbishop of Cologne in the eleventh century, may be referred to O.H.G. *ano*, ancestor. And Hannah (more properly Hanna) is, with the ending in *a*, p. 24, the same as Hanney and Hann, probably from the same stem, the *h* being falsely assumed. Nanny corresponds with an O.G. Nanno, referred to Goth. *nanthian*, audere. Betty, along with which we must take Batty, is to be referred to A.S. *beado*, O.H.G. *bado*, war, found in many ancient names. Sall, along with Sala, is from a stem, p. 62, supposed by Foerstemann to mean dark. Kitty, along with Kitt and Kitto, and also Kidd, corresponding with an A.S. Cydd, p. 98, and a Cyda, in the *Liber Vitæ*, is from a stem *gid, kit*, referred to A.S. *giddian*, to sing. Babb, corresponding with an A.S. Babba, the name of a moneyer, and other ancient names, is from a stem which Foerstemann thinks must have been originally derived from "children's speech." Magg and Meggy, corresponding with an A.S. Mæg and Mecga, and an O.G. Megi, are from a stem referred to Goth. *magan*, posse, valere ; and May, along with Mayo, corresponding with an O.G. Maio, and perhaps with a Maio on Roman pottery, is a softened form of the same. Lucy corresponds with an O.G. Liuzi, a High German form from *liud*, people, and I think must have come to us through the Normans. Nelly, along with Knell, is referred to at p. 161, as probably from O.N. *hnalla*, to beat. Maude stands on a somewhat different footing from the rest, the surname being really in this case from the same origin as the woman's name. But the woman's name, as I shall endeavour to show in the next chapter, owes its origin to an ancient mistake, and is properly a man's name.

Names apparently from Animals.

Many of the names apparently from animals are also to be otherwise explained. A few of the nobler animals, as the bear, the wolf, and the boar, are to be found in the names of · men throughout the

Teutonic system. The lion also and the horse occur, though by no means so commonly. The *urus*, or wild ox, appears to have contributed a few names, of which our *Ure* may be one. I have met with the fox in one single instance, that of a Northman, Füks, on a runic inscription quoted by Stevens, though it is rather probable that Foxes beorh, " Fox's barrow " (Kemble, *Cod. Dip.*), may also be from the name of a man. Among birds, the eagle, the raven, and the swan were common throughout the Teutonic system, the last, among the Germans, more especially in the names of women. To account for this, Weinhold observes that along with the beauty of the swan was contained a warlike sense derived from the swan plumage of the maids of Odin. But among the Danes and the Saxon sea-rovers Swan seems to have been common as a man's name, and in this case the idea was more probably that of the way in which the swan rides the waters as the ideal of a rover's life. The eagle, the raven, the swan, the hawk, and the finch seem to be found in the Earningas, the Ræfningas, the Suaningas, the Haucingas, and the Fincingas, among our early settlers, though the two last do not seem to occur in the Teutonic system generally. I doubt all names that appear to be from fishes, and, with one notable exception, all names that appear to be from reptiles or insects. That exception is the snake, which was in special favour for the names of men among the Danes and Northmen, there being no fewer than twenty-four men called Ormr (worm or snake) in the *Landnamabôk* of Iceland. Hence the name *Orme*, rather common among us, and the Saxon form *Worm*, not by any means common. Among the Germans the snake was, according to Weinhold, who looks upon it as the type of fascination and insinuation, in especial favour for the names of women. The two principal words in use among them were *lind* (O.H.G. *lint*, snake) and *ling* (O.N. *lingvi*, serpent). Hence may be our *Lind* and *Lindo*, corresponding with an O.G. Linto ; and *Ling* and *Lingo*, corresponding with an O.G. Lingo, and an O.N. Lingi. But both of these derivations are somewhat uncertain, and especially the former, for I venture to think that *lind*, gentle, is at least as appropriate for women as *lind*, snake. To come then to the names which I take to be otherwise explained.

CAMEL, LEOPARD, BUCK, PIGG, RABBIT, CAT, RAT, MOUSE, SQUIRRELL. GOOSE, GOSLING, GANDER, DUCK, DUCKLING, OSTRICH, LARK, WREN. FISH, SHARK, DOLPHIN, SALMON, TROUT, WHITING, SMELT, HADDOCK, HERRING, TUNNY, SPRATT, MINNOW, LAMPREY. MOTH, MOTE, FLY, FLEA, EARWIG, EMMETT.

Of the above, Camel is another form of Gamol, signifying old ; there is a Northman called Kamol in a runic inscription in Stevens. Leopard (see p. 151) is a corruption of Liubhard. Buck is found among the early Saxon settlers, also as an O.G. Bucco, and a Buccus, rather probably German, on Roman pottery, and may be taken to be another form of Bugg, p. 3. Pigg, corresponding with an O.G. Pigo, must be referred to the same stem as Pegg, viz. *bichen*, to slash. Rabbit is no doubt the same as a Rabbod, a " Duke of the Frisians " mentioned by Roger of Wendover, a contraction of Radbod, p. 119. Catt, along with Cattey, is another form of Gatty, corresponding with an O.G. Gatto (*gatten*, to unite). Ratt, corresponding with a French Ratte, may be referred to an O.G. Rato (*rad* or *rat*, counsel). Along with Mouse I take Moss, also a present German Muss, and a French Mousse, all of which may be referred to an O.G. Muoza, a High German form of *môd*, *môt*, courage ; this name having rather probably come to us through the Normans. Squirrell I have referred to at p. 160. Goose and Gosling I also take to have probably come to us through the Normans, as representing a High German form of the stem *gaud* (supposed to mean Goth). There are to compare French names Gousse, Gosselin, Josselin, corresponding with Old German names Gauso and Gauzelin, the latter a diminutive. Hence also, as a Christian name, Jocelyn, of Old Frankish origin, come to us through the Normans. Gander is from an A.S. Gandar, referred to in its place as a compound of *gand*, probably signifying wolf. Duck, corresponding with a Duce (hard *c*) in the *Liber Vitæ*, is another form of Tuck, as in the Tucingas, early settlers in Kemble's list, from the stem *dug*, A.S. *dugan*, to be " doughty." And Duckling, corresponding with an A.S. Duceling, p. 98, and an O.G. Dugelin, is a diminutive (like Gosling) from the same stem. Ostrich represents an O.G. Austoric, and an A.S. Estrich (*Auster* or *Easter* orientalis). Wren, along with Rennie and Renno, is from a stem referred to *ran*, rapine ; though it may also be the same name as Rain, from *ragin*, counsel. Lark and Laverock are perhaps a little uncertain ; we find Anglo-Saxon names Lauerc, Lauroca, and Laferca, which might be from the A.S. *laferc*, O.E. *laverock*, lark. On the whole, however, I am rather more disposed to take them to be from Lafer among the early settlers (not I think a compound) with the diminutive ending *ec*, and similarly I would take Leverett to be formed from the same word, *lafer* or *lefer*, with the (perhaps also diminutive) ending *et*.

Coming to names apparently from fishes, I question very much whether Fiske and Fish are from A.S. *fisc*, pisces, though Foerstemann, in default of a better, gives that meaning in an ancient name, Fisculf. I think it is one of the cases in which a meaning is to be got from the Celtic, and take it that the Welsh *ffysg*, impetuous, supplies the sense that is required, of which also some slight traces are to be found in Teutonic dialects. Shark and Sharkey I take to be the same name as Serc in the *Liber Vitæ*, from A.S. *serc*, Sco. "sark," shirt, in the sense of a shirt of mail. It is formed, according to Diefenbach, upon a stem *sar* or *ser*, signifying armatura, p. 62; whence an O.G. Saracho, corresponding with the above. The Sercings are a tribe or family mentioned in the " Traveller's Song," and in connection with the Serings :

"With the Sercings I was, and with the Serings."

The connection between the two, however, is here probably only for the sake of the alliteration. Dolphin is the Danish name Dolgfinnr, p. 48. There was a Dolfin, presumably of Scandinavian origin, governor of Carlisle in the time of Rufus. Herring and Whiting are both from the Anglo-Saxon patronymic, p. 28, and Haddock, with the M.G. Hädicke, is a diminutive from the stem *had*, war, p. 54. Tunny, along with Tunn and Tunno (Tunna, *Lib. Vit.*), is another form of Dunn, a common Anglo-Saxon name. Spratt I class along with Sprout and Sprott, comparing them with an O.G.

N

Sprutho, as from Goth. *sprauto*, nimble, active. And
Minnow, along with Minn and Minney, corresponding
with an O.G. Minna, may be taken to be from A.S.
myn, love, affection. Salmon is the same as an O.G.
Salaman, from, as supposed, *salo*, dark ; and Trout
may be the same as an O.G. Truto, probably signifying beloved. Smelt may be taken to be from A.S.
smelt, gentle ; it occurs once as the name of an Anglo-
Saxon, but does not seem to be a word entering into
the Teutonic system, and may have been originally a
sobriquet. Lamprey I have already referred to, p. 115,
as a probable corruption of Landfred.

Of names apparently from insects, Moth and Mote
(Mote, *Hund. Rolls*) are probably the same as an
O.G. Moata, from *môd*, *môt*, courage, German *muth*.
Fly and Flea are included in a stem, p. 159; and Emmet
may be taken to be from A.S. *emita*, quies, found in
several ancient names. Earwig I have taken, p. 49, to
be a contraction of Evorwig, as Earheart of Everhard,
and Earwaker of Evorwacer.[1] Many other names of
the same sort might be adduced, but those I have
given will I think be sufficient for the purpose.

Names apparently from Office or Occupation :

LORD, EARL, ABBOTT, NUNN, BISHOP, PRIEST,
ALDERMAN, PRENTICE, PRINCE, HAYWARD,
HOWARD, ANGLER, ARCHER, AUTHER, FARRIER,
HURLER, PLAYER, MARINER, WARNER, WALKER,
PLOWMAN, ARKWRIGHT, HARTWRIGHT, SIEVE-
WRIGHT, GOODWRIGHT.

Lord, as noted at p. 158, can hardly be from
A.S. *hlaford*, Eng. lord. Earl, however, along

---

[1] Cf. also Eng. " e'er " for " ever."

with Early, seems to be the same word as Eng. "earl," though as a name entering into the Teutonic system it is only a word of general honorific meaning, and may not represent any man who ever bore the title. Abbott I take to be the same as an A.S. Abbod, p. 96, the stem being, as supposed, from Goth. *aba*, man. Nunn, along with Nunney and Noon, compares with Nun, the name of a kinsman of Ina, king of Wessex, and with O.G. Nunno and Nunni, the meaning of which seems somewhat obscure. Bishop, at least in its origin, can hardly have been from the office, for there is a Biscop in the genealogy of the kings of the Lindisfari, who must of course have been a heathen. The name in this case may be a compound of *bis* (closely allied to *bas*, p. 5) and A.S. *côf*, strenuous, which we find as the ending of some other A.S. names. But after the advent of Christianity, a man, though inheriting the old name, would no doubt wear it with a difference. Priest must, I think, be what it seems, there is a witness to a charter (*Thorpe*, p. 69) whose name is Preost, and whose description is "presbyter"; his original name, whatever it was, must have been so completely superseded by that of his office that at last he accepted it himself, and signed accordingly. Alderman I have taken, p. 116, to be, even in Anglo-Saxon times, a corruption. Such a name, as derived from office, could hardly be borne by an Anglo-Saxon, unless, indeed, as a sobriquet, superseding his original name. So also Prentice, from an A.S. Prentsa, I take to be due to a corruption in Anglo-Saxon times. I am not sure that Prince may not be from the same name, Prentsa, dropping the vowel-ending and becoming Prents. A

N 2

name which has been mistakenly supposed to be from some office of agricultural oversight is Hayward ; it is however an ancient name, more properly Agward or Egward. Howard, which has been sometimes confounded with it, is an entirely different name, the O.N. Hâvardr (*hâ*, high), introduced I think by the Danes or Northmen.

Some names formed with *wright*, as Arkwright, Hartwright, Sievewright, and Goodwright, will be found in their places in Chapter III. as, according to my view, ancient compounds. I might perhaps add Boatwright, from an O.G. Buotrit, and also Cheesewright, for which we have the stem, p. 155, though no ancient form to represent this particular compound. The Wrihtingas, in Kemble's list of early settlers, I take to be properly Ritingas, from a stem *rit*, supposed to be the same as Eng. "ride," though perhaps in an older and more general sense of rapid motion. Many names ending in *er*, as Ambler, Angler, Archer, Auther, &c., are in reality from an ancient ending in *har*, signifying warrior. Ambler represents an O.G. Amalher, p. 42, Angler an O.G. Angilher, p. 42, Archer an O.G. Erchear, p. 42, and Auther an O.G. Authar, p. 42. Farrier, along with Ferrier, may represent an O.G. Feriher, p. 49, and Hurler an O.G. Erlehar, from the stem *erl* already referred to. Gambler represents an O.G. Gamalher, and Player is the same as an A.S. Plegher, from *pleg*, play, probably the play of battle. Then we have Mariner and Marner, which, with French Marinier and Marnier, may be referred to an O.G. Marnehar (*mar*, famous), and in a similar manner Warrener and Warner may be taken to be from an O.G. Warnehar (Warin = Wern). Among names of this class we may also include Walker, of which there is abundant instance as an ancient name. Kemble has Wealceringas among the early settlers, as well as also Wealcingas representing the stem on which it is formed, probably A.S. *wealh*, stranger. There was in after Anglo-Saxon times a Walchere, bishop of Lindisfarne, and Ualcar is found in a runic inscription in Stevens ; while, as O.G. names, we have Walachar and Walchar, and as a present German name we have Walcher. However, in view of the commonness of this name, it is perhaps only reasonable to suppose an admixture from A.S. *wealcere*, a fuller.

I may here observe that this same ending, *har*, so common in ancient names, give us many names which have the appearance of a comparative, such as *Harder*, *Paler*, *Richer*, &c., and in its other form, *hari*, many names such as *Armory*, *Buttery*, *Gunnery*, *Flattery*, which we have also in the other form as *Armor*, *Butter*, *Gunner*, and *Flatter* (*flat*, formosus).

Names apparently from Times and Seasons.

The names of this sort have generally been supposed to be derived from a person having been born at some particular time. That there are names of this sort, such as Christmas, Noel, and Midwinter, we cannot for a moment doubt, but, judging by the early records of our names, they are of very rare occurrence, and I conceive that in the majority of cases names of such appearance are to be otherwise accounted for.

SUNDAY, MONDAY, FRIDAY, HOLIDAY, LOVEDAY,
HOCKADAY, PENTECOST, LAMMAS, LAMAISON,
SUMMER, WINTER, JANUARY.

Sunday may be Sunda, comparing with an O.G.
Sundo, and an A.S. Sunta, perhaps from *sund*, sea.
Similarly Munday may be Munda, to be · referred,
along with Mundy, to *mund*, protection, and comparing
with an O.G. Mundo.   The other four names ending
in *day* seem to represent ancient compounds, and in
what sense these were given it is difficult to say.
Friday corresponds with an O.G. Frittag and with an
A.S. Frigedæg, p. 99, Holiday with an O.G. Haleg-
dag, Loveday (Luiedai in Domesday) with an O.G.
Liopdag (*liub*, love), and Hockaday, with a present
French Hocedé, with an O.G. Hodag (*hoh* or *hoch*,
high).   From the character of these names, compounded with "high," "holy," "peace," and "love,"
they might be supposed to have been given in a
religious sense, and their date, the ninth century,
would be in conformity.   The Anglo-Saxon name
Frigedæg, it will be observed, is from the same word
as our "Friday," and not the same as the Old German
name, which is from *frid*, peace.   But it seems to me
quite possible that the Anglo-Saxons, having received
the name, might mistake its meaning and spell it
according to their own views.   This they seem to do
in some other cases, as, for instance, the stem *wit*,
common to the Teutonic system, and rather probably
from *wid*, wood, they seem to take · as from
wiht, man, and spell it accordingly.   Summer and
Winter are both ancient names ; in the *Cod. Dip.*
Alamanniæ there are two brothers called respectively

Sumar and Winter, A.D. 858. Winter was also the name of one of the companions of Hereward the Saxon. Pentecost I have elsewhere supposed, p. 120, to be a corruption of Pentecast, as an ancient name. I rather doubt Lammas, which is found as Lammasse in the *Hundred Rolls*, and which corresponds with a French Lamas. Lamisso was the name of a Lombard king of the fifth century, and was derived, according to an old chronicler, from *lama*, water, because in his youth the king had been rescued from drowning—a derivation which may perhaps be regarded with some suspicion. Taking Lammas then as the representative of an ancient name, we might get from it our name Lamaison (ending in *en*, p. 27), though if Lammas were from the diminutive ending is, *es*, p. 32, it could not take a German *en* in addition ; in this case the ending must be Romanic, which, from the French form of the name, seems very possible. As to the name January, I am inclined to look upon it as a corruption of another name, Jennery, which, along with Jenner, I take to be the same as the Old German names Genear and Ginheri, from, as supposed, *gan*, magic or fascination.

Names apparently from Parts of the Body.

HEAD, BODY, ARMS, LEGG, LEGGY, LEGLESS, FINGER, HEART, EARHEART, SIDE, BACK, ELBOW, FOOTE, TONGUE. (LAWLESS, BOOKLESS, FAIRLESS, RECKLESS), FAIRFOOT, TRUEFITT.

With the exception of Foote and Tongue, I do not think that any of the above are what they seem. Head seems to be probably the same as A.S. Hedda, which, like another name, Hada, seems to be from *had*, war. Body is clearly from *bodi*, messenger, p. 157, and Arms is from an ancient origin, p. 19. Legg I take to be the same as Law, A.S. *lag*, found in several ancient names. Hence I take Legless to be the same as Lawless, and both to mean "learned in the law," from an ancient ending *leis*, explained by Foerstemann as "learned." (This gives something like a meaning to some other names, as Bookless, "book-learned"; Fairless, "travel-learned"; perhaps Reckless (A.S. *reccan*, to reck, understand). Finger is a Scandinavian name, p. 50, Heart is a false spelling of *hart*, hard, and Earheart is Everard, p. 49. Side is from an A.S. Sida, p. 93, and Back (Bacca and Bacga in the *Lib. Vit.*) is another form of Bagge, *bagan*, to contend. Elbow I take to be Elbo, from *alb* or *alf*, signifying "elf." Foote may be taken to be what it seems, though I think that such a name must have had a vowel-ending, as its meaning must be "footy," *i.e.* nimble, as "handy," from hand. Comparing with our Foote there is a name Fus on Roman pottery, which, see p. 4, it is clear from his little joke, that the owner took to be from *fus*, foot. It does not follow, as a matter of course, that the old potter knew the meaning of his own name ; there is a word *funs*, sometimes *fus*, occurring in O.G. names in the supposed meaning of eager ; this word would more appropriately be used without a vowel-ending than would *fus*, foot. Foerstemann has a name, Fussio, which does not, however, throw any light upon it. Another name, however, also found on Roman pottery, Lytafus, corresponding with our Lightfoot, rather seems to favour the meaning of *fus*, foot. Two other names of a similar kind to Lightfoot are

Fairfoot (properly Farefoot ; *faran*, to go, travel), and
Truefitt (properly Truefoot) a name like Treubodi,
p. 26. The last name, Tongue, corresponds with an
O.G. Tungo, which I take to be from *tung*, lingua,
probably in the sense of eloquence. We must presume the name not to be High German.

Names apparently from Trees.

Names from trees have been generally taken to be
derived from a local origin, as marking the site of a
man's habitation. There are, however, a number of
names which I take in some, or in all cases, to be
from a different origin.

Ash, Aske, Askey, Beech, Birch, Alder,
Oake, Oakey, Ivy, Linden, Thorne, Hasell,
Willow, Sycamore, Chesnut, Rowantree.

Aske or Ashe represents an ancient stem in Teutonic
names, perhaps derived from a mythological origin,
man being feigned to have been created out of an
ash-tree, perhaps from being the wood out of
which spears were made (Cf. *Asquith*, p. 148). The
Ascingas were among the early settlers, and Æsc was
the name of the son of Hengest. Hence I take our
names, Ash, Aske, and Askey, with several compounds.
The Bircingas were also among the early settlers ;
the stem seems to be *birg*, supposed to mean protection, and entering into a number of names throughout the Teutonic system. Alder, which corresponds
with an A.S. Aldher, and an O.G. Althar, is a compound of *ald*, old, and *hari*, warrior. The oak, as
the symbol of strength, would seem suitable for men's

names, but upon the whole it seems more probable
that Oake and Oakey, Aikin (A.S. Acen, p. 96) and
Aikman (A.S. Æcemann, p. 96), are from *ac, ec,*
perhaps " edge," acies.   Ivy is the same as Ive with
a vowel-ending, and compares with an O.G. Ivo, and
an A.S. Iffa, perhaps from O.N. *ýfa,* to rage.   Linden
is from *lind,* p. 175, with the ending in *en,* p. 27.
Hasel and Thorn are both found in the list of early
settlers, the former I take to be properly Asel, corresponding with an O.G. Asilo, from *as* or *os,* semideus ;
the latter, which does not seem to occur in the
Teutonic system generally, I rather suppose to be
a contraction of O.N. *thoran,* boldness.   Willow,
along with Will and Willey, is also found in the
list of early settlers, and corresponds with an O.G.
Willo, perhaps from *will* in the sense of resolution.
Sycamore is from an O.G. Sicumar, p. 162, and
Chestnut is referred to at p. 155.   Rowantree is
no doubt from the tree, and may perhaps have
reference to its supposed magical powers.   Rointru
is also a French name, perhaps a relic of the many
Scotchmen who have at different times taken refuge
in that country, though possibly of older origin.

    There are a few other names which may be
included here.

STUBBE, STUBBING, GROVE (GRUBB), TWIGG,
    SPRIGG (TWINE, TWINING, TWISS, SPRAGUE,
    SPRACK, SPARK, SPRACKLIN, SPRECKLY).

    Stubbe might be taken to be of local origin, for
nothing would be more appropriate to mark a locality
than a stub.   But the patronymic Stubbing points to
an origin of a different kind, and moreover we find

Stubingas among the early settlers. And there was also a Stuf, nephew of Cerdic, and a Northman called Stufr in the *Laxdæla-saga.* The origin is to be found in O.N. *stufr, stubbr,* A.S. *styb,* branch, shoot, probably in the honorific sense of race or lineage. I take Grove, along with which I put Grubb, to be from Germ. *grob,* Dan. *grov,* coarse, clumsy; but no doubt in an older sense more suitable for men's names, and probably cognate with Eng. "gruff," the idea being that of great size and strength. We find Grobb as an Anglo-Saxon name, p. 99, and Griubinc (son of Griub) as an Old German name, of which, however, Foerstemann does not offer any explanation. Gröbe and Grove are pre-sent German names (the latter Low German), and Grub and Grubi are found in France. Here also I may take Twigg, corresponding with an A.S. Twicga, moneyer of St. Edmund, also with a Tuica found in Tuicanham, now Twickenham. I take it to be from the same root as "twig," viz. A.S. *tweg,* two, and to have perhaps the meaning of "twin." (Names of a similar kind may be Twine, with its patronymic Twining, and also Twiss, corresponding with an O.G. Zuiso, A.S. *twis,* twin.) Sprigg I class along with Sprague, Sprack, and Spark, correspond-ing with a Spraga in the *Lib. Vit.,* as from O.N. *sprackr,* Prov. Eng. *spragg, sprack,* smart, active. We have also, as a diminutive, Spracklin, corres-ponding with a Spraclingus in the *Lib. Vit.,* and we have Spreckley, probably the same name as that of Sprakaleg, brother of Sweyn, king of Denmark, from O.N. *spræklegr,* sprightly.

Names apparently from Complexion or Colour of Hair.

Such names as Black, White, Brown, have been no doubt in many, probably in most cases, original surnames. Nevertheless they are also ancient baptismal names, and it is not by any means certain that these are from the same origin as the surnames.

BLACK, BLACKER, BLAKE, BLANK, BLANCHARD, WHITE, BROWN, DUNN, GRAY, GREGG, CRAIG, MURCH, MURCHIE, SMIRKE.

The Blacingas were among the early settlers. Blecca was the name of a governor of Lincoln, A.D. 627 ; Blaca is an early name in the *Liber Vitæ*, and Blac is a name in *Domesday*. I am inclined to take Black, along with Blake, to be (of course as an ancient name) the same word as *blic*, found in some Old German names, and to find the sense concerned in A.S. blican, to shine (which indeed is the root of *black*), hence to give it, like Bright, the sense of "illustrious." Hence I take our Blacker and the French Blacher to be the same as an O.G. Blicker (*hari*, warrior) — the ancient family of Blacker, I believe, trace their origin to Nancy. I further take Blank and Blanchard (*hard*, fortis) to be a nasalised form of the above, and to have the same meaning. The stem will be found in more detail p. 46.

I take White, so far as it may be of ancient origin, not to be from colour ; in some cases it may be from *wid*, wood, and perhaps in others from *wit*, wisdom. In Anglo-Saxon names it is spelt *wiht*, as if from *wiht*, man—Cf. O.G. Witgar, A.S. Wihtgar, O.G. Witleg, A.S. Wihtlæg, O.G. Widrad, A.S. Wihtræd, though, as I take it, it is the same word common to the Teutonic system.

The Brownings (Brûningas) were also among the early settlers, and Brûn frequently occurs in after Anglo-Saxon times; among others there is a Brûn bydel, "Brown the beadle," in a charter of manumission. Bruno also occurs as an Old German name, and Brûni was not an uncommon name among the Northmen. I am rather disposed to question the derivation from brown, *fuscus*, and as in the case of Black, to take the sense contained in the root, which seems to be that of burning or brightness. One of the Northmen, called Brûni, was surnamed "the white," so that in his case, at any rate, the name was not derived from complexion. Dunn is another name that is found among the early settlers, and also in after Anglo-Saxon times. It seems to me to be at least as probably from O.N. *duna*, thunder, as from *dun*, fuscus.

The Grægingas (A.S. *græg*, grey) are also found in the list of early settlers, though the name does not seem to figure much in after Anglo-Saxon times. There are Old German names Grao and Grawo, and various compounds. The root-meaning seems to contain the sense of " horror," which may be that which is present in names, the idea being of course that of one who is a terror to others. As well as Gray, we have Gregg, and perhaps as another form Craig,[1] and the Germans have Grau. The Myrcingas among the early settlers may perhaps be represented in our Murch and Murchie (whence Murchison), possibly also in S(mirke). Whether the name is from A.S. *mirc*, dark, mirk, may be uncertain; Professor Skeat thinks of *marc*, limes,

[1] There seems probably an Anglo-Saxon name Crecga in Crecganford, now Crayford.

for the Myrcingas, who are probably the same as the Myrgingas of the "Traveller's Song."

Names apparently from Scriptural Personages.

While names taken from the eminent characters of Scripture have, ever since the advent of Christianity, been in favour for the names of men, there are among our surnames some names which we must reasonably suppose are to be otherwise explained.

PHAROAH, HEROD, ESAU, CAIN, JAEL, POTIPHAR
PUDDIFER (ABLARD).

Of the above, Pharoah is only a misleading spelling of an O.G. name Faro, perhaps come to us through the Normans. And Esau is a similar perversion of another O.G. name Eso, probably from *as* or *os*, semi-deus. Cain is, along with Gain, from the name Gagin, Cagen, p. 10, probably signifying victory. Herod is, no doubt, the same as an A.S. Herrid in a charter of Wihtræd, from, as supposed, A.S. *herad*, principatus, found also in some Old German names. Jael I take to be most probably a softened form of Gale, from a stem referred to A.S. *galan*, to sing. Potiphar, along with Puddifer, a French Potefer, and perhaps a Low German Bötefur,[1] I take to represent an ancient name not turned up, from *bod*, *bud*, or *pot*, envoy or messenger, and *faran*, to travel, found as an ending in some Old German names. Abel is a name which, as frequently used for a Christian name, might also be found in surnames. But there is a Teutonic word *abal*, signifying strength, which may be more

---

[1] Nomen honestissimæ familiæ Hamburgensis (*Richey*). He evidently takes it as a sobriquet " beet (*i.e.* make up) the fire."

probably that which is found in the French Abeillard. with which we have a name Ablard to correspond.

Names apparently Descriptive of Moral Characteristics.

There are a number of names which, if they had been found as Christian names, might have been supposed to be of Puritan origin, but which as surnames must be otherwise accounted for.

GOODHEART, STONEHEART, GODWARD, LOVEGOD, LOVEGOOD, LOVEMAN, MANLOVE, GOODLIFFE, FULLALOVE, GODLIMAN, GOODENOUGH, THOROUGHGOOD, HUMBLE, SAINT, BADMAN, PAGAN, BIGOT, GODDAM, SWEARS, SWEARING, SCAMP.

Of the above, Goodheart and Stoneheart are compounds of *hart*, hard, pp. 53, 63. So also Godward, Lovegod, Lovegood, Loveman, Manlove, Goodliffe, and Fullalove will be found in their places as ancient compounds in Chap. III. Godliman I take to be a corruption of an O.G. Godalmand (the *l* being introduced in accordance with a principle referred to at p. 114) Goodenough is referred to at p. 119, and Thoroughgood at p. 120. Humble I take to be the same name as the German Humboldt, from an O.G. Hunbald, the ending *bald* often in our names becoming *ble*. Saint I take to be the same as Sant, *sand* or *sant*, verus, the stem on which is formed Sander in the list of early settlers.

Of the names apparently of an opposite character, Badman, corresponding with a Badumon in the *Liber Vitæ*, is a compound of *bad*, war. Goddam stands for Godhelm as William for Willihelm. Swears and Swearing are explained, p. 160. Scamp corresponds with an O.G. Scemphio, derived by Foestemann from O.H.G. *scimph,* jocus. This may possibly be the older sense of the word, and Scamp may have been nothing worse than a wag. Pagan, with its contracted form Paine, I have referred to p. 118. Bigot, along with Pigot, Pickett, and probably Beckett, and a Pigota and Picotus in the *Liber Vitæ,* may be the same as an A.S. Picced, p. 101, which I take to represent the form Pichad or Bighad, from the stem *big,* with *had,* war. There is, however, another explanation suggested by our name Bidgood. This name, for which the ancient equivalent has not turned up, seems to be from *bad,* war, and might have been Bidgod (for *god* and *good* constantly interchange), which would readily contract into Bigod or Bigot.

Names apparently from Nationalities.

While we have a number of names derived from nations or races in accordance with the Teutonic system, there are some others which might seem more obviously than most others to be from such an origin, and yet which must I think be referred to some other source. Three of these, England, Scotland, and Ireland, I have already referred to at p. 9.

ENGLISH, INGLIS, ROMAN, NORMAN, GENESE, TURK, SPAIN.

English I take to be a phonetic corruption of Inglis, which seems to be the same as an Ingliseus in the *Pol. Irm.,* and which I rather suppose to be a transposition of an Anglo-Saxon Ingils, for Ingisil, from the stem *ing,* p. 56. Roman, I doubt not, is contracted from Rodman, p. 61, as Robert is from Rodbert, and Roland from Rodland. I introduce

Norman here as not being, in my view, from "Norman" as we generally understand the term, but as representing more probably the word in its original sense of "Northman." Nordman was a Scandinavian name, and hence it is I think that we have the name, which seems to occur more especially in Scotland and the Danish districts of England. Genese I take to be most probably from the old Frankish name Genesius, perhaps from a stem *gan*, p. 52, with the ending in *es*, p. 33. Turk corresponds with an A.S. Turca, p. 111, which again is probably the same as a Gothic Turicus of the fifth century, a diminutive from the stem *dur* or *tur* found among the early settlers, and of uncertain meaning. Spain I take to be from the A.S. *spanan*, allicere, found in some ancient names, and from which I take to be our name Spenlove, (*leof,* dear) with the corruption, Spendlove. The name Spegen, corresponding with our Spain, occurs in the *Liber Vitæ* more than once—Is its aspirated form due to the Northumbrian dialect?

Of the names which are truly derived from nationality I will here only refer to one as an illustration of successive forms built one upon the other in accordance with the principle referred to in treating of the ending *en*, p. 27.

BOY, BYE, PYE, BOYER, BYARD, BOYMAN, PYMAN, BEYERMAN, BYRON.

There are three forms, the first representing the form *boi*, as found in the name of the Boii, who gave the name to Boioaria or Bavaria, the second representing the extended form found in German *Baviar*, the third the further extended form as found in *Bavarian*.

O

SIMPLE FORM BOI.

O.G. Boio, Beio, Peio, ninth century. A.S. Boia (in a charter of 'Cnut). Eng. Boy, Bye, Pye. Germ. Boye· French, Boy, Boye, Poy, Poyé.

Compounds.

(*Hard*, fortis), Eng. Byard—French Boyard, Poyart— Italian Boiardo. (*Man*, vir), Eng. Boyman, Pyman.

EXTENDED FORM BOYER.

O.G. Baior, Peior, ninth century. English, Boyer, Byer. French, Boyer, Boyreau, Poyer.

Compound.

(*Man*, vir), English Beyerman.

FURTHER EXTENDED FORM — BAVARIAN.

O.G. Beiarin, eighth century. English Byron. French Boiron, Boyron.

Names apparently from abbreviated Christian names of men.

As I began this chapter with names apparently from women, such as Moll, Betty, Pegge, so now I propose to conclude it with names of a similar kind derived apparently from men.

BILL, BILLY, BILLOW, WILL, WILLY, WILLOEE, WILKE, WILKIE, WILKIN. WILLIS, WILLING, DICK, DICKLE, TICKLE, DICKEN, BENN, BENNEY, BENNOCH, BENNELL, TOM, TOMB, TOOMEY, TOMEY, DUME, DUMMELOW, DUMBELL, TOMMELL, TOMLIN, DUMLIN, DUMPLIN, HARRY, JACK, JAGO, JACKLIN, BOBY, BOFFEY, BUBB, BOBBIN.

No one would take our name Billing to be other than from the Anglo-Saxon Billing, of which so many traces are to be found in English place names. And no one, I venture to say, who looks into the subject, would dispute the ancient compounds formed on the stem, p. 45. Why then should any one doubt Bill himself, the father of them all, or Billy, ending in *i*, p. 24, and Billow, ending in *o* and corresponding with an O.G. Bilo? Moreover the name is common to all the races who share with us in a Teutonic ancestry; the Germans have Bille, the Danes have Bille, and the French have Bille and Billey. The same remarks apply to Will, Willey, and Willoe, with the diminutives Wilke, Wilkie, Wilkin, Willis, patronymic Willing, and compounds, p. 66. Dick I take to be the same word as found in Ticcingas, and suggest for it the meaning of power or vigour which seems to lie at the root. Hence Dickle and Tickle are the same as the Diccel found in Diccelingas, and Dicken is the same as an A.S. Ticcen, p. 102, while Dixie (Dicksie) may be from the ending in *es*, p. 33. Benn and Benny represent the stem on which are formed the compounds, p. 45. We have also as diminutives Bennoch, corresponding with an O.G. Bennico, an A.S. Benoc (in the genealogy of Ida, king of Bernicia), and a name Bennic (Bennici manû), on Roman pottery; and Bennell, corresponding with a Gothic Βενίλος, in Procopius, besides other names in correspondence with ancient forms. Tom has its vowel shortened, but I take it to be the same as Tomb, Toomey, Tomey, and Dume, probably from A.S. *dôm*, O.H.G. *tuom*, judgment, "doom," ancient names in correspondence being Toma, p. 111, Tumma *Lib. Vit.*, and Tomy *Roll. Batt Abb.* With regard to the last, I may observe that the French still have corresponding names, as Thomé, Tombe, Thom, Dome, &c. Then, as diminutives, we have Dummelow, Dumbell, and Tommell, corresponding with O.G. Duomelo, Tomila, Tumila ; and we have Tomlin, Dumlin (whence Dumplin), corresponding with O.G. Domlin, names in accordance with both of the above being also found in Germany and France. Harry, along with Harrow, and Harre, I take to represent the stem from which we have so many compounds, p. 55. Jack, along with Jago, and corresponding with an O.G. Jacco, I take to be from O.H.G. *jagon*, to hunt. Hence as a diminutive, we have Jacklin, corresponding with Jagelinus and Jachelinus (*Domesday*), and with present German Jacklin, and French Jacquelin. The stem seems to be somewhat better represented in French names than in English ; among others they have Jacquard (*ward*, guardian), who gave his name to the Jacquard loom. Boby, Boffey, and Bubb I take to be the same as Boba, in a charter of Egbert, and Bofa, dux, in a charter of Ceolwulf of Mercia, also as Old German names, Bobo, Bovo, Boffo, and Bubo, the word concerned being probably to be found in German *bube*, Dutch *boef*, boy. Kemble has both Bobbingas and Bovingas, different forms, I take it, of the same name, in his list of early settlers. Our name Bobbin, which corresponds with an O.G. Bobin, may be taken as an example of the ending in *en*, p. 27.

I trust that I have succeeded in making it clear, from the definite place which the foregoing are shown to occupy in the Teutonic system, that they are not, as they have been generally supposed to be, familiar contractions of Christian names.

CHAPTER XI.

THE names of women, so far as they are of German origin, enter into the Teutonic system precisely as do the names of men, and there is, as far as I know, no instance of a stem used exclusively for the names of women. But in regard to the second part of the compound, which is that which governs the name, there are certain words which are only used for women. Some of these are such as from their meaning would not be suitable for anything else, such as *trud*, from which we have *Gertrude* and *Ermentrude*, both of which seem to be of Frankish origin, and to have come to us through the Normans. The Anglo-Saxon form appears to be *dryth* or *thryth*, as in Mildthryth, from which comes our *Mildred*, the only name, as far as I know, in that form. Another feminine ending among the Anglo-Saxons was *gith*, which, as elsewhere noted, I have supposed to mean woman or goddess. The only name we have with this ending is *Edith*, unless, as seems not impossible, an Anglo-Saxon *Godgith* (Godith, *Lib. Vit.*) has got mixed up

The principal part of this chapter appeared in the *Antiquary* for March, 1882.

with *Judith.* Another specially female ending was
fled, in H.G. *flat,* the meaning of which seems to be
beauty. As a prefix this word enters into the names
of men, and we may have some names from it, as
Flatt, Flattery, Flatman, &c. As an ending there
may have been some word corresponding with O.N·
fliôd, a beautiful woman, which has caused its special
application. Then there are certain words, such as
hild, war, and *burg,* in which the meaning (condere,
servare) may perhaps imply in such case modesty or
chastity ; which, as endings, are used almost exclusively
for names of women. But as a general rule the same
range of words forms indifferently names of men and
women, the latter being distinguished only by having
the ending in *a.*

My object in this chapter is only to deal with a few
names, in regard to which I desire to correct some
wrong impressions, or to throw some new light upon
the subject. And in the first place I have to refer to
the connection between Isabel and Elizabeth, and to
the manner in which I suppose the former name to
have originated.

ISABEL *another form of* ELIZABETH, *and how it
came to be so.*

Miss Yonge in her *History of Christian Names,* is
no doubt right in taking Isabel to be another form of
Elizabeth, with which it is historically shown to have
interchanged. But the etymological process by which
this has been brought about has been always somewhat of a puzzle, and it is upon this point that I have
to suggest an explanation. Now the key to the
puzzle is this: that the early Frankish converts in he

time of Charlemagne, introduced the name, not only in its Latin form of Elizabeth, but also, and indeed more frequently, in its Hebrew form of Elischeba—it was Elischeba that was made into Isabel and not Elizabeth. Protected by its strong ending, Elizabeth has retained its form unchanged. Elischeba has been entirely lost to sight under a cloud of transformations. Slightly modified to suit Frankish pronunciation, it was introduced in the first instance as Elisaba, Elisabia, Alisabia, and Elisavia, all names of women in the *Polyptique de l'Abbé Irminon* and the *Polyptique de Saint Remi de Reims*. In the fourteenth century (if, indeed, it did not take place earlier) we find this old Frankish form El(isaba) abbreviated into Isabeau, its ending being made to conform to French ideas of spelling. Isabeau was the name of the wife of Charles VI. of France, and the name was still recognised as being the same as Elizabeth. We have got to forge the connecting link between Isabeau and Isabel, but the process is not a violent one. It would not be difficult to suppose that the French idea of the fitness of things in the case of a woman's name would lead them to change this masculine-seeming ending, *beau*, into what they would conceive to be its appropriate feminine, and so make Isabeau into Isabelle. We need not suppose that this took place all at once, or that because one man changed Isabeau into Isabel, everybody else forthwith proceeded to follow his example. It is more probable that the two names existed side-by-side, together, for some time before the struggle for existence terminated in the survival of (what seemed) the fitter. Throughout all these changes the identity of the name with Elizabeth had always

been recognised ; but when Isabel had finally succeeded
in establishing its claim as the representative, the de-
posed Isabeau, its origin having been forgotten, might
have become a man's name, and so capable of trans-
mitting surnames, which would account for Isabeau as
a family name in France at the present day.

But these are not the only changes which have
come over this unfortunate name, for we find Elisavia,
another of the old Frankish forms before noted, forthwith abbreviated into Lisvia, and further corrupted
into ·Lisavir and Lisabir, all names of women in the
two old Frankish chronicles before referred to.   And
if we can again suppose the name Lisavir (or rather
Elisavir), its origin having been forgotten, to have become a man's name (towards which its masculine-
looking ending, *vir*, might have assisted) it might well
give the origin of the name Elzevir, of the famous
printers at Amsterdam.   Not that the name would
necessarily be of Frankish origin, for the Hebrew
form seems also to have been introduced into Germany, where we find the woman's name, Elisba, in
the ninth century ; and, it might be also into Holland,
while the phonetic principles which regulate such
changes are more or less of general application.
Again, it seems not improbable that the Spanish
woman's name, Elvira, for which no derivation at all
satisfactory has been suggested, might be properly
Elzvira, and so again another form derived from
Elischeba.   The question might naturally be asked
how it is, seeing the various contractions which Elischeba has undergone, that Elizabeth has not been
treated in the same way.   In point of fact it seems
probable that it has, for we find a solitary name

Isabeth in the *Liber Vitæ* about the thirteenth century. This was before Elizabeth had come into use in England, and the name might probably be an importation. But abbreviate Elizabeth as you will you cannot disguise it, and this is what I meant in referring to it as "protected by its strong ending." And now, having dealt with the diversified forms that have grown up around Elisabeth, I shall have, in a succeeding note, to endeavour to show that Eliza, which might more certainly than any other form be supposed to be derived from it, is, in fact, of entirely different origin, and a name that was in use long before Elizabeth was introduced; though at the same time we cannot doubt that as soon as ever that potent name came in, Eliza would be at once appropriated by it.

ANNABELLA, ARABELLA, CLARIBEL, CRISTABEL, ROSABEL.

But in the meantime I may refer to some other names which seem cast in the same form as Isabel ; as for instance, Annabella, Arabella, Claribel, Christabel, and Rosabel. With regard to these names, I am disposed to come to the conclusion, that though moulded into the same shape, they are not by any means all of a similar origin. Annabella would be a very natural corruption of Amabilla, a name in the *Liber Vitæ* of Durham. The same record contains, as names of women, Amabilis, Amabel, and Mabilla, of course from Latin *amabilis*—whence our Mabel, on this theory the same name as Annabella. Arabella, again, might be a corruption of the old Frankish Heribolda—*bold*, as an ending often changing into

bel, as in our surnames Grimble and Wimble, from
Grimbald and Winibald, and Tremble (most in-
felicitously), from Trumbald (A.S. *trum*, firm, strong)·
So, also, Claribel might be from an old Frankish
Clarebalda, of which, however, we have only on
record the masculine form, Clarebald.   This appears
to be from Latin *clarus*, illustrious, and is not the only
case in which the old Franks at that period mixed
up Latin and German in the same name.   It is
possible that Christabel might be from a similar
origin ; for the early Frankish converts at that period
freely adopted the name of Christ, and mixed it up
with German compounds, such as Cristhildis, a
woman's name, from *hild*, war.   But on the whole I
am rather disposed to suggest a different origin for
Christabel.   Finding among the Franks at that
period such names as Firmatus, Stabilis, Constabulis,[1]
and the woman's name, Constabilla, in the sense, no
doubt, of "established in the faith," it might not
be unreasonable to suggest such a compound as
Christabila, "established in Christ," as the origin of
Christabel.[2]   As to the last named, Rosabel, the
ordinarily-received expression of " fair rose " would

---

[1] Possibly, at least in some cases, the origin of the surname
Constable.

[2] The earliest mention of this name that I have seen, occurs
A.D. 1431, in the *Liber Vitæ*, when one John Duckett, having
died at the remarkable age of 127, his children, one of whom
was called Cristabel, presented offerings at the shrine of St.
Cuthbert.   These would seem to be of the nature of pro-
pitiatory offerings on behalf of the dead, of which there are
various instances recorded.   One of these is that of one Maria
del Hay, who in a large-hearted spirit, seems to have included
in her offering, not only all who had gone before, but all who
were to come after her.   The entry is, "Maria del Hay, cum
omnibus suis progenitoribus et successoribus."

be a natural and graceful name for women if the French had to form names at a later period. But there is a woman's name, Rosibia, in the *Pol. Irminon,* which suggests a possible process like that in the case of Isabel—viz., a corruption into Rosibeau, and then a change into Rosibel. However, as in this case the connecting links are wanting, I can only put this forward as a conjecture.

MAUD *properly a man's name. Its interchange with* MATILDA *an ancient mistake.*

As Isabel interchanged in former times with Elizabeth, so did Maud with Matilda, among other instances being that of the daughter of Henry I., who was called by both names. Yet, etymologically, Maud can no more be derived from Matilda than can Giles from Ægidius, by which it used formerly to be always Latinized. And the interchange is rendered all the more curious by the fact that Maud, when traced up to its origin, seems to be properly a man's name. There has evidently been some ancient mistake or misappropriation, the origin of which I hope to be able to account for. The names Mald, Maald, Mauld (all names of women), found in the *Liber Vitæ* before the introduction of surnames, and the Christian name Maulde, found in the fifteenth century, show the form from which our Maud is immediately derived. Then we have the older forms, Mahald, Mahalt, and Maholt, all also apparently names of women. And in one case, about the twelfth or thirteenth century, the name stands as " Mahald vel Matilda." Now no one who has given attention to the subject can doubt that Mahald, Mahalt, and

the French form, Mahault, are the same as an Old
Frankish Magoald, eighth century, from Gothic *magan*,
posse, valere, and *wald* power. This is distinctly a
man's name; indeed, *wald*, as an ending, is almost
exclusively confined to men's names, as the ending
hild, as in Matilda, is to those of women. There is
but one way that I can see out of the difficulty, and
it is this. There is in the *Liber Vitæ* another name,
Mahild, which is no doubt the same as an Old
Frankish Mahilda, which Foerstemann (*Altdeutsches
Namenbuch*) takes to be a contraction of Matilda. It
would seem, then, that some mistake or confusion has
in old times arisen between these two names, and
that Mahild, which really represents Matilda, has
been set aside in favour of Mahald, an entirely
different name. The fact, however, of our having
Maude as a surname would rather seem to show that
this misappropriation was not universal, for surnames
are not—unless it be in some very exceptional cases—
taken from the names of women.

ALICE, ALICIA, ELIZA, ADELIZA, ALISON.

ALICE *properly a man's name, and* ELIZA *its proper
Feminine.*

I have seen it stated, though I cannot at present
recall the authority, that in one of our ancient
families Alice is a name given to the sons and not
to the daughters. This would at any rate be etymologically correct, for Alice is properly a man's name,
and not a woman's. It is, there seems little doubt,
derived from the Anglo-Saxon Adelgis, of which the
female form was Adelgisa. It is clear that Alice
(Aliss) represents Adelgis, and not Adelgisa, and that

the proper female form would be Alisa, or, for euphony,
Aliza. I venture to suggest that our Eliza, generally
and very naturally assumed to be an abbreviation of
Elizabeth, is in fact this missing name. Now, for
the proofs of Aliza as the representative of Adelgisa,
we must refer to the *Liber Vitæ* of Durham, in which
we can trace the changes that have taken place in
Adelgisa since the first noble lady of that name laid
her gift upon the altar. First we find it contracted
into Adeliza, and then, from about the twelfth century
into Aaliza and Aliza, the latter name being hence-
forward rather a common one. The former of these
two contracted forms, Adeliza, though not a name in
common use, is one still given to the daughters of
certain of our noble families; the latter form, Aliza,
I take to be the origin of our Eliza. (The initial
vowel is of no account, the ancient name beginning
indifferently with *a* or *e*, and Alice in some families
appearing as Ellice). But concurrently with the
above forms in the *Liber Vitæ*, we have also Adaliz,
Adliz, and Alis, at an early date, some of them at
least being certainly names of women, so that the
misappropriation is at any rate an ancient one.

Towards the close of the record, and about the end
of the fourteenth century, another form, Alicia, begins
to make its appearance in the *Liber Vitæ*, and appears
to have become at once a very favourite name. Then,
as now, fashion seems to have ruled, and when a new
name came in, there seems to have been a run upon
it. But by this time Elizabeth had come into use,
and as soon as ever that took place, the two names,
Eliza and Elizabeth, would begin to get mixed up
together as they are now, so that a new female form

would, so to speak, be required for Alice. Alicia (or more properly Alisia), is an attempt to supply the euphony which is lacking in Alisa, by supplementing it with a vowel, just as, for the same reason, Amala has been made into Amelia.

About the beginning of the fifteenth century another Christian name for women, Alison, begins to make its appearance in the *Liber Vitæ*. This name, however, I take to be from an entirely different origin. There is an old Frankish woman's name, Alesinda, Elesind, Alesint, of the eighth century, from which, dropping the final *d*, it would naturally come, and which is derived by Grimm from Gothic *alja*, alius (in the probable sense of stranger or foreigner), and *sind* in the sense of companion or attendant.

JANET : *Not from* JANE *or any female form of* JOHN.

It may seem rather a paradox to suggest that Janet has nothing to do with Jane, and yet I think that a pretty good case can be made out. We find Geneta as a woman's name in the *Liber Vitæ* in the thirteenth century, before Jane or Joan or Johanna were in use. And in the two following centuries we have Gennet, Janeta, Janette, and Janet, of common occurrence as Christian names. (One of these cases is a very curious one. It is that of one Willelmus Richerdson and his wife Christina, who having a family of eighteen children, seem to have been so completely at their wits' end for names to give them, that two of the sons are called Johannes, two Willelmus, after their father, two of the daughters Christine, after their mother, and no fewer than three called Janet. Such reduplication of Christian names does not, however,

seem to have been unusual at that time.) Now it
seems clear that the above name, Geneta, is the same
as our Janet, and equally clear that it is not derived
from any female form of John. Foerstemann (*Altdeutsches Namenbuch*) has an old Frankish woman's
name, Genida, tenth century, from a Codex of
Lorraine. And I find also the woman's name, Genitia,
in the *Pol. Rem.*, one of the old Frankish chronicles
before referred to. These old Frankish names might
well leave a woman's name behind in France, which
in after times might get mixed up with Jean, and
from which our name may also have been derived. I
may observe that we have also Gennet and Jennett as
surnames, and the Germans have also Genett. But
these, though from the same stem, must be taken to
be from another form of it—viz., from Genad, eighth
century, a man's name. From the same stem Foerstemann derives the woman's name, Genoveva, sixth
century; whence, through the French, our Genevieve.
As to the etymology of *gen*, the Germans are not
agreed, Leo suggesting a borrowed Celtic word, with the
meaning of love or affection, while Foerstemann seems
to prefer Old High German *gan*, magic or fascination.

EMMA : *Its Place in the Teutonic System.*

The ordinary derivation of Emma from a Teutonic
word signifying grandmother, or nurse, becomes
impossible in face of the fact that among the Old
Franks, from whom, through the Normans, we
received it, the man's name Emmo was quite as
common as the woman's, Emma. But in point of
fact the stem, of which the older form seems to have
been *im*, was one common to the whole Teutonic

system, including the Low Germans settled in England. And the Immingas, descendants or followers of Imma, are ranged by Kemble among the early settlers. But among the Anglo-Saxons, with whom the ending of men's names (other than compounds) was generally in *a*, Imma would obviously not be suitable for names of women; and in point of fact it always appears in England, at that time, as a man's name. And probably, for this reason, the Frankish princess Emma, on becoming the wife of Cnut of England, considered it necessary to assume a Saxon name in addition to her own, and so become known as Ælfgifu Imma. But a few centuries later, when the simple old Saxon names in *a* had very much died out, Emma coming in as something quite new, and with the stamp of Norman prestige, became at once, as appears from the *Liber Vitæ*, a name in favour. As to the etymology, which is considered by the Germans to be obscure, I have elsewhere ventured to suggest Old Northern *ymia*, stridere ; whence the name of the giant Ymir, in Northern mythology. The sense is that of a harsh and loud voice, which suggests huge stature. So, from Gaelic *fuaim*, noise, strepitus, comes *fuaimhair*, a giant, of which we may possibly have a lingering tradition in the nursery—" Fee, Fa, *Fum*," representing the giant's dreaded war-cry. And from what follows, " I smell the blood of an *Englishman*," one might almost think of the nurse as a Saxon, and the ogre as one of the earlier Celtic race, who might in those days be dangerous neighbours.

I give below the stem, with its branches, so far as it forms names of women. It also enters into some compounds, one of which, Americo, bequeathed by the Franks or Lombards to Italy, has the honour of giving the name to America.

Stem *im* or *em*.

Names of men.—O.G. Immo, Himmo, Emmo (among others, three bishops in the seventh and ninth centuries). A.S. Imma, found in Imman beorh, "Imma's barrow, or grave." Imma, Hemma, Hemmi, about the tenth century in the *Liber Vitæ*. Eama, Anglo-Saxon moneyer.

Names of women.—O.G. Imma, Emma (among others Emma, daughter of Charlemagne).

Present surnames.—Eng. Him (?), Yem (?). Germ. Imm, Ihm. French, Eme, Emy.

With the ending in *en*, p. 27.

Names of men.—O.G. Imino, Emino, eighth century. A.S. Immine, a Mercian general, seventh century. Emino, *Liber Vitæ*.

Names of women.—O.G. Immina, Emmina, eighth century. Early Eng. Ymana, Ymaine, *Liber Vitæ*.

Present surnames.—Eng. Emeney. Fr. Emmon.

Ending in *lin*, p. 31.

Names of women. — O.G. Emelina, eleventh century. Emalina, twelfth century, *Liber Vitæ*.

Present Christian name.—Eng. Emmeline.

ETHEL, ADELA, ADELINE, ADELAIDE.

Ethel and Adela are different forms of the same word, *adal, athal, ethel,* signifying noble. But while Adela is a correctly formed feminine, Ethel can hardly be said to be so. Both as a man's name and as a woman's it had usually a vowel-ending, and though this was not invariably the case, yet a name appearing without it would be rather assumed to be a man's name. Adeline is a diminutive like Eveline and

P

Caroline; it represents the old name Adalina, eighth century, and Adalina, about the twelfth century, in the *Liber Vitæ*, and comes probably through the French, the ending in *e* preserving the feminine by lengthening the syllable. Adelaide is from *adal*, as above, and H.G. *haid*, corresponding with Saxon *hood*, as in manhood. Hence the name seems to contain the abstract sense of nobility. The name must have come to us through the Normans ; indeed, a woman's name could hardly be so formed among the Anglo-Saxons, for, curiously enough, this ending was a feminine one among the High Germans, and a masculine one among the Saxons. Hence perhaps it is that we have as surnames such names as *Manhood* and *Mahood*, the latter perhaps signifying boyhood, A.S. *mæg*, boy.

EDITH.

Edith is the only representative in women's names of A.S. *ead*, happiness, prosperity, from which we have so many men's names, as Edward, Edwin, Edmund, Edgar. It represents an A.S. Editha, a contraction of Eadgitha, and the question, which is not without a little difficulty, is, What is the origin of *githa ?* Is it a phonetic variation of *gifa* (A.S. *gifu*, gift), so common in Anglo-Saxon names of women, as in God-gifa (Godiva), Sungefa (Suneva), &c., or is it a separate word ? I am disposed to come to the conclusion, upon the whole, that it is a separate word, and though the traces of it as such are not strong, yet there are some traces. . There is a woman's name Githa in the *Liber Vitæ*, and this seems to be the same as an Old Norse woman's name Gyda in the *Landnamabôk*. There was also a Gytha, daughter of Swend, king of Denmark.

Then there are two Old German names of women with the endings respectively of *gid* and (H.G.) *kid*. And the origin of all I should take to be found in O.N. *gydia*, goddess, the exalted conception of womanhood.

EVELYN, EVELINA, EVELINE.

There.does not seem to be sufficient ground for Miss Yonge's suggestion that Eveline, a name which we have from the Normans, was borrowed by them from the Celts. On the contrary, they seem to have derived it from their Frankish ancestors, among whom we find it in the eleventh century in the form Avelina. This appears to be the original form, for we find it as Avelina in the *Liber Vitæ* about the twelfth century. And again in the thirteenth century we find that one of the Earls of Albemarle married a lady named Aveline. It is probably a diminutive from the stem *av*, which Foerstemann refers to Goth. *avo*, in the probable sense of ancestor. The names Evelyn and Eveline should be kept sharply distinct, the former being a man's name, and the latter a woman's, being the French form of Evelina, as is Louise of Louisa.

From the same stem, *av*, is formed also the female name Avice, now become very rare. It appears as Auiza and Avicia in the *Liber Vitæ*, and its original form I take to be found in Avagisa, eighth century, in the *Altdeutsches Namenbuch*, from *gis*, hostage. From a similar origin, but from the masculine form Avagis, may probably be *Avis*, included by Mr. Lower among Latinized surnames.

Another name from the same stem which seems to have been formerly rather common, but which now seems quite obsolete, is Avina.

HAVEYS, HAWOISE.

This is another woman's name which has become almost extinct, and, seeing how uncomfortable a name it is to pronounce, I do not wonder that it should be so. It appears in the *Liber Vitæ* as Hawysa, and in the *Pol. Irminon* as Hauis, but its proper form is to be traced up to the older name Hathewiza in the *Liber Vitæ*, from *hath*, war, and *wisa*, leader. A surname corresponding, though of course from the masculine form of the name, may probably be the well-known one of *Haweis.*

Some other Obsolete or Obsolescent Names.

The name Helwis occurs in the *Liber Vitæ* about the thirteenth century, and a more perfect form, Helewiza, about two centuries earlier. It seems rather probable, however, that its proper form would be Hildwisa, from *hild*, war, and *wisa*, leader. It occurs as Helois in the *Pol. Irm.*, and is the same as the French Heloise (= Helwise). This name I take to be quite obsolete with us.

A name given by Miss Yonge as still in use is Amice or Amicia. It may probably be the same as the woman's name Amisa, Ameza, or Emeza of the eighth century in the *Altd. Nam.*, which Foerstemann takes to be from A.S. *emeta*, quies. In that case it would probably be the same name in another form as Emmota, formerly not uncommon as a woman's name.

Another name which I rather suppose to be obsolete is Agace, Agaze, or Igusa, found in the *Liber Vitæ* up to the fourteenth century, and probably the same as an O.G. Eggiza, eleventh century, from a stem *ag*, supposed to mean point or edge.

LIST OF THE PRINCIPAL WORKS
CONSULTED.

FOERSTEMANN.—Altdeutsches Namenbuch.—Vol. I. Personen-
namen.—Vol. II. Ortsnamen. London, Williams Norgate.
POTT.—Personennamen. Leipzig, 1853.
STARK.—Beitrage zur kunde Germanischer Personennamen.
Vienna, 1857.—Die Kosenamen der Germanen. Vienna,
1868.
WEINHOLD.—Die Deutschen Frauen in dem Mittelalter.
Vienna, 1851.
GLUCK.—Die bei C. Julius Cæsar vorkommenden Keltischen
Namen. Vienna, 1857.
WASSENBERG.—Verhandeling over de Eigennaamen der Friesen.
Franeker, 1774.
Islands Landnamabôk. Copenhagen.
Scriptores Rerum Langobardicarum et Italicarum, Sæc. 6-9.
Hanover, 1878.
Polyptique de l'Abbé Irminon, ou denombrement des manses,
des serfs, et des revenus de l'Abbaye de Saint Germain-
des-Prés sous le regne de Charlemagne. Paris, 1844.
Polyptique de l'Abbaye de Saint Remi de Reims, ou denom-
brement des manses, des serfs, et des revenus de cette
abbaye vers le milieu du neuvième siècle. Paris, 1853.
₊ The above two Old Frankish records contain a list of the
names of all the [serfs and dependants of the respective
abbeys, with the names also of their wives and children.
KEMBLE.—Codex diplomaticus Ævi Saxonici. London, 1845-48.

THORPE.—Diplomatorium Anglicum Ævi Saxonici. London, 1865.

TAYLOR.—Names and Places. London, 1864.

STEPHENS.—The Old Runic Monuments of Scandinavia and England. London.

MISS YONGE.—History of Christian Names. London, 1863.

LOWER.—Patronymica Britannica. London, 1860.

BOWDITCH.—Suffolk Surnames. Boston, U.S.A.

Liber Vitæ Ecclesiæ Dunelmensis. Published by the Surtees Society, London, 1841.

ADDITIONS AND CORRECTIONS.

Page 17.

We have also *Tray* as a man's name, and from the same origin as that which I have supposed for the dog's name, though the one is from the German and the other from the Celtic. The stem in men's names is referred to Goth. *tragjan,* to run, and may probably include also *Trail* (= Tragel) and *Train* (= Tragen), with the respective endings in *el* and *en.* Also, from the interchange of *d* and *t,* we may include *Dray* and *Drain.*

Page 20.

Among names of the first century is that of Ingomar, uncle of Arminius, which is represented in America by the dreadful name *Inkhammer,* though whether of English or of German origin seems uncertain.

Page 29.

From *Shilling,* as a man's name, is derived *Shillingsworth,* as a name of local origin (A.S. *weorth,* property), a name like Wordsworth, Dodsworth, &c.

Page 120.

Some doubt may be thrown upon the derivation I have suggested for *Pentecost* by the name Osbern Pentecost, which comes before us in Anglo-Saxon times. The name seems here to be a surname, and if so would be derived most naturally from the festival.

Page 159.

From this stem, as found in an A.S. Flogg, may be formed the Anglo-Saxon name Flohere ˙ (*Thorpe*, p. 636), from *hari*, warrior, whence may be our surnames *Floyer*, *Flower*, and *Flowry*.

Page 171.

Among other names apparently from women are *Ella*, *Eva*, and *Louisa*, in *Suffolk Surnames*. Of these, the first is a regular Saxon man's name, and the second is, I doubt not, the same, corresponding with Eafa found in Eafingas, and with Eafha, the name of a Mercian alderman. Louisa I should suppose to be the name Louis with a Romanic, perhaps Spanish, but not female, ending.

INDEX OF NAMES.

₊ *All foreign names are printed in italic type, with the letters distinguishing their nationality within parentheses after them, thus—(D.) Dutch ; (Dan.) Danish ; (F.) French ; (G.) German ; (I.) Italian ; (S.) Spanish.*

ABBA, 25
Abbe, 25
Abbey, 25
Abbiss, 32
Abbott, 96, 178, 179
Abingdon, 106
Ablard, 190
Accolti (I.), 147
Ackerman, 115
Ackermann (G.), 115
Ackman, 96
Acres, 79
Adcock, 35
Addicott, 34, 35, 43
Adela, 209
Adelaide, 209, 210
Adèle (F.), 123
Adeline, 209
Adeliza, 204, 206
Adier, 43
Adimari (I.), 146
Adlam, 40
Adlard, 40
Adolph, 43
Adolphe (F.), 123
Adolphus, 146
Agar, 40
Ager, 79
Agmondesham, 106
Aikin, 96, 185

Aikman, 40, 96, 185
Ailger, 41
Ailman, 41
Alamanni (I.), 147
Albert, 96
Albert (F.), 123
Alberti (I.), 148
Alberto (I.), 143
Albery, 41, 152
Albutt, 43
Alcock, 34, 35
Alcott, 35
Aldebert, 41
Alder, 41, 96, 98, 185
Alderdice, 115
Alderman, 98, 115, 178, 180
Aldighiero (I.), 148
Aldobrandini (I.), 147
Aldred, 41
Aldrich, 41
Aldritt, 41
Alfieri (I.), 152
Alfonse (F.), 123
Alfred, 41, 96
Alfreton, 106
Algar, 96
Algardi (I.), 148
Algarotti (I.), 147
Alger, 42
Alice, 204-206
Alicia, 204-206

Alighieri (I.), 149
Alison, 204-206
Allard, 42
Allaway, 43
Allcard, 96
Allday, 79
Alley, 26, 79
Allfrey, 42, 96
Allgood, 43
Allnut, 42
Allo, 79
Alloisi (I.), 148
Alloway, 118
Allt, 79
Allward, 42
Allwin, 43
Allwood, 42
Almar, 42
Alment, 42
Almiger, 41
Almond, 42, 98
Alpha, 79
Alphonso (I.), 146
Altman, 41, 98
Altree, 41
Alvary, 41, 96
Alvert, 41
Amabel, 201
Amalteo (I.), 152
Amalthius (I.), 152
Amalungi (I.), 151
Ambler, 41, 180

Q

I.

IBBETT, 32
Ihm (G.), 209
Imm (G.), 209
Impey, 167
Inchbald, 56
Inchboard, 56
Ingledew, 42
Inglesent, 42
Inglis, 192
Ingold, 56
Ingram, 56
Ingrey, 56
Inkhammer, 215
Ipswich, 108
Ireland, 9
Iremonger, 19
Irminger, 19, 44
Irwine, 99
Isabel, 198
Isabelle (F.), 199
Isburg, 56
Ismer, 56
Isnard, 56
Isnell, 165
Isner, 56
Ive, 83
Ivy, 83, 185, 186
Izod, 56

J.

JACK, 194, 196
Jacklin, 194, 196
Jacklin (G.), 196
Jacquard (F.), 196
Jacquelin (F.), 196
Jael, 190
Jago, 194, 196
Jane, 206, 207
Janet, 206, 207
January, 182, 183
Jarman, 51
Jeannerett, 52
Jeffcock, 35
Jeffcott, 35
Jellicoe, 31
Jenner, 183

Jennery, 52, 183
Jennett, 207
Jervis, 51
Jocelyn, 176
Jordaens (D.), 135
Jordan, 135
Jordan (F.), 135
Josselin (F.), 176
Jourdain (F.), 135
Jourdan (F.), 135
Judith, 196

K.

KAY, 9, 10, 80
Keble, 98
Kedge, 9, 10
Kegg, 9, 10
Keho, 11
Kelk, 98, 170
Kelvedon, 107
Kemerton, 71, 107
Kenilworth, 107
Kennard, 56
Kennaway, 56, 118
Kenrick, 56, 98
Kensal, 168
Kensett, 168
Kenward, 56, 98
Keogh, 11
Kettering, 105
Kettle, 97
Kettleby, 107
Key, 9, 10, 80
Keysoe, 107
Kidd, 98, 173
Kiddy, 155
Killer, 53
Killman, 53, 98
Kilsby, 109
Kindred, 117
Kinmonth, 56
Kinnaird, 56
Kinney, 26
Kitt, 100, 173
Kitto, 173
Kitty, 155, 170
Klyne, 160
Knapp, 100, 161

Knapping, 161
Knall, 161, 173
Kneller, 161
Knibb, 99, 161
Knife, 161
Knipe, 99, 161
Knipping, 161
Knott, 81
Knyvett, 161
Kupfernagel (G.), 166

L.

LAMAISON, 182
Lamas (F.), 183
Lambert, 56
Lamberti (I.), 147
Lambeth, 109
Lambrook, 56
Lammas, 182, 183
Lamprey, 56, 115, 175, 178
Lanaway, 57
Lander, 56
Landfear, 56
Landlord, 57
Landridge, 57
Landward, 57
Lanfear, 56
Langstaff, 164
Lanoway, 118
Lanwer, 57
Lanzi (I.), 147
Lark, 175, 176
Lascelles, 139
Lateward, 57
Laundry, 57
Lauringen (G.), 72
Lavenham, 109
Laver, 83
Laverick, 100
Laverock, 176
Lawless, 183, 184
Laycock, 34
Leamington, 73
Leathart, 57
Leather, 57
Leboeuf (F.), 139
Lecoq (F.), 34

Q 2

Rattham, 60
Rattray, 60
Raven, 85
Raybauld, 60
Raybolt, 60
Rayment, 60, 120
Raymond, 60
Raynbold, 60
Raynham, 60
Read, 83
Reading, 105
Readwin, 60, 101
Reckless, 183
Redband, 60
Reddaway, 60
Reddish, 33
Redgill, 60
Redman, 60, 61
Redmarley, 110
Redmond, 60
Redmore, 60
Redwar, 60
Regal, 85
Reginald, 13
Regnard, 60
Rennie, 86, 176
Renno, 176
Reulver, 110
Reynard, 60
Reyner, 60
Reynolds, 60
Riccard, 61
Rich, 85
Richard, 61
Richarde (F.), 123
Richbell, 61
Richer, 61, 181
Riches, 32
Richey, 85
Richez (F.), 32
Richman, 61
Richmond, 61
Richold, 61
Rickinghall, 110
Rickman, 61
Ridding, 85
Riddle, 86
Riddy, 85
Ridgway, 61
Ridgyard, 61

Ridolphi (I.), 143
Ringer, 61
Ringold, 61, 100
Ringstead, 110
Ripley, 83
Ritta, 85
Robert, 61
Robert (F.), 123
Roberti (I.), 147
Rock, 85
Rodber, 61
Rodbourn, 61
Rodborough, 110
Rodd, 85
Rodgard, 61
Rodger, 61
Rodman, 61, 192
Rodney, 61
Rodrick, 61
Rodyard, 61
Rointru (F.), 186
Roland, 118
Rolandini (I.), 147
Rolfe, 61, 118
Rolland, 61
Rolle, 85
Rollesby, 110
Rolleston, 110
Roman, 61, 118, 192
Roothing, 105
Rosbert, 61
Roskell, 61
Rosnagel (G.), 166
Ross, 85
Rotherham, 61
Rothery, 61
Rowantree, 185, 186
Rubery, 101
Ruck, 85
Rudd, 85
Rudder, 61
Rudding, 85
Rudolfe (F.), 123
Rudwick, 61
Rugg, 85
Rumbold, 62, 101
Rummer, 62
Runwell, 137
Rush, 85
Rutledge, 61

S.

Sacchi (I.), 147
Saint, 191
Sala, 86
Salaman, 178
Sale, 86
Salloway, 62
Salmon, 62, 175, 178
Sander, 85
Sargood, 66
Sarle, 85
Sarratt, 62
Satchell, 83
Scales, 86
Scally, 86
Scamp, 191
Scard, 83
Scarth, 85
Schilling (G.), 29
Scotland, 8
Scott, 6
Scotten, 8
Scotting, 8
Scotto, 8
Seaber, 63
Seaborn, 63
Seabright, 63, 102n
Seabrook, 63
Seabury, 63
Searight, 63
Searle, 85
Seawall, 63
Seaward, 63
Sedgeberrow, 110
Sedgewick, 62 ·
Sefowl, 63
Segar, 62, 102
Seguin, 62
Self, 85
Sellar, 62
Selvey, 86
Sempringham, 88
Serbutt, 62
Sermon, 62
Seward, 63
Seyfried, 62
Seymore, 15, 20, 62, 118
Seymour, 102

THE END.

LONDON :

R. CLAY, SONS, AND TAYLOR,

BREAD STREET HILL, E.C.

LONGFELLOW'S POETICAL WORKS.

Author's Copyright Editions.

N.B. - Routledge's Editions of Longfellow's Poems are the only complete
ones that can be issued in the United Kingdom.

		s	d.
POEMS.	THE ILLUSTRATED QUARTO EDITION, with 180 Designs by Sir JOHN GILBERT, R.A., and Portrait	21	0
Do.	THE ILLUSTRATED OCTAVO EDITION, with 53 Designs by Sir JOHN GILBERT, R.A., and Portrait (7s. 6d. Gift Books)	7	6
Do.	The THREE-AND-SIXPENNY POETS COMPLETE EDITION, with 6 full-page Plates by Sir JOHN GILBERT, R.A. Crown 8vo.	3	6
Do.	THE STANDARD LIBRARY COMPLETE EDITION; 640 pages, crown 8vo. This Edition contains 53 Copyright Poems	3	6
Do.	THE EXCELSIOR EDITION, 726 pages, paper cover, 1s. 6d.; ditto, cloth	2	0
Do.	PEARL EDITION, with Portrait, 16mo, paper cover, 1s.; ditto, cloth	1	6
Do.	POCKET-VOLUME EDITION. 11 vols. In a box, gilt	21	0

Separate Volumes, paper covers, 1s. *each, or cloth gilt,* 1s. 6d.

1. Voices of the Night.	7. The Divine Tragedy.
2. Evangeline and Miles Standish.	8. The Golden Legend.
3. Hiawatha.	9. New England Tragedies.
4. The Spanish Student.	10. Birds of Passage.
5. Translations and Songs and Sonnets.	11. Flower de Luce, Masque of Pandora,
6. Tales of a Wayside Inn.	Kéramos, &c.

PROSE WORKS: HYPERION—KAVANAGH—OUTRE MER. With 6
Illustrations by Sir JOHN GILBERT, R.A. Crown 8vo. cloth. (Standard
Library.) **3 6**

Ditto, cloth, gilt edges **3 6**

The COMPLETE WORKS of H. W. LONGFELLOW—Poetry, Prose, Dante.
3 vols. crown 8vo. **10 6**

SEPARATE WORKS.

THE HANGING OF THE CRANE. Illustrated Edition. 4to, gilt
edges **10 6**

THE MASQUE OF PANDORA. Fcap. 8vo. **3 6**

KÉRAMOS and other Poems. Fcap. 8vo. **3 6**

AFTERMATH. Fcap. 8vo. **3 6**

THREE BOOKS OF SONG. Fcap. 8vo. cloth **3 6**

THE DIVINE TRAGEDY. Fcap. 8vo. **3 6**

NEW ENGLAND TRAGEDIES. Fcap. 8vo. **3 6**

DANTE'S DIVINE COMEDY. Mr. Longfellow's Translation. Crown
8vo. (Standard Library) **3 6**

EXCELSIOR. Illustrated Edition. 4to, gilt edges **3 6**

TALES OF A WAYSIDE INN. Complete Edition, with 8 Illustrations by Sir JOHN GILBERT, R.A. Crown 8vo., gilt edges **3 6**

COURTSHIP OF MILES STANDISH. 24mo. cloth, red edges ... **1 0**

EVANGELINE. 24mo. cloth, red edges **1 0**

FAVOURITE POEMS. 24mo. cloth, red edges **1 0**

ULTIMA THULE. Fcap. 8vo., paper cover **1 0**

IN THE HARBOR. Fcap. 8vo. cloth **3 6**

GEORGE ROUTLEDGE AND SONS, BROADWAY,
LUDGATE HILL.

THE BLACKFRIARS POETS.

In Imperial 16mo., cloth. 3s. 6d. each.

SHAKSPERE.
Edited by CHARLES KNIGHT. With 32 full-page Illustrations by Sir JOHN GILBERT, R.A.

BYRON.
Edited by W. B. SCOTT. With Portrait and 15 full-page Illustrations.

SCOTT.
Edited by W. B. SCOTT. With 16 full-page Illustrations by Sir JOHN GILBERT, R.A., and other Artists.

BURNS.
Edited by CHARLES KENT. With 16 full-page Illustrations by Sir JOHN GILBERT, R.A., and other Artists.

MOORE.
Edited by CHARLES KENT. With 16 full-page Illustrations by GEORGE H. THOMAS and other Artists.

LONGFELLOW.
Author's complete Copyright Edition, containing 70 Poems in no other Edition printed in England. With 16 full-page Illustrations by Sir JOHN GILBERT, R.A.

GEORGE ROUTLEDGE AND SONS, BROADWAY, LUDGATE HILL.

ROUTLEDGE'S STANDARD LIBRARY.

In post 8vo, toned paper, cloth, 3s. 6d. each.

The Arabian Nights.

Don Quixote.

Gil Blas.

Curiosities of Literature. By ISAAC D'ISRAELI.

One Thousand and One Gems OF BRITISH POETRY.

The Blackfriars Shakespeare.

Cruden's Concordance.

Boswell's Life of Dr. Johnson.

The Works of Oliver Gold-SMITH.

The Family Doctor.

Sterne's Works.

Ten Thousand Wonderful THINGS.

Extraordinary Popular De-LUSIONS.

Bartlett's Familiar Quota-TIONS.

The Spectator (unabridged).

Routledge's Modern Speaker.

One Thousand and One Gems OF PROSE.

Pope's Homer's Iliad and ODYSSEY.

Josephus. Trans. by WHISTON.

Book of Proverbs, Phrases, QUOTATIONS, and MOTTOES.

The Book of Modern Anec-DOTES — Theatrical, Legal, and American.

Book of Table Talk. By W. C. RUSSELL.

Letters of Junius. Woodfall's Edition.

Charles Lamb's Works.

Froissart's Chronicles.

D'Aubigne's History of the REFORMATION.

The Rev. James White's His-TORY OF ENGLAND.

Macaulay—Selected Essays AND MISCELLANEOUS WRIT-INGS.

Carleton's Traits and Stories OF THE IRISH PEASANTRY. First Series.

Carleton's Traits and Stories OF THE IRISH PEASANTRY. Second Series.

Essays by Sydney Smith.

Dante. Longfellow's Translation.

Prescott's Ferdinand and ISABELLA. Vol. 1.

Prescott's Ferdinand and ISABELLA. Vol. 2.

Prescott's Ferdinand and ISABELLA. Vol. 3.

Prescott's Conquest of Mex-ICO. Vol. 1.

GEORGE ROUTLEDGE AND SONS, BROADWAY,
LUDGATE HILL.

Prescott's Conquest of Mexico. Vol. 2.

Prescott's Conquest of Mexico. Vol. 3.

Prescott's Conquest of Peru. Vol. 1.

Prescott's Conquest of Peru. Vol. 2.

Prescott's Conquest of Peru. Vol. 3.

Prescott's Charles the Fifth. Vol. 1.

Prescott's Charles the Fifth. Vol. 2.

Prescott's History of Philip II. Vol. 1.

Prescott's History of Philip II. Vol. 2.

Prescott's History of Philip II. Vol. 3.

Prescott's Biographical and CRITICAL ESSAYS.

Napier's History of the PENINSULAR WAR. 1807-10.

Napier's History of the PENINSULAR WAR. 1810-12.

White's Natural History of SELBORNE.

Dean Milman's History of THE JEWS.

Percy's Reliques of Ancient POETRY.

Chaucer's Poetical Works.

Longfellow's Prose Works.

Spenser's Poetical Works.

Asmodeus. By LE SAGE.

The Book of British Ballads.

Plutarch's Lives (LANGHORNE'S Translation).

The Book of Epigrams. By W. DAVENPORT ADAMS.

Longfellow's Poetical Works (Complete Copyright Edition).

Lempriere's Classical Dictionary.

Adam Smith's Wealth of NATIONS.

The Works of Father Prout. Edited by CHARLES KENT.

Carleton's Traits and Stories OF THE IRISH PEASANTRY. The Two Series Complete in One Volume.

Walker's Rhyming Dictionary.

Macfarlane's History of British India, down to Relief of Candahar.

Defoe's Journal of the Plague AND THE GREAT FIRE OF LONDON. With Illustrations on Steel by GEORGE CRUIKSHANK.

Glimpses of the Past. By CHARLES KNIGHT.

Michaud's History of the CRUSADES. Vol. 1.

Michaud's History of the CRUSADES. Vol. 2.

Michaud's History of the CRUSADES. Vol. 3.

GEORGE ROUTLEDGE AND SONS, BROADWAY,
·LUDGATE HILL.